I love Sarah Harnisch's book, Gameplan! It's her personal story and YOUR road map on how to be successful in Young Living Essential Oils. She lays out everything for you in her no-nonsense fashion, from finding your why to developing your skills to using social media to learning the Compensation Plan to scripts and closes ... every nuance of what's necessary to advance up the ranks as she has done. A lot of my downline are teaching from this book and loving it! When you read it, YOU GET IT!!

Diane Mora

Young Living Crown Diamond

To be successful in this business you need three things: passion, consistency and strategy. Gameplan gives you the strategy you need to make your business grow. It is simple, easy, and duplicatable for the whole team. I have watched Gameplan turn struggling, frustrated distributors into successful business owners. If you want strategy and easy duplication, get Gameplan. It works!

Mary Starr Carter

Young Living Diamond

This is the best book on the market, giving you the tools you need to rock your business. Whether you are a new or a seasoned business builder, you will be able to take this book and apply it to help you and your team grow. If you ever get the chance to meet Sarah in person, don't pass it up!

Lorene Allen

Young Living Platinum

TO:

_____

FROM:

_____

DATE:

_____

GAMEPLAN

UPDATED SECOND EDITION

The Complete
Strategy Guide
to go from
Starter Kit to Silver

Sarah Harnisch
Young Living Diamond

DEDICATION

The dedication for this book is incredibly easy to write. I knew before I put the first word on the page that every thought was focused on you and you alone, Young Living Distributor.

I know what it felt like to start my business without a script, a vision, or a lot of direction. I have been in a place where I plateaued—and I didn't know my next move. Heck, I went through the first six months of my business not even realizing I had a business at all. I had no idea how to inspire and train leaders. I have had moments of panic as I watched my volume dip. Unintentionally, I have made just about every mistake imaginable with the FDA. I got over the initial fear of the unknown with my first class, then had ten-thousand questions on what happened next. I have been lost, overwhelmed, exasperated, and elated, invigorated, and blown away all on the same day. I have been disappointed in leaders, in my own leadership, and then stood back and saw that, despite our mistakes, we were catapulting to Platinum. I realized there is a strategy—there is a method, a way of doing this business. If someone wrote that down, it would bless thousands and thousands of people trying to navigate the network marketing world.

If you're brand new, great! You have just as much of a chance at making Diamond as someone who is a Platinum. If you're a Diamond and on the cusp of losing rank, this will give your leaders new energy and focus. Wherever you are, this book is dedicated to your tenacity, your hard work, your diligence, your fight, your climb, your drive and focus, your days of weariness and desire to quit, and your days of fist-bumping your team in raging success in the final minutes at the end of the month. This book is for all of it, your high days and your low days and your in-between days. I am standing there, rallying right beside you. Because some days, it takes a little shouting with joy for us to move.

I'd never have found my "shout" if it hadn't been for my Lord and Savior, Jesus, who gave His life for me on the cross. If you hear joy in these pages, my joy comes from Him. If you hear passion and hope, my Hope is in the Lord. May this book inspire you to grow a business and grow your faith. I know it's done both for me. And because of that, because God is my center, this book is also for Him.

Thank you for your commitment to ingest all that's on these pages. If you can grab a 3-page script and read it on your couch with another person, you have what it takes to go all the way to the top in this business. I want you to know that whether you're on my team or not, you are worth fighting for. Your dreams matter. Today is the day you stop chasing them, and you start to see them through. It's Gameplan time.

CONTENTS

STRATEGIES FOR GROWTH: STAR AND BEYOND

STRATEGIES FOR BUILDING YOUR TEAM

EXPAND YOUR INFLUENCE: SECRETS TO GREAT LEADERSHIP

IT WORKS: THE VIEW FROM THE TOP

APPENDIXES: SARAH'S SCRIPTS AND MORE

Sarah Harnisch has distilled the essence of what it takes to build a successful Young Living business! Her wonderful book Gameplan gives simple and practical steps to building a team to Silver and beyond, taking out the guesswork that may otherwise slow your business. Gameplan is a real game changer for those seeking to create abundance in Young Living.

David Stewart, PhD

Young Living Diamond,
Founder of *CARE International,*
Author of *Healing Oils of the Bible*
and *Chemistry of Essential Oils Made Simple*

FORWORD

BY DR. OLIVIER WENKER

I was a Gold distributor when I picked up this book. I am now a Young Living Crown Diamond.

Two years ago, my wife Ellen gave me and everyone else in the family the same Christmas gift: Sarah Harnisch's book "Gameplan".

I immediately started reading it, as did our children, and during Christmas break we had lively discussions around the dinner table, as we were all astounded and excited about the things that we learned while studying this book.

We are a true Young Living family. We believe in everything that this company produces and live the lifestyle. We use all the products and are excited about the business opportunity, however, despite our enthusiasm, our team building seemed to have hit a wall.

After reading Sarah's book, we all felt re-energized and full of new ideas and we decided that all of our team leaders should experience the same and have a chance to use Sarah's ideas and strategies as well. So, shortly after the holidays we ordered a whole bundle of her Gameplan books (and sweet Sarah added a lot more to it after she heard the Christmas gift story!) We sent them to all of our team leaders. The feedback was enormous and overwhelmingly positive, and this enthusiasm caused ripples of growth throughout our whole team. Our leaders were sharing and recommending the book and we soon felt the tremendous impact that this had on our growth.

After sharing our own experience with Sarah and meeting her in person at the Young Living Convention, we are more inspired by her then ever. She is not just a great teacher but also an incredibly generous and caring human being, a true example of the principles of Young Living: sharing, caring, doing, helping and encouraging others to switch to a health supporting lifestyle while building an opportunity to add or even fully support your family as well as the causes dear to your heart.

For us personally, this translated into a chance to not only have a secure retirement income but also to make to make our dearest dream come true, building a rescue sanctuary for unwanted and abandoned dogs. This dream is slowly taking shape, and we owe Sarah a debt of gratitude for having a part in it.

If you are reading this, congratulations, you are obviously ready to take your Young Living organization to the next level by applying and sharing the Gameplan strategies that Sarah so generously shares with all members.

Olivier Wenker, *MD, MBA, DEAA, ABAARM*
Young Living Crown Diamond

INTRODUCTION

WHAT'S NEW IN THE SECOND EDITION?

Hey there guys! So much has happened in the 18 months since Gameplan was released!!! The Gameplan series has sold over 1.5 million copies. You put a woman at the top of the entrepreneur charts for 10 straight months—the only woman in the top 20 on the world's largest bookseller, Amazon. We beat Donald Trump and Dr. Seuss! Gameplan bootcamp has been viewed by hundreds of thousands of people. You took a homeschool mom on her couch and made Young Living training go viral on the web! It has been a year of awe for my family as we watched the whole thing unfold like a Cinderella fairy tale—from the projects to Diamond, from pauper to giver. I wish you could see the other end of it, and how your personal recommendation of the book—your sharing on the web—has helped so many families. I have had a front row seat to watch people plucked out of poverty, just as I was, because of their pursuit of this incredible company.

Young Living has grown to surpass the 1.5 billion dollar mark because of YOUR tenacity and fight! That is an amazing feat for a network marketing company. I have had the honor of meeting thousands of you and hearing your stories of ranking up using Gameplan. We have sprinkled many of your words, including those from Singapore and Australia, to California and New York, throughout this new edition. You are Gameplan.

I have also had a chance to hear your heart and your deepest struggles. I've added about 50 pages of content based on the Gameplan roundtable, which I've done every single Tuesday night since February of 2018, on the Oil Ability with Sarah Facebook page. Hidden in the pages of this book, you will find your burdens, your exhaustion, and your frustration. It's the things you whisper, alone, when you're ready to quit. It's your story. And it's how to fight your way out. You CAN do this. May this new edition give you new fire, new hope, new purpose, new ideas, and new tools to rise all the way to Royal Crown.

What's new?

- A full explanation of the Rising Star bonus and the new Elite Express with strategies to help you make the most of Young Living's amazing compensation plan!

- Exact wording for conversations that lead to kit sales and people coming to your classes!

- Deeper, diamond-level insight into placement and team structure.

- Updated section on sharing through social media and how to rock Facebook Live for sharing and team training.

- The famous purple bag: how to build and use the most powerful sharing tool in the Gameplan system!

- The art of the relationship, and how to lead people to a lifestyle of oiling.

- The secret to building with vendor events.

- A brand new 101 script, updated and revised with the new Premium Starter kit oils and new language for purity, as well as the latest stats on Young Living as a company.

- Plus an index to help you keep all this awesome right at your fingertips!

Are you excited yet??

Here is one thing I have not done: delete content. If you were in love with the first edition of the Gameplan book, and use it with your leaders, you'll be madly in love with this edition. It just got better.

HOW TO USE THIS BOOK

You've picked up this book up for one of four reasons:

1) You're brand new and want to learn how to get your oils for free (that's very doable!).

2) You are a seasoned oiler that is now interested in the business. You love earning free oils, but now you want to start making some money!

3) You are a business builder that has been taking it seriously for months or years but don't understand why you aren't growing as quickly as those around you.

4) You have already been successful at the business, but reached a plateau and you're not quite sure where to go next.

This book is for every single one of you. The title is deceiving. I began writing it as a resource for newbies who want to get to Silver, but I have seen even Diamonds benefit from it because we can all learn from each other. When you stop learning, you stop growing. As I sit and write this, I'm constantly gleaning new ideas from odd places and from every rank to use on my own team.

If you're just getting started

To the new oiler or new business builder: if you are just getting started, promise me something. Teach at least one class before you try to digest this whole book. Most of your fear is simply fear of the unknown. Grab the simple 101 Script in the appendix of this book, gather a few friends and read it aloud. Go through the motions of what a class looks like. Once you have gone through one business cycle of inviting to a class, sharing the 101 Script, closing confidently, and touching base afterward, return to the book.

Before you've held a class, the information in this book will seem overwhelming. But what I found was after that first class experience, there were a thousand legitimate questions:

"How do I navigate the Virtual Office?"

"Someone wants to sign up, but where do I place them?"

"No one is coming to class!"

"How do I deal with no's?"

"Where do I find leaders?"

"How do I get people on Essential Rewards?"

Once you are asking those questions, you are ready for this book. It's a game plan. It's a strategy guide. It's not a feel-good, vision casting book—it's a nuts and bolts, how-to book. It's here to help you navigate the chessboard of network marketing. You absolutely can succeed at this, because it simply requires will. If you have will, even distractions and crises cannot keep you from your end game long-term. This book is to show you it can be done by anyone who sees where Young Living goes, despite personality, income, time, resources, location, or friend circles.

This book is not fluffy inspiration—it's a proven set of instructions that work. But it's not overwhelming—most chapters are just a couple of pages, and written in a down-to-earth, easy-to-understand format. Take it at your pace, apply what you learn, and utilize the appendixes. (I always skip the appendixes in other books, but that's where the gold is in this book!) Then find an accountability partner, fill out the monthly accountability worksheets and you're off and running.

If you're tired or stuck

If you have leveled off in your growth and need new perspective or fresh wind—this book is written for you, too. You will be energized by the many tips and tricks assembled here from a very active, diverse, and creative team.

A word of caution: Gameplan is extremely dense. I'm a researcher and compiler by nature, and 17 years as a news anchor perfected my ability to pack the most essential info into the shortest amount of time. I'm trained to do election coverage, to listen to seven hours of tape on every

major network, ingest it, and condense all of it into 30 second stories that are easy on the ear.

When I went to train my oils team for the first time, I found there were many incredible resources, but they were in too many places. If I wanted to get someone off the ground, I had to purchase several dozen books for them!

This book is a summary of what I've experienced at my personal classes, what I've learned from my own leaders, crossline friend's tips for growth, what I have gleaned from my Diamond and Platinum friends on Young Living trips, what I have read for personal growth, and more. It is the best of the best, every page packed with practical action points intended make the transition into a Young Living business fast and successful.

The Gameplan system will keep you on track if you stick with it. When life knocks you over, get back up, pick the book back up and start again where you left off. The only time you lose at network marketing is when you get off the horse and don't return. Stay on the horse.

If you're Silver or higher

If you are in higher leadership, take this book and run. Read it, digest it, apply what you need, and fly. You have been doing this long enough that you know the drill and you know what it takes to rock this thing. But maybe there aren't good training materials on your team; this book provides you with a proven system to train your leaders. My upline Diamond leadership and crossline Diamond friends have used it successfully with their teams, and we have had a powerful outcome from Gameplan on the Oil Ability Team.

Maybe you're a rock star who truly has it all totally together. You have ranked at record speed, your classes have standing room only, you pick up leaders everywhere and set them on fire, and you are a master at getting people on Essential Rewards. But here's the thing: every leader has a breaking point. We all have a place where we're worn so thin, and there are a thousand things we want to share with someone, but there is no space in our life to do it.

That's what this book is for. It's for the things you want to tell your brand new budding Diamond, on level 47, but you don't have two weeks to spend with them alone on an island uninterrupted. This is your time saver. This allows you to pour into every leader with the same tenacity and content without killing yourself or robbing your family of time.

Whatever the reason is that you are reading this, thank you for picking up Gameplan! My goal is to see as many individuals and families rise to Diamond as possible. My vision is to break the cycle of poverty, whether you're on my team or a crossline team. We're all part of the same Young Living family!

I can't wait to walk alongside you in the following pages and pour my heart into your business. Thank you for the honor of your time. This book is rich and dense and full of my mistakes to save you time, and I pass it off with prayers of blessing, multiplication, application, favor, and fun. This is your year to explode! As I say to my Oil Ability leaders, you are a #diamondrising!!!

———*Sarah*

PART ONE

GETTING STARTED: WHAT YOU NEED TO BEGIN

I read Gameplan the same week I decided I would give this business a try. I picked my class date and started the Bootcamp. My first class turned into two...back to back because I had so many people want to attend. It was the beginning of my financial freedom. This month I reached Silver in 5 and I credit it mainly to the Gameplan! Last month I hit 100 people in my downline and decided it was time to finally do the Gameplan with them. We started last week with 7 girls. Three just hit Senior Star and 3 Star! Who would've known that I had three business leaders sitting right there in those first two classes? Not me. Train two to train two works. Thank you for giving me direction and confidence!

Janel Chiccini Hirsch

I oiled for a full year with no intention of ever sharing about oils, then I read your book and lightbulbs went off as to the chemicals I had in my house that were harming my family...I knew I had to share with loved ones and friends. I was a star, skipped right passed Senior Star and went to Executive in one month, then earned Silver in 4. I proceeded to rank 44th in Race to Finish and earn a trip to Hawaii...to say I have been blessed is an understatement!!!! THANK YOU!!!

Tracie Gallant

CHAPTER 1

WHY LAUNCH A YOUNG LIVING BUSINESS?

Welcome! My name is Sarah Harnisch. I'm a Young Living Diamond and a leader on the Oil Ability Team.

For more than a decade and a half, I was a full-time news anchor, which meant depleting my body of sleep and robbing my husband and children of my time. Although I love radio, and never took a day in the anchor chair for granted, it was extremely hard on my body, like running a marathon every single day. I retired from full-time radio on August 27, 2015—after just 14 months with Young Living.

With God's complete grace, I attained Platinum rank in Young Living 17 months after getting my Starter Kit, and Diamond a little over a year later. I did this while also homeschooling my five children; rearing a special needs son; anchoring news full-time starting at 4:00 a.m.; and cooking gluten-free, sugar-free, and dairy-free meals for seven people with allergies.

When I launched my Young Living business, I lived in a new state, in an extremely rural and impoverished area with poor internet, and had no circle of friends. I'd love to say that running a network marking company is easy, but the road has been full of curves and obstacles, and I'm still learning, every single day.

I do believe that with Christ as the center of your business, and tenacity, *anyone* can run a Young Living business. It has nothing to do with who you know, how famous you are, how you look, what your personality is, where you live, or how much income or time you have. If I can pull this off—*you* can pull this off.

This book is about showing you the things I've picked up on my journey.

WHY START A YOUNG LIVING BUSINESS?

That's the question I get more than any other. Here's the short answer: it's better than any job you've ever had, including a job you love. (I love anchoring news!) Why?

Freedom.

If you can show your leaders and potential business builders that this is better then what they are doing right now, you will have a lifelong business builder. They have to see that how they are spending their time at this moment will not get anything crossed off their bucket list in the next five years. The minute they spot that, they have vision.

I didn't see the business right away. In fact, it took a good six months before my husband, John, finally sat me down and asked, "What are you doing? You're making more with these little weekly oils classes than you are at your full time job!"

That's when I realized I needed to take it seriously. The Lord had put something in my path to pull me out of the bondage of my 4 a.m. high-stress anchoring job, and I didn't even see it. It took my husband's wisdom for me to snap out of my routine and my patterns to realize this was a viable job that could really bless our family.

Once I saw it, I made a list of pro's to doing my Young Living business based on what I'd seen over our first six months. Was it truly worth it? When I weighed the options, that's when Young Living blew me away. This is that list.

Sarah's Why Do A Young Living Business Pro's List

1. THERE IS NO INCOME CEILING

In four months flat, I made more with Young Living than in 16 years of anchoring news. Two years out, I have multiplied the highest income I ever made in my life by five—and the best is yet to come.

If you look at the Income Disclosure Guide in a couple of pages, you'll see the average Diamond's monthly income is well over what most people usually make in a year. I know the people that are living that dream, dozens of them are our close friends. John and I are living that dream. It's possible. The only ones that don't get to the top are the ones that give up.

2. THE TIMING HAS NEVER BEEN BETTER

Many people say that timing is everything, and that you can't be successful in a network marketing company unless you get into the business early. But my story, and many others, disproves that. I didn't get into Young Living until the company was almost 20 years old! But in months, I had surpassed nearly every person ahead of me, save my Diamond upline. There are hundreds of Diamonds, hundreds of Platinums, thousands of Golds, and thousands upon thousands of Silvers; and the company continues to experience radical growth even as you read this. It's rare for any network marketing company to cross the one-billion-dollar threshold in sales. Young Living has blown past that threshold and continues to grow.

The date that you sign up for your Premium Starter Kit has no bearing on where Young Living will go for you. How do I know? Because the current market has never been more open to what you have to offer. In just the past five years, Panera Bread has cut all chemicals from their salad dressings. Kraft Mac and Cheese has cut all dyes from their sauce. Chipotle has vowed to cut all GMO's from their menu. People are demanding better food and better products. You're seeing more and more items on store shelves that are "simple" or "natural" versions—peanut butter with peanuts and salt instead of hydrogenated oils and soy products. And the stuff is selling.

This world has started to dramatically change. No longer do we accept at face value that everything in a store is safe simply because the product made it past the government. We are starting to read labels on the bottles and boxes of the foods that we consume, the things we clean our home with, and the personal care products we scrub our teeth with and slather on our armpits and say, "I think there's a better way to do this."

The companies that are keeping up with that trend are thriving. Those that don't will lose. Young Living is ahead of the game in every single field: personal care, oils, cleaning supplies, supplements, and more. They are a total wellness company. Wellness means you stay above the line of disease.

Do you ever get frustrated that it seems doctors are always treating the symptoms instead of the cause? That they chase inflammation, pain, headaches, and a plethora of other ailments instead of finding out what's underneath all that and stopping it? You're not alone.

That's what Young Living is about. It's about stopping the cause before it happens by supporting all the systems in your body without chemically overloading them. It's not about treating disease; it's about staying ahead of it: preventative maintenance.

The average woman applies 80 chemicals to her body daily before breakfast through four types of products: makeup, hair care, skin care, and soap. Then we wonder why our livers are taxed and we are tired and have hormonal issues! It's the yuck in our life. We are in constant chemical exhaustion.

This means that if you meet any person who has not banned that stuff from the threshold of their doors, any person who is not label-reading every product in their home—you have just found a potential oiler. You have a market that is 100% wide open, because literally every person you know needs oils. It's not like a pan or lipstick or a book or a skirt. It's about your health. It's about your life and your family's lives. That's what makes this company the best.

I believe with all my heart that Young Living will continue to absolutely boom—because they have what everyone wants: health freedom. It is what wellness is all about, getting ahead of your health by saying "no" to the things you allow across the threshold of the door to your home. You are the gatekeeper. And if you will teach others to be a gatekeeper, you have the secret to unlocking an explosive business with unlimited customers.

3. YOU ARE YOUR OWN BOSS AND SET YOUR OWN HOURS

I had no idea how much I appreciated this until I had no boss! I dictate my own schedule every single day. And to a weary momma who has been getting up hours before the sun rises for years, you can't put a price tag on that.

One of my best moments was a few days after I retired. I woke up to the sun in my face, and stumbled out into the living room to watch the sun rise over the fields behind our home. I had not seen the sun rise in nearly ten years. I had my weekends off, but from sheer exhaustion, I always slept well past the sun coming up. Now I get to be home with my kids and see the sun rise every day. Some of the smallest things bring the greatest joy. To me, a sunrise means freedom.

4. WILLABLE INCOME (THE BEST PERK EVER!)

Once you hit a certain income threshold, then connect with Young Living and fill out their paperwork, the income your business generates will go to your heirs *forever*. So, say you have five kids, and are making $15,000 a month as a Platinum—that's $3,000 a month for each child! My kids will never grow up without food in their stomach or a roof over their head. Young Living brings peace of mind. That's the biggest perk to me. It's a legacy income, not a 401K that disappears when the cash is gone.

Outside of network marketing, there is no job on the earth where you can pull that off. If I passed away while working in radio, two weeks after my death, my final news anchor check would show up. My family would be out of luck. The $17,000 I saved in my 401K over nine years would be gone in about six months. A Young Living business doesn't work like that. This isn't some account somewhere with cash in it—it's a real, living, growing business that generates capitol—cash that goes to your family every single month.

Young Living is like setting up a storefront in your hometown and having employees run it for you. It keeps generating income even after you're gone. If you have a will, your rank in the Young Living hierarchy doesn't disappear after your death; it goes to your family.

5. YOU CAN TAKE TIME OFF AND STILL GET PAID!

If you were in a car accident tomorrow and missed three months of work, your paycheck at a regular job would drop off within a few weeks, right? Even with disability insurance it would be a fraction of what it usually is. But with network marketing, if you are in a season where you can't share the oils, the powerful team beneath you is still working.

This was one of my wow moments, where I really grasped the power of network marketing for the first time. John and I have a special needs son on the autism spectrum. When he was 14, we had to have him placed in a school on the other side of the country. We had homeschooled all five of our kids together for 12 years, and it was extremely painful to split the Harnisch herd up. Gabe was at that school for an entire year. For 12 months, save a visit at Christmas, we did not see him, and had to get by with a 20-minute weekly phone call. At Christmas the next year, he came home. It was a huge milestone for our family. We had missed him terribly!!

These are our two oldest sons, minutes after Isaiah saw his older brother.

When Gabe returned, I felt convicted that all of my time needed to be spent on assimilating him back into the family. So I committed to taking 30 straight days off Young Living: no phone calls, no training, no classes, not even Facebook posts. I put all my attention on him, and reintegrating him into the house and our routines. From December 6th until January 9th 2015, I didn't do a thing for my business. I figured it would be a period of famine for us that year, but it was more important to focus on Gabe than on work. We'd just have to get through.

But four days before Christmas, I got a Young Living check in the mail that was higher than my monthly income from my full-time job. I scratched my head, took it to John, and told him, "I didn't do anything this month!" I hadn't anchored news either, and I had no paycheck come from the radio station. I had only been doing Young Living for five months and hadn't even taught any classes in December, but I still got paid because the team underneath me was still out there selling. This was the power of network marketing at work for our family! When I was at my low point, my team (and my paycheck) were still there!

I came back more excited than ever, and started a firestorm of teaching after January 9th when Gabe was comfortable at home and had enrolled in college. That firestorm led us to Gold rank just 12 weeks after his return.

There will be seasons in your life that make it tough to work your Young Living business well. It's okay. When the season passes, keep going. In the interim, you have the strength of the team under you. It's the best structure of any job there is.

6. RELATIONSHIPS: THE SURPRISE BENEFIT

I had no idea how small my circle of friends was until I got involved in network marketing. You get into a groove with a nine-to-five job, or with homeschooling, or public schooling, or with running your home; and simply forget that the Lord created us for relationships, that we thrive when we're in community. Some of us need many, many friends, while others are fine with just a couple of them. But we need to take time to connect with the women and men that inspire us and make us better people.

Until two years ago, I had very little contact with the outside world save trivial relationships, because I was either anchoring or homeschooling. That has completely changed for me now because of Young Living. In 30 months, I have a team of over 6000 in all 50 states and several countries, and have developed some serious relationships that I know will last my lifetime. Hundreds of them would drop everything and open their home to me in an emergency. I look forward to my girl time at our Oil Ability Silver and Above Retreats and Oil Ability Beach House Retreats, and our adventures at convention. Even outside of my own team, I have true friendships around the entire world. And best yet, I get to see them at corporate events, Silver retreats, Gold retreats, Platinum retreats, leadership events, training seminars, Oil Ability team events, and convention. We grow and laugh and make memories together each time we see one other.

There are members on my team that run their business for the sole reason of developing deeper relationships. And that's a great "why." Young Living has an incredible way of networking us with people when we need to be poured into, and allows us to be a spigot to pour into others. This is an aspect of the business I completely underestimated which has blessed me more than I can put on paper.

7. GUARANTEED BONUSES

Young Living is a generous company that has built in bonuses and perks for every level in the business. If you do the work, you will be rewarded. What are some of these perks?

Stars and Senior Stars get a bigger paycheck.

Executives get a pin, a certificate, and a larger check.

Anyone who holds Silver rank for three consecutive months goes to the largest essential oils farm in the world (Young Living at Mona, Utah) for three days. The company pays to fly you there, puts you up in a posh hotel, loves on you with a swag bag worth a few hundred dollars, and feeds you like a king. You'll make friends from around the world and catch the vision of where Young Living goes.

Golds get the same thing, except their trip is to the first Young Living farm, in Saint Maries, Idaho.

Platinums head to the farm in Ecuador and see Ylang Ylang, Oregano, Dorado Azul, and Copaiba—and the work of the Young Living Foundation, which has built a 200-million-dollar school for impoverished kids.

There are trophies for every new rank from Silver and up each year at convention.

Diamond retreats are in different locations every year. They also get new products before they are released, front row seating at convention, and are paid a hefty Diamond bonus every month for maintaning the rank. Young Living wants their top leaders there and gives generously to have them come. They also get regular conference calls from Young Living to get the latest inside information from the company (which is my favorite Diamond perk!).

And if none of those reasons rock your world, how about this one: you can earn a ridiculous paycheck!! Check out the 2016 income disclosure guide. These are average incomes from all Young Living distributors!

YOUNG LIVING 2016 U.S. INCOME DISCLOSURE STATEMENT

As a direct selling company selling essential oils, supplements, and other lifestyle products, Young Living offers opportunities for our members to build a business or simply receive discounts on our products.

Whatever your interest in the company, we hope to count you among the more than 2 million Young Living members joining us in our mission to bring Young Living essential oils to every home in the world.

What are my earning opportunities?

Members can earn commissions and bonuses as outlined in our Compensation Plan. As members move up in the ranks of Young Living, they become eligible for additional earning opportunities.

This document provides statistical, fiscal data about the average member income and information about achieving various ranks.

RANK	PERCENTAGE OF ALL MEMBERS	MONTHLY INCOME				ANNUALIZE AVERAGE INCOME	MONTHS TO ACHIEVE THIS RANK		
		Lowest	Highest	Median	Average		Low	Average	High
Distributor	93.5%	$0	$341	$0	$1	$12	N/A	N/A	N/A
Star	3.5%	$0	$811	$60	$77	$924	1	15	258
Senior Star	1.3%	$1	$5,457	$147	$240	$2,880	1	22	290
Executive	0.6%	$50	$12,139	$434	$514	$6,168	1	29	253
Silver	0.2%	$102	$25,504	$1,783	$2,227	$26,724	2	38	291
Gold	0.1%	$1,781	$46,820	$4,874	$6,067	$72,804	7	54	240
Platinum	<0.1%	$5,166	$85,992	$12,188	$15,328	$183,888	3	61	278
Diamond	<0.1%	$14,898	$140,333	$33,078	$39,566	$424,792	10	75	231
Crown Diamond	<0.1%	$17,397	$232,351	$64,256	$74,188	$890,256	14	83	274
Royal Crown Diamond	<0.1%	$58,392	$362,864	$155,246	$152,377	$1,828,524	17	106	230

The income statistics in this statement are for incomes earned by all active U.S. members in 2016. An "active" member is a member who made at least one product purchase in products in the previous 12 months. The average annual income for all members in this time was $25, and the median annual income for all members was $0. 51% of all members who enrolled in 2015 did not make a purchase with Young Living in 2016. 57% of all members who enrolled in 2014 did not continue with Young Living in 2016.

Note that the compensation paid to members summarized in this disclosure do not include expenses incurred by a member in the operation or promotion of his or her business, which can vary widely and might include advertising or promotional expenses, product samples, training, rent, travel, telephone and Internet costs, and miscellaneous expenses. The earnings of the members in this chart are not necessarily representative of the income, if any, that a Young Living member can or will earn through the Young Living Compensation Plan. These figures should not be considered as guarantees or projections of your actual earnings or profits. Your success will depend on individual diligence, work, effort, sales skill, and market conditions. Young Living does not guarantee any income or rank success.

Based on a count of all active members in 2016.
Because a distributor's rank may change from during the year, these percentages are not based on individual distributor ranks throughout the entire year, but based on the average distribution of distributor ranks during the entire year.
Because a distributor's rank may change from during the year, these incomes are not based on individual distributor incomes throughout the entire year, but based on earnings of all distributors qualifying for each rank during the entire year.
This is calculated by multiplying the average monthly incomes by 12.
These statistics include all historical ranking data for each rank, and thus is not limited to people who achieved these ranks in 2016.
These statistics include income earned from January 1, 2016, and December 31, 2016, but which was paid between February 2016 and January 2017.
Members who do not make at least one product purchase in the previous 12 months have their membership terminated.

8. FINANCIAL FREEDOM

Young Living is a vehicle to financial freedom. But it's about so much more than the money. Let me explain.

Not only are my husband and I debt free (including $70,000 in student loans), but I have had the honor of watching many of my closest friends and family members do the same thing with their Young Living paycheck. If you're going to get rich, do it beside your friends and family! It's been incredible to watch friends pay cash for their wedding; watch my mom buy a home; see my downline members invest in missions, become debt free, give to the needy, let jobs go and stay home with their kids, retire their spouses, go on family vacations before their teens leave for college, cross things off their lifelong bucket lists, travel, and chase their dreams.

Many of my friends have asked me if Young Living is a prosperity gospel or a get-rich-quick scheme. No, it's not. If you think it's a get-rich-scheme, you're making the assumption that a Young Living business is handed to you. Let me tell you, new business builder, you will work and you will work hard! If anyone tells you otherwise, you're being fed a lie. There is no outstretching of your hands and waiting for the cash to fall from the sky. Sometimes it's difficult. People won't come to your classes. Leaders will drive you batty. But my worst day in Young Living has been better than my best day at 40 other jobs I've held.

Are you willing to stick it out and see where it goes? Do you have the tenacity to pull this off? If you look at that Young Living Income Disclosure chart—and truly believe where it goes—isn't it worth the push to keep going? Heck, I would work at a Dollar Store for ten years if I knew I could make $30,000 a month eventually! That's what this is. No other job I've ever worked has had a chart like that. It's raw truth. Those are the stats. That's where people land when they push through the tough times with Young Living;the months where sales are down; the times when people said no to Essential Rewards. But every no means you were out there working, you were doing it, and there are yes's on the horizon. Stick it out and create your dream! Keep fighting and never give up. Some will make it to Diamond in two years, and some in twenty years. But Diamond is Diamond. And it's worth every no, every no-show, and every dissident leader. Don't give up too soon! Be so busy teaching classes that you don't have time to notice the no's.

So many people are afraid of abundance. I scratch my head on that one! When the Lord gives you more, it means you are able to give more. It means you've been trusted with wealth. Some of God's favorite people were wealthy: David, Solomon, Abraham, and Job. Wealth is a blessing that gives you time, peace of mind, resources, and the ability to love more generously on others. And if we fear it, that's not of the Lord. He's the one that owns the cattle on a thousand hills; my Lord is the creator of wealth. And He loves to love on His children. You just have to accept His gift and be willing to roll up your sleeves in obedience when He calls on you to act. I am really enjoying this season of giving when I see a need, and knowing I'll still be able to put dinner on my table that night. There is something beautiful in coming beside someone hurting or in financial pain and making a difference, even anonymously. That is waiting for you with this business: the ability to silently bless.

You Can't Free Others When You're in Bondage

God wants abundance for His people. How are you supposed to take care of the widows, the sick, and the poor when you have a blown head gasket on your car, $100 in your account, and are short for your electric bill this month?

We love Dave Ramsey's financial advice and have taken Financial Peace University. He says to save $1,000, make a list of all your debts from the smallest to largest, and start paying them off, beginning with the smallest debt first. We had done that so many times. But the reality is that when you and your husband are working four minimum wage, full-time jobs just to make ends meet, you don't have the income to pull it off. We'd save that thousand, then blow the transmission in our car. We'd save it again, then the water heater would go out in our home. We found that we could never, ever get ahead, and that's how we lived for nearly two decades. Save it, lose it. Save it, lose it. How can you help others when you are in that place?

You can't serve when you can't even stand.

That is why we are here—to serve. You can't serve when you can't even stand. John and I were technically middle class, but we were drowning. We are not drowning any more, and we will never drown again. We live by Dave Ramsey now and can actually do his debt reduction strategy, because the crisis period in our lives has ended. Even as a middle class family in the richest nation on earth, we could not breathe with our regular jobs. You'll hear me say it so many times in this book: Young Living is a way out. The Lord has sent you a boat. Get on it and get off that island where you're financially stranded.

It's Not About Fame and Fortune

As a radio anchor, I've had my name in millions of homes, so I know what it's like to be famous. I've had my name and face on many a banner and billboard. As a Diamond in Young Living, I've received recognition, been on stage, and traveled the world. But I'll tell you, freedom is better than being famous. Why? Because I can be home with my kids. I have time to take care of my husband and take care of my body. I have the ability to run with my teenagers in the woods in the morning and stay up late watching their soccer games and talking into the night about their relationships and their faith, without having to rise at 3 a.m. to anchor news. I have the ability to wake up and have a candlelight breakfast with my husband and do devotions without interruption. I have the ability to give, and that drives me. I have the ability to see others set free—especially struggling families. Those are my "whys."

Money doesn't drive me. Freedom does.

Let me tell you how I found my "why." I fell in love with oils the first week I got my kit and saw them work. My primary focus in starting to teach was selfish. I just wanted to get them into my home and use them on my own children and husband. I had no other reason. But when I saw them work, I started wanting my friends and family to have them, too, so I taught. My husband said if I wanted every oil in the catalog, the only way that was going to happen was if I was out teaching. So I taught some more. And pretty soon, my "why"—my purpose for sharing the oils—was to hear the stories of people who had used them successfully. It was incredible! I was on a high, having a front row seat to see the Lord work right in front of me. But honestly, that's not why I do it now.

Sharing Freedom

Now I share Young Living to break the cycle of poverty in which I see so many families living. How can you do what you were called and created to do when you're constantly in survival mode? You can't. And that is where the business comes in. That little ripple in the pond of my oils business became a tsunami throughout New York and Pennsylvania, and I started seeing something I didn't expect to see as I got out there and taught. People weren't just experiencing wellness, they were becoming financially free!

First, it was a mom on my team able to stop working and stay home with her children.

Then my own mom's check surpassed her full-time job.

Then a Silver on my team, married to a legally blind husband, was able to quit her $10/hour desk job that she'd had at different offices for 15 years.

My own sister, who had worked three jobs for 20 years, retired from one job, then two. Then a month before her wedding, retired from her third and final job.

One by one, people were seeing freedom. At the beginning, it was just a few people sharing the oils. Then in 18 months, we had 800 leaders. One in every five people on my team was sharing. Most were just getting their oils for free, but many were able to make game-changer decisions with their life: retire themselves, retire their spouse, or pay off copious amounts of debt.

At the time of publishing this book, dozens of leaders on our team have either cut back or fully retired from their jobs. Those families have been forever changed because of a news-anchor homeschooling mom of five freak who was exhausted, living in a rural area, and thought she couldn't make a difference for anyone.

Raising Diamonds

Now, my "why" is to raise as many Diamonds as I can. If you are on my team, that's a blessing; because you may be a close friend or a family member and I have the honor of getting to watch amazing things happen in your life. But if you are not on my team, that's part of my purpose too. You matter. It's because Young Living isn't just about me or my family. I got outside that circle with my very first class. It's about abundance, wellness, and purpose.

Abundance means you're financially free *and* have the time economy to do the things the Lord has called and created you to do. How do you do that when you are tied down at a 40-hour/week job and have nothing in the bank? That's not freedom. That's slavery. I am no longer a slave!

Wellness means you are educated on the Young Living products and living a life where you make conscious choices to take care of yourself.

Purpose means you take that healthy self of yours and pour into the people around you with the same passion that was poured into you. Keep the spark going. Show others how to be free. You are a hope-bringer. You are a path-changer. You were born for Diamond.

My goal with Gameplan is to show you how to get your own freedom. I'm here to train you how to start that ripple in your pond, and then how to fight for it. I want to see as many Diamonds packed onto that Young Living stage as possible.

IT'S TIME TO START

Remember the Income Disclosure Chart earlier in this chapter? John and I are Diamonds on that chart! Crazy, huh?? And it happened in less than three years. This is doable. You just have to understand the strategy of how to pull it off and that's what this book is about. It's a meat and potatoes, get-from-point-A-to-point-B book.

Read it, re-read it, highlight it, and make your own personal game plan by filling in the Gameplan workbook (which customizes this entire book for your team) and the Accountability Worksheet in the appendixes of this book. Read Gameplan once a year to regroup. Read it again if you plateau. Order Gameplan books (at oilabilityteam.com) for your leaders and get them on the same page. Use the scripts in the appendixes to rock this thing. This is your guide book. This will fill your head with ideas and you will see network marketing from a different, doable perspective.

That's what this book is—thousands of hours of study, trial, and error in our own business and fool proof tips that work; all in an easy to understand format. You'll find tips on how to fill classes, how to do this if you're shy, how to find new friend circles, how to do follow up, and how to raise leaders. All of this information is in one simple place. You don't need ten books to learn how to start this trade. Just one. This one.

A Young Living business is a mathematical certainty because the oils work

---

A Young Living business is a mathematical certainty because the oils work. The only thing that is uncertain is your commitment and dedication to see it through. The neat thing is that you are the one who controls commitment. You control your ability to dig out. So share the oils with people! A few will get a kit. Share again. A few more will get a kit. Share again the same month and follow up with the first few you talked with, and you'll have more people on your team; even a few who will share the oils with others. It grows and grows. Hold onto your hat, mentally prepare yourself for the abundance that's coming, and brace yourself for what's ahead!

You were made to be free. So call it out, speak life over yourself, and run! It's time to move. The place you are now is not giving you the results you're looking for. Your bucket list will remain unchanged in five years if you don't regroup, refocus, and make a plan. You are the only one with the power to alter the outcome.

This is your year to get your game on.

CHAPTER 2

SARAH'S STORY

So what does it take to rock a Young Living business? Do you have to already be successful in sales, have a huge circle of influence, or a background in natural health? I hope not, 'cause I don't have any of those.

You simply need a strong enough why.

For you to see the power of a personal why, you need to hear my story. To see why I'm so passionate about leading others to wellness and financial freedom, you have to understand a bit about where I came from. And maybe as you read you will begin to see that your past does not have to define you, but can be the fuel that drives you to succeed in this business.

A Rough Start

I grew up in suburban Chicago in a townhouse in a poor family. My father was an alcoholic and car mechanic, and my mother pretty much raised my three siblings and me single-handedly. My dad has been in more DUI crashes then I can count, is a convicted felon, and has lost his driver's license for life. The abuse was hard. I was the oldest of four children, and when the yelling got bad, I'd take my siblings into my bedroom and we'd have Amy Grant concerts, singing into a plastic ice cream cone as a microphone and cranking up the music so we could not hear. Many times I remember my mom waking us up, putting us in the car, and driving away; I wasn't sure if I'd see my dad again. Once, when I was in 4th grade, we stayed away for a full six months, living with my grandparents and aunt, and I had to enroll in a different school. But we always returned.

The neighborhood we lived in wasn't the greatest, either. Our subdivision was the drug trading ground for two gangs on either side of our community. I remember coming home from school one day to a drug raid going on in our subdivision. We had to sit there on the bus for 45 minutes as a helicopter flew overhead and SWAT teams entered the house.

I became engaged to my husband John when I was 16 years old, and we were married three years later. For the first ten years of our marriage, we had babies every two years, while holding down four minimum wage jobs and full-time college courses. We lived off student loans, racking up $70,000 in debt.

The first year of our marriage, John worked eight hours a day for minimum wage at a gas station. He also worked another full-time job at a competing gas station across the street eight hours on the overnight shift. He'd leave for one shift at 7 a.m., work until 5 p.m., come home and sleep four hours, and then go work another eight hour shift overnight. Then he would repeat it.

I typed addresses eight hours a day for a book publishing company (it's still the least favorite job I've ever had) and worked part-time for a Christian bookstore at night. I had a 21-hour course load in college as night classes, and was pregnant with our first son. That was our first year of marriage.

Below the Poverty Line

Just about every month, we got an eviction notice. Even with four jobs, we could not maintain our rental, so we moved in with my parents and hunkered down for three years. Then we lived in government housing in Dixon, Illinois, and then in government housing in DeKalb, Illinois.

We were on public aid for everything: our medical card, LIHEAP heating assistance, the LINK food card, three food pantries, WIC food, government housing assistance, cards through our church for gas. Even with four jobs, we were still getting disconnect notices. When you make $5/hour, it's really hard to make an $800/month rent. If anything, we knew it wasn't a handout. We physically could not take on more than four jobs between us. For a 12-year period we lived in extreme poverty, balancing full-time college coursework with multiple jobs, toddlers, and nursing.

During that time, I had 11 different jobs in the world of food service, until I caused the evacuation of a restaurant after setting a microwave on fire. *Twice.* (Food was not my niche!) Amidst all of that, I was prompted by a friend to apply for a job at a local radio station. I was hired there to work every other Saturday for three hour shifts, at $4/hour. My first month's check was $21 after taxes. (I kept my day job!)

John and I adjusted to poverty, even while I was entering the world of radio. At the first government housing projects where we lived in Dixon, there were "water bugs" (cockroaches) crawling on the floors. We had almost no furniture, and the kids slept on mattresses on the floor because we could not afford beds for them.

Feasting From the Food Pantry

We went through the transmissions in four used cars in six months. We'd go a few days with no food in the house; digging for a quarter to get a loaf of bread so the kids could eat, while John and I went hungry. We'd literally not have a morsel of food in the house, because when you have to choose between food or gas in your car to get to work, you pick the gasoline. I remember running out of meat for two weeks, waiting for the next food pantry to open. When I arrived, they were out of meat also, but had plenty of chocolate pudding. So, we ate chocolate pudding for a couple of days until our next food card went through.

We lived from food pantry to food pantry. We had more eviction notices and utility disconnect warnings then I can count, but the Lord always came through. A check from a relative would come within hours of our power being shut off. We'd use birthday card money to stave off eviction. After a few years of college and a few years in radio at a tiny station in a trailer in a corn field, I was offered a job in downtown Chicago anchoring news for an all-news station. It had an audience of seven million people. I thought I had arrived! My income was $35,000 a year!

What I didn't count on was that taxes, gas to drive 72 miles one-way into work each day, tolls, and parking in Chicago would take half my paycheck, and our family of seven would be living off $16,000 a year, and still on food stamps. I was on the air with personalities who were making millions of dollars a year, and we didn't have enough food for our children.

We had done it right. John worked full time and put me through college. I worked full time and put him through college. We both graduated with honors and took white collar jobs and started repaying $70,000 in student loans. We had followed the system, and we were drowning. 12 years after I had graduated from college, I still owed $18,000 on my student loan, and my oldest son has already started college himself. This is the American life??! This is living the dream??

Weary worker, I know you have been there. Many of your stories are even harder than ours. That's why you *have* to take this seriously. You don't need to work this hard.

Dream Job

After John and I graduated, I was offered a position with a Christian radio network in upstate New York.

It was a wonderful ministry, but it meant leaving everything we knew behind: our family, our friends, our church, and the doctors who had delivered our babies. It was crazy hard. But there was the possibility of work for my husband, who had looked for a job for 15 months in Chicago without a single serious offer. And I had prayed for 11 years to work in Christian radio on morning drive so I could be home during the day to homeschool my kids. This was my dream job.

I remember a few nights before Christmas, days before the move from Chicago to upstate New York, I'd tossed my name into a lottery with the Salvation Army. We hadn't had a paycheck in six weeks and had borrowed from the station for the move. Food was scarce. Christmas wasn't even on the radar. We had just a few dollars in our bank account. That morning, I got a call that our family's name had been chosen in a lottery, and I was to come in and pick out new gifts for our kids.

I walked into that high school gym and saw all the things people had donated—brand new gifts—piled high three-quarters of the way up the gym wall. I was allowed to pick out a new jacket, boots, hats, gloves, a board game, and three presents for each child. I walked out with three 44-gallon garbage bags of the best toys my kids had ever owned and a turkey for Christmas dinner.

I sat in my car with all those new gifts in the backseat and lost it. Twelve years of poverty caught up with me. I wept harder then I'd ever had: tears of joy at the gifts of strangers, and how they'd made our Christmas that year, and tears of fear, that I didn't know how long our money famine was going to continue. We worked so hard, yet there we were, with $70,000 in student loans, a car payment, a van payment, credit card debt, and absolutely nothing to show for it at the end of the day but an empty stomach, five little blue-eyed faces trusting us to take care of them, and a government-subsidized townhouse. I was so overwhelmed.

Praying Like Moses

That was when I prayed a prayer I'll never forget. I took several minutes and thanked God for every single gift in that car, for the turkey on my front seat, and for all that He had provided. We always had just enough. And we made it because of Him and Him alone. I thanked Him for how He loved us. But then I got bold, and I asked for something more. I asked to be totally rich—beyond my wildest dreams. I asked to make more than I could spend. I prayed for the Moses blessing. Moses waited for 40 days on that mountain to see God, and when He appeared, His glory was so great that Moses was face down on the ground. He never even got to see Him. I asked for the blessing to be so great, we couldn't even use it all or see the swath of what the Lord had given.

It wasn't because John and I wanted to own our own jet or mansion; it was because every single person we knew lived just like us. There was no way out. There was no hope. For 12 years of our marriage, all we'd done was take from people out of desperation. I was asking the Lord to be the giver. I wanted to be able to give as much as people had given to me, and I couldn't do that when we barely had food. I wanted to live on 10% of my income and give the rest of it away.

Seven years later, God answered that prayer. For my 36th birthday in 2014, a Young Living premium starter kit showed up on my door. This is the box that started it all!

A New Adventure

My husband told me if I wanted to get oils every month, I'd have to teach a class and have a few people sign up under me. So without any strategy and without any sales background, I started teaching oils classes. I grabbed a bunch of aromatherapy encyclopedias and from them wrote a little 3-page 101 script chronicling all the things I'd love to know about oils: the who, what, when, where, why and how of oils. Then I gathered a few friends on the couch in my living room and read it. I have given that script 206 times all over the country now; it is the number one reason we hold the rank we hold. (The script is in the appendix of this book!)

But for my first class, on July 18, 2014, I was completely terrified. I'd done radio for nearly two decades, but that meant staring at a wall six hours a day in a room all by myself. I never had to look at the people I was talking to, so this was a whole new ball game! Gone were the days of wearing pajamas to work and anchoring news barefoot. (People looked at me quite strangely when I tried to pull that off in an oils class!) If you had seen my knees knocking, you would have thought it was comical with my work background. (So don't beat yourself up if you have butterflies! Even famous people that talk to millions of people get them! You're not human if you don't have a little fear!) How did I get through it? I doused myself in Valor oil (Stress Away works, too!), prayed a lot, and just read the script.

After I taught my first class, three people signed up. I was in total shock. I didn't think anyone would listen to a word I had to say! Three others who couldn't make it for the class met me for lunch and by the end of the month I was off and running. I had a team of six and was a Young Living Star. My goal that month was to make $50 so I could get on Essential Rewards and get my oils for free. But my first paycheck was enough to pay my husband back for the starter kit, get on Essential Rewards, and still have nearly half my check to invest in the business!

I realized pretty fast that I wasn't going to be able to teach during the week, because I was still anchoring news at 4 a.m. every day. A 7 p.m. class was impossible for me because that was my bedtime. So I decided to teach a class Friday night and Saturday morning, then take the next weekend off. In August, I taught four classes total. That was a commitment of eight hours a month. I did another two hours of follow-up calls to people. That month, my check paid my $800 mortgage payment—and my oils!

Eight weeks into my business, I made Executive. Eighteen days after Executive, I made Silver. In 12 weeks, I had surpassed 16 years of anchoring income by working less than a quarter of the hours. Five months later, I was Gold. Eight months after that, Platinum! A little more than a year later, Diamond. How? By teaching classes slow and steady, and committing to treat this opportunity as a business, not a hobby.

Retired From Radio

In January, six months after receiving my kit, my husband asked me when I was going to start taking the business seriously, and I told him, "I don't know, Harnisch. You told me to teach oils classes to get my oils for free, so I'm teaching classes, just like you told me!"

But my soft-spoken, gentle-spirited husband replied with, "Are you paying attention? You are making more and working less! I know how much you love it, but it's time to let go of your anchoring job." It took me nine months to get up the courage to step off full-time radio. (I still fill in, just because I love radio so much.) But almost exactly a year after I started Young Living, I was able to retire even though I had no previous network marketing experience. I took a photo of my face the last day I anchored full-time and a photo of my face three weeks later—with eight hours of sleep each night. I look like a totally different person!

Less stress, more family time, better balance in my mommy life.

Please understand, never will I take my years anchoring news for granted. Never do I take the generosity of the radio ministry for granted, or their graciousness in allowing me to step off morning drive and yet still fill in. Never will I take any job for granted, really—no matter where the Lord leads me. But to have such a large prayer answered—I have no answer for that, save the grace of God.

I learned so much in that first year. I made a lot of mistakes. I've been discouraged, and I've been blown away. I've grown and been stretched and have been loved and hated. I'm starting to learn what matters and what to let go. I've picked up pieces and put them together again and then dropped it all on the floor once more. I have ten thousand mistakes and ten thousand victories ahead of me. This book would have saved me over and over and over again, had it been written. This is my game plan. This is how I ranked.

Reaching Diamond

When I started Young Living, we were living in a 1,300 square foot house with a finished off garage bay as extra bedrooms for our children. Since we hit Diamond, we have been able to pay off over $250,000 in debt and buy our new home debt free. We were also able to hold onto our old home to provide a home for my father. Below are some photos of my kids seeing their new bedrooms for the very first time. The first photo is a picture of the garage bay of our old home in May of 2017, where we had three bedrooms. We had used bookcases as dividing walls and sheets for doorways.

Our lives have turned 180 degrees from the direction we were facing. Before Young Living, we had no hope. We had no way out. We had no focus. I was doing the same things I had been doing for years that were not yielding results. My heart's desires and bucket lists and dream lists sat untouched. My oldest son was 18, and we had still never been on a family vacation. We were drowning in debt and drowning in stress. I had not been able to share some of my childhood memories with my kids, because we didn't have the means. I could not feed them the way I wanted to or make sure I was taking care of my own body.

Now, I am able to cross things off that list. We are thriving! I can truly say "poverty over." I have created a legacy income for my children; knowing that they will never live in the projects, they will always have food in their stomachs, they will always have the lights on and heat in their homes. At a Diamond income, they are cared for forever. It's so much better than a life insurance policy that's gone in a year or a lifetime of saving in a 401k that leaves no legacy. I get to spend the rest of my life watching the same thing happen to all of my leaders — and to all of you.

All I can say is, it was worth it. It was worth it. It was worth it. It was worth it.

NOW IT'S YOUR TURN

I know that each person is unique and has different gifts and talents. I know my road may not be your road; that my pace may not be your pace, and my tactics may not work for you. I won't claim that Gameplan can get you to Diamond—that's all you! I advocate for any system developed by any Young Living Diamond, because if they have made it to Diamond, they have guaranteed results. Gameplan is only one way to get from Point A to Point B.

But I also know there are tools in this book that will save you a lot of time. There are resources here that took me quite a while to find, and if I couldn't find them, I wrote them. If I can save you time, you may have a shorter path to Diamond than I did. One of my life goals is to help every person I possibly can to become financially free. When you are financially free, you have time economy and wealth to invest in the lives of those around you. The best way I can help other people to avoid the life I had is to give them the tools to stand.

Read, be blessed, pass this book on, and teach others what you have learned. Don't let the secrets of this book sit on a shelf. Share it. Hand it off to a budding leader. Hand it off to someone who needs inspiration, a team member who is frustrated, stuck, desperate, or who needs a way out. One of the things that makes Young Living so wonderful is that it's about helping other people. You thrive when your team soars. I have had so many people ask me who this book was written for. It's not just for my team or my friends' teams. It's not even just for those in Young Living. It's for anyone who has a dream and wants to see that their dream is possible. Any team, any person, any dream, anywhere.

So take this book and fly!

Never lose your fight. Remember who you are: you are a #DIAMONDRISING!

I just wanted to tell you, I'm sitting outside in the sunlight reading the Gameplan book. I just read the first two chapters and started crying. I'm sitting outside because my electric was just shut off. I was doing a great job for years putting on a front to everyone that everything is just great. Lately I've been just too exhausted to keep up the front. My husband is permanently disabled and many days can't get out of bed, therefore needs someone here pretty much 24/7. He has been falling a lot lately and has fewer and fewer good days where he can actually walk with his walker. It's sad, but everything comes down to money. He'd have a better life, my four kids would have a better life and I would as well. Anyway, as I'm reading your story I just lost it and cried. Just knowing I'm not the only one who has gone through this, that I'm not a bad mom even though my kids don't have everything they need, that I'm not a bad person. Reading this has given me so much hope, a light at the end of the tunnel. If I work for it, it WILL pay off. Not in 20 years, but now. So I just wanted to thank you, thank you for sharing your story. Now on to chapter 3! I need to learn the right way, most effective and efficient way to work this business! Thank you, again.

Nancy

CHAPTER 3

A YOUNG LIVING QUICK-START TRAINING GUIDE

I told you earlier that the number one question I'm asked is, "Why do a Young Living business?" If that's the most common question, the second thing I hear is, "how?"

This is going to be the quickest training you've ever seen! It's just two steps.

1) Photocopy the 101 Script out of the Gameplan Appendix. Read it a few times.

2) Open your calendar, schedule a class, get a few people to your couch, and read the 101 Script.

You are off and running! Book over! (Just kidding!) If you like, we can add a third step: "rinse and repeat."

It's the repeat that will get you to Diamond. So it's simple, but it will require diligence. Let's dig deeper into what that day-to-day diligence looks like.

RINSE AND REPEAT

I tell my business builders, if you do the above steps four to six times a month, that's generally enough volume to reach the rank of Silver in six months, depending on your class size. It takes me less than 30 minutes to read the script top down, and about two hours from start to finish with questions and time to build relationships (though if your classes run longer, don't sweat it—you are personally investing in people!) Just for the sake of math, if your classes last two hours with setup and tear-down, that's a commitment of 12 hours a month. A Silver income is usually $2,000 to $3,000 a month. Fewer than three hours of work a week for that check is not a bad deal! If you can commit 40 hours a week—160 hours a month—to a job that will not give you freedom, surely you can commit 12 hours a month to a weekly 2-hour class and follow up for a business that will grow and set you up for retirement.

At the beginning, it's tough. You're pushing a snowball up a hill. You're launching your team, and you're going to have to run your Young Living business alongside your life. You'll have to wiggle it in where it best fits. For me, that meant no weeknight classes, because my job had me up at 3 a.m. to prep for the start of that 4 a.m. shift. But as your check grows, you can start kicking a few things off your plate.

A year into my Young Living journey, one of the things I was able to let go of was my full-time job. There are people on my team who dropped second and third jobs. Some add services to save time; for example, one woman on my team added a cleaning service at $25/week. Some have used the extra income to have organic food delivered twice a week so they can answer emails instead of cook. Others have paid mommy helpers $20 a week so they have time carved out for their business.

Ultimately, any such choice creates more space for Young Living. Once you reach Silver, that snowball is starting to roll down the hill on its own. It means more time to step away, to be with your family, train leaders, rest, and regroup.

I now limit myself to three classes a month and a leadership training every Tuesday night online. That's six hours of work, plus a couple hours a week of follow up and answering emails. It's pretty sweet for a Diamond income! Admittedly I work harder during Oil Ability retreats, bootcamps, or when I'm doing things like writing a Gameplan book; but those are short, rare bursts of work. My average workweek now is about 10-15 hours. My average anchoring week was closer to 40, with 60-hour spikes. I believe I got the better deal with Young Living.

KNOW YOUR WHY

The critical thing to nail down as you begin is your "why." In layman's terms, you have to know why it is that you're doing this. Sit down and think through your reasons. If it's to replace an entire income, you should be teaching four to six classes a month. If it's to get your oils for free or double your grocery budget or go on a vacation, one class a month would be enough. If you treat this business as a business, you'll get paid as a business. If you treat it as a hobby, you'll get paid as a hobby. Make a commitment, set your hours, and run with it! Then watch it grow. A word of caution: it grows *fast*.

If you treat this business as a business, you'll get paid as a business.

Here's your action step for this chapter: sit down, grab a sheet of paper, and write out why you want this. If you're crafty, clip a few photos out of some magazines and make a photo collage vision board to show where you want to end up. (It sounds like a waste of time, but it truly does work! It's about keeping tangible goals front and center, every single day.) You can even run to a Walmart, or Michaels, or Hobby Lobby, and pick up a canvas board to glue your pictures on, but it doesn't have to be fancy.

I'd encourage you to put specific, tangible goals on the board; goals for your OGV, for your rank, and for your paycheck. Don't just cut out photos—pick words of life that you want spoken over your business, and add them to the board, too.

Put your vision board in a place where you'll see it, like a bathroom or bedroom wall. Pray over it. Revisit it a few months into your business and see if your why has changed.

As I shared in Chapter One, my first why was simply to afford oils. Then it became paying off debt. Then my goal was to get my kids on the Global Leadership Cruise to Venice. Since all of those things have happened (the things I put on that board *always* seem to happen!) now, my vision board is about seeing all of my friends become financially free. My vision board keeps changing because I keep reaching the goals!

You will meet your goals if you see them every day and work every day toward your goal. There is power in the spoken word. It changes the direction of your feet and your mind when you deliberately speak life over yourself out loud.

PART TWO

Making Your First
Class Successful

I read Gameplan and went through the Gameplan bootcamp in the very first month of my business. I felt like starting off with all of that information and tips, as well as my upline's mentorship, helped me achieve Silver in my second month of the business. I didn't waste anytime figuring things out, I studied and knew exactly what I needed to do. Classes, education, get people on ER and do it again and again! We are on the verge of hitting Gold now and Gameplan is the first book I recommend to all of my builders, or even those slightly interested!

Nicole Matteson

*Being a little bit on the quieter side, the scripts in Gameplan helped me sell four kits at my **first** class! Thank you Sarah!*

Dawn Courtney

Having Gameplan in my hands is like having a leader from my upline right there with me! From determining my next move, class prep, great class scripts, to a powerful close... BOOM! It's all in your book—and so much more! Thank you for sharing a solid, concise business plan-of-action to take us from starter kit to success!

Joy Cooke

CHAPTER 4

Avoiding Pitfalls:
The Six Mistakes Every Stagnant
Business Builder Makes

Why are we talking about mistakes before we've hardly started? Because if I point them out, you can avoid these pitfalls from the very beginning of your business.

In the first 18 months, I launched my business and hand-trained about 800 business builders. Some are now Gold rank and beyond. Many are Silvers. Many more are Executives and Senior Stars. When you train that many people, a pattern forms. Every time one of my business builders is stagnant, they fall into one of these six categories:

1) They don't have a strong close to wrap up their lecture. ("Tell me how to buy Young Living!") This book is full of training and scripts to help you share the oils with confidence and have a strong close.

2) They keep tapping into the same friend circles. I tell you how to avoid this mistake in Chapter Eight.

3) They don't market enough, or give enough lead time be-fore a class. Again, Chapter Eight has your answers with a complete plan for marketing your classes.

4) They don't have a system for following up with people who came to class or bought a kit. Check out Chapter Ten for all the tools you need.

5) They don't treat their business as a business. They vision cast, read leadership books, and go to events, but never get out and actually teach.

   You can't grow a business without teaching in some form, even if it's handing out CD's or DVD's. Step outside your comfort zone. (See Chapter Five on how to teach that first class! It's as hard as grabbing a three-page script, reading it in front of faces, and rinsing and repeating. You CAN do this!)

6) They get distracted. This one is so important that I wrote a whole chapter on it at the end of this book. Check out Chapter 23. Distraction will kill your business.

   Wake up every day with a list of three business goals and attack them. Don't bite off more than you can chew. Learn to gently say no to things that rob your time. Commit time to your business every day, even if it's an hour. And don't pour into things that don't grow your business.

   What is distraction? Making a store instead of raising leaders. Attending tons of leadership training but never actually holding classes. Going for an aromatherapy cer-tification. Getting on Facebook to connect with your team and then wasting time scrolling through your timeline instead. Doing crossline classes but never growing your own legs. Those are distractions, and I have done them all! Are the things you're doing actually pouring into your business or pulling from it? How do you spend your time? Is it productive?

   Make a list of what you need to do to reach the next rank, and then do it—and nothing else.

If you can avoid the six things listed above (and this book teaches you how), you can have a flourishing business.

Now don't get me wrong—this list isn't about when you have to take a break. If you have a major family emergency, you are living through a crisis. Just as you would at a regular job, you take time off. In the same breath, I'll tell you that if you don't go to work every week at your 40-hour-a-week job, you get no paycheck. When the crisis ends, return to your Young Living business. How can you grow a paycheck without working your business? Don't wait for it to come to you. Fight for it!

But for people who are actively holding classes and not seeing growth, it's usually because of one or more of the six items above. So identify your weakness and follow the plan to avoid those pitfalls!

CHAPTER 5

OVERCOMING EXCUSES AND FINDING YOUR NICHE

I cannot tell you how many times people come up to me and make one or more of the following excuses:

"I don't know any people."

"I live in a rural area."

"I am not a news anchor."

"I don't have the influence you have."

"I don't have the time you have."

"I don't have the money to start a business."

"I can't stand in front of people."

"I have children and no babysitter."

"I work too many hours."

"I don't want anyone in my house."

"I don't like to sell stuff."

Yes, I pulled out my inner momma bear and I used the word "excuses." Because that's exactly what those are. When you want something, you find a way around the mountain without complaint. You find someone who did it before you and learn from them. If their way doesn't work for you, find another person with a way that does. You fight for it, and you dig out of where you are.

Let's tackle these challenges head on.

LOCATION

My strongest teams live in extremely rural areas with limited resources. My Eldred, PA team regularly draws 100-person crowds for classes, but you have to drive 12 miles from the highway to get a cell signal there. It's in the middle of the Alleghany forest, which runs half the length of western Pennsylvania.

On the opposite end of the coin, I regularly hear that people can't hold classes in a certain town because of "saturation." Saturation??? That's what happens when you put too much butter on your popcorn. It's not a concept that affects your Young Living business. I've been told that they can't teach in a certain area because too many people in that town are holding classes.

One woman, who lives in a town of 12,000, gave me the same story. I told her there are 3,000 people on my team, and that as soon as we cross 12,000 and every member on my team was from that town, then it's officially saturated. The issue is tapping into new friend circles, not market saturation. We'll attack that in a later chapter.

I also have had quite a few people tell me they really don't want anyone in their home. That's fine. Either find a free location within 20 minutes or so (libraries, fire halls, community centers, churches)—or ask a friend to loan you their living room. If you want this, you will find creative ways to make it work. One woman on our team even used the local state park's picnic pavilions for six months, when it was warm enough, until she had found a better location.

MONEY

There's no overhead with Young Living, save a starter kit. It's the cheapest business on the planet to start! Franchises cost about $200,000 to $500,000 per store. Not Young Living. There's no store front, no rent to pay, no employees to pay, no insurance, no utilities—the oils literally go straight from the Young Living farms and warehouses to people's homes. There's just you, your starter kit, and your 101 Script. That's all this takes.

I'll be honest with you: it took me about five weeks to save for my kit. A bunch of times, I kept asking myself why I was putting cash into a box for oils instead of getting more food for the house or taking my van in to find out what the knocking sound was. I'll tell you now that Young Living was the best financial decision I've made in my life! I wish I'd made it when I was 20 years old.

The investment of the kit is a fraction of what you'd pay to launch any other small business. I had one friend in a different multi-level marketing company that had to stock $5,000 of product in her home, then transport it from site to site for her classes. That's crazy! All the ordering is done through Young Living's site. You don't need to stock a thing for anyone else—just show up with your own personal kit. Your job is to get that kit in front of as many people as you can. No inventory required.

Do whatever it takes to get that starter kit in your hand; hold a yard sale, tuck $30 a week away out of groceries (that's what I did), pick up some babysitting or some extra house cleaning jobs—just pull it off. You'll be so glad you did.

INFLUENCE

Right now, this month, I have more than 800 active business builders who aren't news anchors, and they are doing just fine. They're all growing at their own pace. Some are Gold and some are Stars, but their rank doesn't matter much to me. The fact that they are out there running their business without being famous is what matters. Some of my top leaders are the most soft-spoken people on my team.

It's not fame that grows a business. It's rolling up your sleeves and holding classes! I don't know people, either. I moved from Chicago to rural upstate New York, and the largest population center in my town is the county jail. Again, it comes down to friend circles—not who you know. It's who your friends know. Our Oil Ability system for filling classes works (see Chapter Seven and Chapter Eight). Influence is not necessary. Tenacity is.

TIME

So many people come to me and tell me they want to do this. I hand train them and then four months go by and they've added two people. When I contact them and ask what's up, they tell me, "I just don't have the time." Seriously? Young Living is *your way out*. Look at all the things going on in your life right now that consume all you have. Young Living is time economy.

I tell people all the time when I train them that the Lord isn't going to bless you with more time if you aren't using the time you have now wisely. It's a gift. It's one of the greatest gifts, actually. If you're not a good steward of your time, you'll always need more time.

Look at your schedule, find two hours for a class each week, and make it happen. Cut other things out to make it fit. Bring your kids with you if you have to (my oldest four have taught 206 classes faithfully by my side!)

As your team and your income grow, you'll be able to re-evaluate other places where you can save yourself more time. Yes, it's a juggling act. This mom of five who was working 40 hours a week and homeschooling gets it. If you want out, you have to make your doorway and walk through it. No excuses.

Here's the deal: you can either start the business or not start the business. If you speak life into your business, you'll flourish and grow. If you speak death and talk of all the reasons you can't pull it off, you'll never get off the ground. Start each day by knowing where you're going and run for it. Make a plan. Then do it. No excuses. (In the same breath, don't over-plan. Jay Carter, my Diamond upline, makes a list of three business items each morning. When those three are done, he's done for the day. Make it manageable.)

"I DON'T WANT TO SELL STUFF"

This is the statement that irritates me the most. I've never sold a starter kit in my life! From day one, from the very first class in my living room, to today—when I speak to auditoriums of thousands of people, it's always been about education. I have a passion to help people live a chemical free life. Every oil they're using is a chemical they're not using.

Let me share why chemical-free living means so much to me.

When I was 12 years old, I had my first migraine headache. It was debilitating. By age 22, I was having them monthly, and they lasted ten days, and followed the bell curve of my cycle. With each child I had in my 20's, they got worse and worse. I worked with 13 neurologists and was on 16 families of migraine medicines over the space of twenty-four years. By age 32, the headaches were so crippling that I would lie in bed, grabbing my knees writhing in pain in a room of total darkness. I went into cycles of vomiting and tremoring from the pain and would get dehydrated.

Most months, I went to the local emergency room for a migraine cocktail, a trio of three drugs given intravenously—a pain medicine, an anti-inflammatory and a drug to stop throwing up. They started doing yearly MRI's on me, and found that every time I had a migraine, the blood vessels in my head would swell and cause tiny, pin-prick brain bleeds. Each year, I had about 30-40 more spots of dead tissue on the surface of my brain. And every month, the right side of my face would droop and half my body would go numb until the migraine was gone.

The last neurologist I saw wanted me on six medications: all the ones listed above as well as a steroid and two medicines to counteract the side effects of the first four medications I'd be on. The steroid alone had two pages of warnings, most heart-related. I told the neurologist I felt like I was choosing between a heart attack and a stroke. He said, "You are. But if it was me, I'd choose the heart attack. If you have a stroke, you'll watch your kids grow up but will never be able to communicate with them. That would be worse than just being gone." I remember driving away thinking, *"How dare you make that choice for me?"*

I took the medications home and lined them up on my counter. I was going to be on drugs every two hours for the rest of my life. John and I are not anti-pharmaceutical, and I have over 45 nurses on my oils team, but something about this specific situation just didn't sit right. I did not have peace.

So I started using what I knew about researching news and applied it to researching my own health. Was there anyone out there who had been cured of migraine headaches? I stumbled on a neurologist named Natasha Campbell-McBride. She had cured thousands of people in her office of neurological and digestive disorders simply by changing their diet and cutting all sugar, gluten, and dairy. Her website is called gapsdiet.com. I started her diet (which I'm convinced is the most masochistic thing on the earth) in January of 2013.

The first month, I still had the drooping in my face and the numbness on my right side; but I had no pain. I remember telling my husband, "if this is as good as it gets—it's good enough for me! I don't remember what a life of no pain feels like!"

The second month I had no drooping, no weakness and no pain. I'm proud to say that I've been completely migraine free for nearly four years. I have not taken a single medication since 2013, after over 20 years on meds. I did it solely by changing what I was eating.

The foods I'd been eating were loaded with processed garbage, hydrogenated oils, soy, nitrates, dyes, preservatives, synthetic, enriched vitamins and chemicals. Those ingredients, over time, punctured holes in my gut lining until my body couldn't function the way it was designed. For me, it metastasized as migraine headaches. For others, it's food allergies, IBS, Crone's Disease, unexplained inflammation or pain, or a host of other illnesses. What I was eating was literally killing me.

I'd love to say that oils had a hand in eradicating my migraines, but I was healed of them long before I got my starter kit. What it did do, though, was open my eyes to what's out there. Not everything that's in a store is safe. Not everything that has "FDA approval" is safe. If gluten, sugar, and dairy (we're talking a bowl of ice cream and a sandwich), could puncture holes in my gut lining; what about the bright blue chemical-laden dish soap that I wash my dishes with and then eat off of? What about the chemical cleaning supplies with ingredients I can't even begin to pronounce, that I wipe my butcher block with, in the name of sanitizing? Then I read the bottle and it says, "Don't eat, poisonous, not for human consumption." Three days later, I am dicing strawberries and eating them right off the same butcher block that smells like chemical cleaner. We're oblivious. And we're poisoning ourselves.

This is why it's so critical that you take oils seriously, and you share them with every person that you meet. Start the swap from chemical cleaning supplies first if you're not sure where to begin. Young Living's Thieves cleaner alone replaced every cleaner under my kitchen sink—and it's made of plants! There's no yuck!

I am passionate about oils because I have lived through the other side of slowly poisoning myself and my family. I will do everything I can, even teach a million classes, if it saves one family from what I have gone through. For me, it's all about education—it's never been about sales. I'm bold and tell them where I started my journey and I have no fear of walking them through ordering a Young Living starter kit. There's passion behind the purpose: it's to save them. This is serious, and there is a haste to it, because with each passing day someone out there is getting hurt. You can't do what you were called and created to do if you have lost your health.

Always know the place where your student is coming from—the place you were when you first got your kit. Return to that place and walk them through so they see the dangers in their own home. This isn't about selling. It's absolutely always about education.

Now with those excuses out of the way, I'll give you one get-out-of-jail-free pass.

THE ONE LEGITIMATE EXCUSE

There is one legitimate excuse, and it's the, "I can't stand in front of people" line. God made us all with unique talents. We're different, and that means we all have creative ways of sharing Young Living. If you would rather *die* than stand in front of a room full of people, let me encourage you with some of the stories from my team, and give you some creative ideas to help you find your unique way of sharing Young Living.

Myrna grew her team to 10,000 OGV a month (a Silver in Six)—simply by mailing our Oil Ability 101 DVD to her friends and doing great follow up one-on-one. We now offer an audio CD of the 101 class that people can listen to in their cars. Here's what Oil Ability leader Bethany says about the CD:

> "Sarah, I LOVE your CD's!!!! In my opinion, hands down, the best tool you've given us yet! I sold a kit today with one...I gave it to a lady at church and by the time I got home she had ordered her kit!!! People can listen in their car.... it's so easy to do!!"

(Pick the audio CD's up at oilabilityteam.com).

Robyn runs her entire business by looking for people she can bless. Her focus is on those who need the income the most. She has never taught an in-person class, but every time I do a Teacher Training in her area, it's loaded with potential business builders. She has an eye for talent, and for those in need.

Stephanie grows by putting the oils on people. She loves handing out samples and letting people see how the oils can support their systems. Her team cracked Star in a month using only this method. She is also a genius at seeing a need for people to have a good income and raises as many leaders as she does 101 classes. She is extremely gifted at edifying her leaders and recognition of them. People will go to the end of the world for Stephanie because of her strong leadership.

Rachael works three jobs and is new to the area. She held 11 classes and no one came to the last five classes. So she started meeting people one-on-one over lunch. Using that method only, she rose to a Senior Star. When I did our marketing training with her, she implemented it and had a class with eight people and a class with 20. She also raised up four new leaders in a week, and they are now off the ground with their own Young Living businesses. By August of 2016 she was able to retire from all three jobs! Rachael is now a strong Silver on her way to Gold!

Joel just moved to North Carolina and he's a brand new first time dad. He's young—just 21 years old. But he's determined to beat Adam Green (sorry, Adam!) and become the youngest Royal Crown Diamond in Young

Living history (by age 24). He grows fast by putting up flyers in health food stores and bulk food stores and Salvation Army stores. He makes contacts with chiropractors to have places to teach across the area and markets to areas already clean-living driven, areas that will get excited about Young Living. He enrolled nine people his first month.

Theresa does vendor events where she can talk to people one-on-one, because she's personable and loves sharing knowledge. Her goal is to help people understand how they can use the oils. She is education driven. She's also a very gifted writer and her blog has taken off on-line. She thrives on seeing others "get" concepts and then apply them to live a chemical-free lifestyle. But her greatest strength is leadership. She writes a weekly newsletter and connects with her team on the oils and oily products on Young Living's site. She raises leaders and builds intimate relationships with them. When I met her, she was living in a trailer with her family and had to make a choice between medicine for her non-verbal autistic son and club foot surgery for another son. She had no stove in her home. She is now a solid Silver with a powerful and dynamic team of leaders, en route to Gold, and she is planning for her husband's retirement. This was a total game changer for her family. Poverty: 0–Theresa's family: 1.

Sharon is a genius at follow up. Though shy, she's incredible at hand-written notes and resources. She spends hours at her desk each week putting something personable together for her team members. She mails out Oil Ability DVD's with hand written notes. Her OGV just cracked 30,000 and despite her quiet personality, she's on her way to Gold this year. She was married for 40 years to an abusive, alcoholic husband with multiple DUI's. After a year and a half in her Young Living business, Sharon is now financially free and dependent on him for nothing. Her Young Living check is now twice her pay at her full time job! She just purchased her own home after renting for more than eight years.

Aaron plays to his gifts. A natural salesman, with a decade and a half in sales, but he had a hard time making the jump from a brick and mortar store to network marketing. He markets to businesses, because he understands business. It took him a while to warm up to the oils and then to warm up to the business side. But his warm personality allowed him to start sharing the oils with his inner friend circle and then his circle of clients from his brick and mortar job. Now he is catapulting into the world of network marketing. His heart's desire is to be home with his wife and two babies so they can enjoy more family time. On average, he spent 12 hours daily at the sales job, and 16 hours during peak sales times. His Young Living "why" is freedom.

Angela holds 101 classes, but her focus is on prayer and where God can use the money. She prays heavily and mightily over her business. She just made Silver in Six and donated her entire check to a cancer patient for treatment and to a family in poverty (and a few other charities!). When you keep Christ as the center of your business and lean on Him for every decision, He multiplies your efforts.

By the way, I used each person's real name (with permission). These are real people like you and me. They are all members of the Oil Ability team. Most have just started in the past six months, and they're thriving in Young Living.

Here's the trick: each person has a niche. Maybe it's teaching—either lecture style, in front of people, or by playing hostess and simply popping my 101 DVD in the T.V. and letting me teach for you. It could be in front of one or ten or 50 people. Maybe it's strong follow up, with hand written cards and personalized letters and notes. Maybe it's vendor events or make-and-take classes. Maybe it's one-on-one's over lunch. Maybe it's online work—building your business through social media, blogging, and video. Maybe it's a theme—you love animal aromatherapy, or biblical aromatherapy, or beauty school classes and full orchid facials with Young Living products.

Take the skills you already have and use that as your starting place to launch your business. If you are gifted with people, begin there. If you are a gifted writer, begin sharing in that way. If you are technically gifted or gifted online, start from that place. Don't try to develop new skills you have never had when you are first launching your business (like starting a blog when you have never run one before)—lean on what you already know and share from that place. That's where your fire is.

Whatever your gift is, play to it. Delegate your weaknesses to others. But above all, pray, give your business to the Lord, and keep Him as your center. Then watch it grow!

CHAPTER 6

Your Greatest Tool:
A Detailed Tour of the
Young Living Virtual Office

This is the part of the book where we really start getting into the meat and potatoes. How do you actually run a Young Living business? By this point, you should have found the 101 notes at the end of this book (or at oilabilityteam.com) and picked a location and date for your first class. After you hold it and get past that fear of the unknown, read the next few chapters of this book. I will walk you through one entire cycle of a Young Living business: marketing, filling classes, holding classes, and follow up. By the time you're done, you'll be a pro!

This chapter is pretty neat, because Young Living has done a lot of the work for you online. You don't really need any costly business tools, just about all of it is offered through the Virtual Office. This is where you track your online presence, your team, your rank, and more. All of it can be viewed online by going to www.youngliving.com, clicking on "Sign In," and using the username and password you set up when you got your starter kit. If you're not sure what those are, you can phone Young Living and they will send you new ones.

Once you have logged in, you'll be looking at your Dashboard, which looks something like this:

There are three tabs across the top. Those are Summary (which takes you back to the main page), Rank Qualification, and Getting Started. Then there are a bunch of buttons down the left side of the page. I'd really encourage you to spend an afternoon just exploring all the information and resources here! I'll give you a little explanation of each, but I'll go in depth on the two most important buttons—how to watch yourself, and how to watch your team. Let's start with the top tabs.

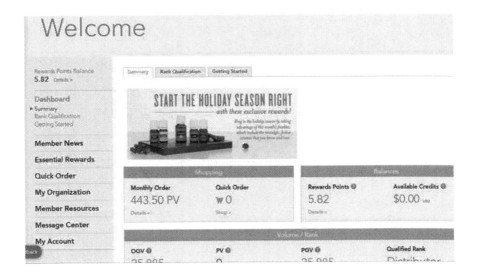

"GETTING STARTED"

The "Getting Started" tab is fantastic and gives you a series of short, 3-minute videos that tell you exactly who Young Living is and what we stand for. Watch them all. My favorite is the Seed to Seal page with videos on why Young Living is so different from other oils companies. It's what sets us apart.

"RANK QUALIFICATION"

Next, click on Rank Qualification. This is the all important "How to Watch Yourself" button. It looks like this:

Distributor	Star	Senior Star	Executive	Silver	Gold	Platinum	Diamond	Crown Diamond	Royal Crown Diamond
100 PV	100 PV	100 PV	100 PV	100 PV	100 PV	100 PV	100 PV	100 PV	100 PV
	500 OGV	2K OGV	4K OGV	10K OGV	35K OGV	100K OGV	250K OGV	750K OGV	1.5M OGV
			2 x 1K OGV Legs	2 x 4K OGV Legs	3 x 6K OGV Legs	4 x 8K OGV Legs	5 x 15K OGV Legs	6 x 20K OGV Legs	6 x 35K OGV Legs
				1,000 PGV	1,000 PGV	1,000 PGV	1,000 PGV	1,000 PGV	1,000 PGV
				19,381.75	19,381.75	19,381.75	19,381.75	19,381.75	19,381.75

If you look across the top, you'll see all the ranks that were in the income disclosure guide at the front of this book. These are the ranks in Young Living: Distributor, Star, Senior Star, Executive, Silver, Gold, Platinum, Diamond, Crown Diamond, and Royal Crown Diamond.

Understanding How You Rank

There are four requirements to move up to the next rank. Two are crazy easy to get, and the other two require persistence and strategy.

Line 1: PV

If you want your full paycheck, you need to spend 100 PV a month. The good news is that you never need to spend more just because your check goes up—it stays at 100 PV all the way to Royal Crown Diamond.

People ask me all the time why Young Living requires them to purchase 100 PV in product to get a paycheck. Honestly, I'm grateful for it. The products I've ordered have made me much more familiar with the company and what they offer. I could never talk knowledgeably about Pure Protein Complete if I hadn't had it in my glass of raw milk this morning. You can't talk about what you don't know. It also supports your team and your check. If all your leaders are spending 100 PV, it contributes greatly to the team volume.

One word of caution: I have had people on my team place an order under 100PV, and are poised to lose their check at the end of the month. Make sure you're always checking your leaders the last week of the month to see if they have spent their 100PV so they get paid. Sometimes, it's just a lack of knowledge at what's required. Many leaders on your team will only sell one or two kits in their Young Living lifetime, and just don't know the rules. It's your job to do the PV scan at the end of the month and take care of your leaders. Shoot them a quick message and let them know their hard work won't be rewarded unless they meet the minimum requirements for their check: 100PV.

A tip for leaders: I never place my order for the 28th or 29th of the month, because if something is out of stock, you don't have time to fix your order and could lose your check. Another wonderful resource in the Virtual Office is PV assistant. If an item is out of stock and your Essential Rewards order is below the threshold you set, it will add products, which you have chosen, to raise the PV to ensure that you get paid and receive promotions.

By the way, as a bonus for getting through this chapter, which is the most technically challenging in the book, I'll pause for a moment and give you a knockout smoothie recipe using Young Living's Pure Protein Complete Vanilla Spice powder. Best. Breakfast. Ever.

SARAH'S FAVORITE MANGO CREAM SMOOTHIE:

In a Ninja, Vitamix, or Blendtech blender, combine:
2 cups frozen fruit (I like mangoes best, but strawberries are good too)
2 cups ice
When mixed, add:
½ quart of Stoneyfield organic whole-milk French Vanilla yogurt (it has to be this brand, this flavor. Oh my word it's good. Don't ever buy low-fat anything—they replace the fat with chemicals.)
2-4 Tablespoons of raw honey (no corn syrup synthetic yuck)
2-4 ounces of Young Living's NingXia
3 scoops Young Living's Vanilla Pure Protein Complete
2 tablespoons pure vanilla
1 cup water or unseasoned bone broth until it's your desired thickness. I like my spoon to stand in this sucker!
1 pinch of Himalayan or Celtic sea salt for minerals (no iodized salt!)
If you're up for it, break up a little organic kale and toss it in. Blend it all until it's amazing goodness. Oh. My. Word. It's so much better than sugar-laden cereal. Even organic cereals can have about four days' worth of sugar. Eggs are great, but Pure Protein Complete has 25 grams of protein in it. That's like having steak, hamburgers, fish, eggs, chicken, and more steak for breakfast. Protein helps you think clearly and lose weight. It's a win-win.

Now go make yourself one so you can finish this chapter!!!

We were talking about the four lines in the Virtual office tab under "Rank Qualification." Once you understand this tab, you know how to rank. Now that you've eaten your power smoothie, you can take on the world. Here we go with Line 2!

Line 2: OGV

Organizational Group Volume. These are your purchases and the purchases of everyone under you. To rank as a Star, your OGV must be at least 500. A Senior Star must have an OGV of 2,000; an Executive, an OGV of 4,000, a Silver, 10,000 OGV. Every month, it resets to zero. At first, you will cry when the first of the month appears, but as you rise in rank, it starts getting really fun to watch it. I remember rolling my eyes when a Platinum in line in front of me at convention said he reached Gold by the third day of the month. Now we are there too, and it's awesome to see your leaders lead and be blessed financially. Your work raising them up blesses you and them!

Line 3: Legs

This is where the strategy comes in. This third requirement is all about legs. A "Leg" is one person with a bunch of people underneath them. To rank as an Executive, you need two people under you, and each of their legs must have an OGV of 1,000. The overall volume of your entire team (your purchases and everyone else's) must be at least 4,000 OGV.

Why do you need legs at this rank? It sets the stage for you to grow long-term. You don't just make a big paycheck at the beginning and then lose it. You don't have to work 15 years to get a decent check. The growth is consistent as you build your team, first deep and then wide. Young Living is a company with tenure. The average network marketing company fails within seven years, but Young Living has been around more than three times that length. With this business model, you are building a business legacy, one that will last far beyond your lifetime.

We'll go deeper into strategy for building legs in Chapter 18. Just remember, you should always be thinking two legs ahead. If you're a Star, be thinking as an Executive. If you're a Silver, be planning as a Platinum—with 4 legs. You never want to have your OGV and be caught without your legs.

Line 4: PGV

Personal Group Volume. PGV is how much of your OGV belongs to you—it is the volume of your organization which is not on your qualifying legs and does not belong to any Silver or higher rank on your team. When your leaders rank Silver, they will break off into their own teams, and that volume is not counted in your PGV. Any volume on your legs which qualify you for your rank are also not included in your PGV.

You need 1,000 PGV to qualify for Silver and above.

This one is easy to get. It happens organically if you are sharing the oils. If you have four or five people on Essential Rewards that are not building their own team, you'll always hit this. My PGV comes from people I signed at my first class over two years ago.

Overview of Rank Qualification

Is that all as clear as mud? Let me break it down one last time in uber simple terms:

Line 1: PV—spend 100 PV to get a paycheck.

Line 2: OGV—your purchase and the purchase of everyone under you.

Line 3: Legs (people)—for Executive: two legs at 1,000 OGV each; for Silver: two legs at 4,000 OGV each; for Gold: three legs at 6,000 OGV each; for Platinum: four legs at 8,000 OGV each. Got it?

Line 4: PGV—at least 1,000 PV of your entire volume must be from outside your legs. You can't get carried along in the system from someone else's work. That's why it takes more than one strong leg to rank. You'll have to take time building each of those with your own gifts and talents.

Honestly, I check the rank qualification page at least once a day. If you scroll under the green chart, you'll see all the perks you get for that rank. Below that, it breaks down your OGV. I love that because it tells you exactly how much more is sitting in people's carts, so you can see if you're close to hitting the next rank.

2 ORGANIZATION VOLUME 250,000 OGV

56,371.83 OGV completed orders

37,184.75 OGV pending auto-ship orders

3 LEG VOLUME Build your organization to **4 Or more legs** to **8,000** OGV

1	ANDERSON, ANGELA BETH	32,526.83 OGV	21,315.75 OGV Scheduled
2	(name)	8,002 OGV	4,908 OGV Scheduled
3	SPENCER, SHARON ★	7,314.75 OGV	4,737.25 OGV Scheduled
4	YUSON, THERELL	4,078.50 OGV	3,191 OGV Scheduled

You can see from this peek at my Virtual Office that at the time of this screen shot, I needed four legs at 8,000 OGV to reach Platinum. My first two were already there. My third leg was at 7,300, but that's nothing to worry about because there's still 4,700 sitting in people's carts as Essential Rewards. My last leg, my Platinum leg, looks great—it's only halfway through the month and it's sitting at 7,200 with processed and unprocessed orders. I have 12 leaders on that team and they still have three weeks to sell eight kits. I didn't have to worry about Platinum this month. This month showed me it was time to focus on my Diamond team and let my leaders lead.

Now you know how to keep an eye on your rank—watch your numbers, watch the volume on Essential Rewards, and strategize on how to grow your team—all through the Rank Qualification button.

We've hit all three buttons across the top of the page, so let's zoom in on the boxes in the middle of your screen.

"SHOPPING"

Monthly order:

The amount you have sitting in your essential rewards order right now (which will not process until the day you have selected).

Quick order:

The amount you have sitting in your cart under quick order right now (which won't process until you log in and complete the order).

"BALANCES"

Rewards points:

How many points you have accrued in Essential Rewards

Available credits:

These are credits to your account that have accrued through many ways: for example, if your check was under $25, it would be credited to your account. If you are unsure what it is from, give Young Living a call.

While we are on that topic, you may notice under your "My Account" tab, that there are adjustments to your commission. Young Living has a fee that goes through each month (just a few dollars) that covers the cost of your check being mailed or direct deposit. It is called a "maintenance" fee.

Total Earnings	$11.04 USD
▼ Commission Adjustments	$-11.04 USD
Credit on Account	$-10.04 USD
Maintenance Fee	$-1.00 USD
Young Living Foundation	$0.00 USD
Check Total	$0.00 USD

"VOLUME/RANK"

OGV:

Is your Organization Group Volume, the amount of total sales from your purchases and all those under you.

PV:

Is Personal Volume. It's how much you spent. It's the number I gently sneak past my husband each month.

PGV:

Is Personal Group Volume. It's how much volume is outside your legs. You need 1,000 PGV to attain the rank of Silver or higher.

Qualified rank:

Is what your rank is at this moment. If you have not spent your 100 PV, you will be listed as a distributor. Once you have spent at least 100 PV, your rank will be displayed. I like to place my Essential Rewards order early in this month just for that reason!

OGV history:

This shows the history of your business in a bar graph. If you are holding four to six classes a month, and getting people on essential rewards, your peaks and valleys will be much smaller. There is always a bit of an up-and-down in network marketing, but the overall trend is up. Don't ever compare one month to the next, compare this October to last October. If you are up, you are doing something right.

"MY ORGANIZATION"

Downline accounts:

This tells you how many people are in your organization.

Leaders:

This tells you how many leaders have ranked Silver or above for the month. It will change as the month goes on, especially the last week, as your leaders rank.

New members:

Tells you how many people have been signed to your team, by you or your distributors, since the first of the month.

About to go inactive:

If you sell someone a starter kit and they never purchase again, one year after that kit sale, their account will go inactive and their name will disappear from your downline. To keep them active, have them place an order of 50 PV or greater.

Now let's do a brief tour of the buttons down the left side of your dashboard.

"MEMBER NEWS"

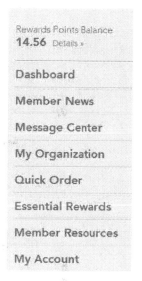

Here's where you'll find the latest Young Living news. It may be a new book, a new oil, a new promotion, the Essential Rewards promos for that month, a new contest, or a philanthropic trip. My favorite feature on this button is the "Products Currently Out Of Stock" button. It will tell you which Young Living products aren't available, why, when they'll be back in, and what you can use instead.

"MESSAGE CENTER"

This is for your leaders or Young Living to write to you directly in your Virtual Office.

"MY ORGANIZATION"

This is the other super important button we're going to look at most closely. This is the "How to Watch Your Team" button.

At the top, you can see the number of members on your team. At the time of this screen shot, ours was at 1,599.

On the right, you can change the month you're looking at and go all the way back to the start of your business.

The top line is you. You'll see your rank to the left of your name—mine was P for Platinum. You'll see your Member ID number, so if someone needs you to look up their member number, this is where you'd look. PV is what you have spent. OGV is what the whole team has spent. PGV is what has been spent outside your legs.

Autoship shows you who is on Essential Rewards. The number is the day of the month that they have chosen for their order to automatically process. All the little boxes are people on Essential Rewards. When it's got a green check mark, their order has been processed. A healthy, growing team has at least 30% of their members on Essential Rewards. If you have lots of kits and no checked boxes, you're not doing good follow up with your team and training them how to use the oils.

On the far right side, you'll see an envelope that allows you to write your team members. I usually just use my personal email, because many don't know how to log into their Virtual Office to see the messages.

The green square with the person's head in it is invaluable; that's how you do follow up. It lists their email, name, address, and phone number. All the information you need to touch base with your team.

The two heads together shows you that person's personally enrolled—all the people they have enrolled, regardless of where they have been placed in their organization.

The three bars show you their rank qualification. It's identical to the Rank Qualification tab on your dashboard, but displays that person's qualification.

If you look at the left side of the page, you'll see a little plus sign next to each person's name. That allows you to expand the team and look under each of those leaders to look more closely at their team.

There are just a few buttons left, and our Virtual Office training is over!

"QUICK ORDER"

Using the **Quick Order** button is one way you can place an order. I recommend placing as much of your order as possible under the Essential Rewards button each month, so you get the maximum ER points. But, if you love the promo, did you know that you can cash in on it twice? Do that by placing a 300 PV order under the Essential Rewards button and a 300 PV order under the Quick Order button. I love doing that when the promos are so good I know it will be a double blessing to get them twice. Some items may be for ER only, so watch carefully as you place the order.

Other times you would use the Quick Order button: When you've already proceesed your ER order for the month and you need something else, or Young Living announces a sale. Quick Order is also how you will redeem your Essential Rewards points or account credits you receive.

"ESSENTIAL REWARDS"

Getting free oils is pretty sweet! Young Living has paid for every oil I've ever purchased—since the very first day my starter kit showed up at my door—either with my paycheck, or the monthly promotions, or ER points. How does it work? You earn a percentage back on each order placed through Essential Rewards. It starts at 10% right away which means if you spend 100 PV, you're getting 10 PV back in free oils. That's nearly a bottle of Lime oil or some Cedarwood, just for restocking your laundry soap! You get 20% back after four months and 25% after 25 months. You're literally getting paid to buy your laundry soap and Thieves cleaner! Double score! Place your order for the month in one shot instead of several smaller orders, so you can do it on Essential Rewards and get the most points.

This graphic lays it out visually if you need to see Essential Rewards in clear language:

Essential Rewards

Young Living's optional monthly autoship program
(monthly order minimum: 50 PV)

Why Join?

- discounted shipping
- change your order monthly
- cancel at any time
- earn extra monthly promos
- receive gifts at 3, 6, 9, and 12 months
- earn points to redeem for free products

How to Join:

1. Sign into your account.
2. Click on "Virtual Office" then "Essential Rewards."
3. Set up your customized order.
4. Smile! You're one step closer to a toxin-free home!

Months 1-3 earn	Months 4-24 earn	Months 25+ earn
10% of your order PV	20% of your order PV	25% of your order PV

For a more indepth look at Essential Rewards see Chapter 19 "The Key to Reaching and Maintaining Rank" on page 195

"MEMBER RESOURCES"

This is the button I told you at the beginning of the chapter to lose yourself in on a lazy Sunday afternoon. It's chock full of resources.

Start with YL Central. It's loaded with videos, scripts, PowerPoints, shareable graphics, essential oils training, and business training. The content is directly from Young Living and it's knockout good! The page is divided into several sections: Essential Oils, Products (the top 30 Young Living products), Dive Deeper, and Share YL. There is also information on Essential Rewards and the monthly promos.

Then browse the Policies and Procedures button and immerse yourself in the ins and outs of network marketing. It'll explain all the rules and all the isms you may have never known before. Did you know you can't enroll your spouse and build a team under him/her? It's just good to know this stuff. Click on each button and absorb. When I am training my leaders, this (along with the Getting Started tab) is one of the buttons that I require them to read all the way through.

"MY ACCOUNT"

This is a pretty essential button! It allows you to set up direct deposit, to track your orders and see if they've shipped (and click on the tracking number to see how close it is). You can click on your commissions, see the breakdown of your paycheck, and who of your team you were paid on. I'd recommend you do that at least once, just to understand the breakdown of your check.

That wraps up your Virtual Office tour! Why do you want to use your Virtual Office? First off, it's a free resource, and as a frugal momma of five, I'm all about free. Secondly, it's an opportunity to see everything in one place: your goals, your team, orders shipped, the breakdown of your paycheck, training videos, and addresses for follow up. Log into it daily and watch your team expand!

CHAPTER 7

Young Living Marketing 101: How to Share Oils

I used to think that I could never do network marketing because I'd come off as salesy to my friends. I'd be begging my closest comrades to buy things off of me weekly, things I knew they couldn't afford. That's what we all think, right? That if you have a friend in an MLM you can expect to host parties, buy pans, makeup, and books—and be harassed constantly. I'm going to debunk all of that in this chapter and make you unafraid of all things MLM, but especially about sharing Young Living.

THE TRUTH ABOUT MULTI-LEVEL-MARKETING

Let's start by talking about MLM's. When you walk into a grocery store chain, you're supporting that CEO's third house. When you buy from an MLM, you are putting food on your friend's table and gas in their car. It's the epitome of a small business, but without a storefront. It's no different from going to the downtown area of your hometown and buying something in the store of your local gift shop.

I have had people tell me they can't take part in an MLM because it's a pyramid scheme. A pyramid scheme is illegal in the United States. It means you pay for something and it never shows up. To date, after two years with Young Living, I've never had an oil not show up at my door, which means this is *not* a pyramid scheme.

Amway was sued by the federal government in 1978, and was told that network marketing was not a valid business model. They won in court, and to this date, MLM's have thrived across the United States. The goal is to put as much cash in the distributor's hands as possible, and cut out the middle man. Instead of paying for lights, electric, health insurance for employees, and rent for a storefront—all that cash goes to the person selling. To debunk the entire argument against MLM's, I'll give you a video to watch. Go to YouTube and type in "I Still Think It's A Pyramid Scheme" by Pat Petrini. For three minutes, enjoy a pig and a bear, and then return to this chapter.

OVERCOMING OTHERS' OBJECTIONS TO MLM'S

While I was writing this book, I spoke with a woman who threw back her head and laughed when she heard I was with Young Living. She said she "didn't do those pyramid things."

I'll tell you, those "pyramid things" are genius! They are endorsed by dozens of the top financial advisors around the world.

She said that it was a get rich quick scheme.

I told her that I multiplied my income by five in a year and a half, and I worked my tush off to do it. It definitely wasn't a scheme, and it definitely wasn't easy.

She said you had to get in early to make cash.

I told her that Young Living had been around for 22 years, and that I'd been a part of it for a year and a half and was able to climb to be in the top 1% of income earners in the entire company. We sure hadn't been doing it 22 years.

Then she said I was an exception to the rule and that the only reason I'd gotten that far was because I was a news anchor and everyone knew me.

I told her I took a survey of my team when we were Gold rank, and only 5% of our team knew me from the radio. The rest were friends of friends of friends. Many were out of state. Several had no idea who I even was.

I also told her that we now have 800 leaders on our team and dozens have retired because of Young Living. More than 100 have experienced lifestyle changes where they can drop things off their plate and make their lives a bit simpler because of the extra income. Hundreds more on our team are getting their oils and their NingXia for free simply by holding one class a month. If that's a pyramid scheme, *sign me up!*

WHY YOUNG LIVING?

She then proceeded to tell me that Young Living can't possibly be the only pure oils company in the world.

I'll agree. It's not the only pure company. But I believe it is the *best* pure company, and I know it is a pioneer. I have far more oils to choose from than anywhere else that I go. I believe in what they do and how they do it, and that's enough for me.

I have so much respect for Gary Young and the groundwork that he's laid in studying the greats in France and then bringing that knowledge to the United States. His methods of distillation are copied all over the world.

There is a wonderful book about the path that Young Living took to become a 1.5 billion dollar essential oils company. It's called "D. Gary Young: The World Leader In Essential Oils." Get your hands on it and devour it, and you'll never look at Young Living the same way again. If you have any doubts as to Young Living as a company, you'll lose them in that book.

Young Living has the largest essential oils farms on the planet. I have used many other oils side by side without the same results, and the only explanation I can give is that the Young Living oils are distilled correctly; at the right temperatures, at the peak of the harvest, and without any chemicals. They are hand weeded. There is integrity in the process.

There are over 140 single oils and blends Gary has developed, many by trudging through forests in the Amazon and smelling for aromatic plants. His passion for purity and integrity blows me away with every new farm I visit!

One of the other things I love about Young Living is that it's a totally transparent company. As a news anchor, I'm naturally curious. I remember as a grade-schooler, my mom had taken my three siblings and me to an ice cream shop. By the time she got the kids out of the car, she could not find me. I was downstairs in the basement of the ice cream shop interviewing the owner and asking for a tour of the ice cream storage area. I have carried that far into the newsroom, interviewing presidents, governors, activists, Olympians, and hundreds of famous people over my career. (If you want to hear my interview with Young Living Ambassador and Olympic Gold Medalist Bryan Clay, go to oilabilityteam.com, click on "Share > Corporate Interviews." Enjoy!)

I love that when I step onto a Young Living farm, there are no secrets. At every Young Living farm I attend, I get the same responses and the same answers from dozens of employees. "I've been here 'x' number of years, I love working for Gary. I love his mission for purity. This company is honest and good. They do oils the right way."

I love how simple the process is. Step out into a wide lavender field that is never touched with weed killers or pesticides, pluck the plant at its peak value (they check it every hour around the clock as it gets close to harvest time, which you just can't do at a mom and pop oils distillery because you don't have the manpower), distill it at the right temperature (that's where most companies make their mistake), and use no solvents distilling, even though it is more expensive to distill without solvents. It's beautiful and simple and true. And the oils work.

When you stand in those fields and see it yourself, it takes your breath away! I was swept away at all the Lord has created. He really gets the glory for it all! He created the plants before He made us. They have been around since the dawn of time. It's only the last 150 years that we've forgotten how to use oils. It's time to take that knowledge back.

I am over the fear of MLM's and over the fear of Young Living as a powerhouse. They have earned that title and my respect. Multi-level marketing works or I wouldn't have been able to write this book.

PROUD TO BE AN ENTREPRENEUR

Let me put one more resource in your hands, because I'm a numbers cruncher and a fact hunter. Eric Worre has a wonderful DVD called, "Rise of the Entrepreneur" that breaks down the numbers in network marketing. If you need facts and statistics that this truly works to show your spouse, your best friend, or to convince yourself that this is worth it; that's the place to go. You can find it at ericworre.com.

Even after you believe in the product, the company, and that MLM's are a legitimate vehicle for entrepreneurs to reach financial freedom; you may still struggle with the fear of selling. That's an easy one to tackle. I already shared my story for using oils: It's to live a chemical-free lifestyle. Now let me tell you how I share it in a compliant way.

WE'RE NOT SELLING OILS!

Never once have I sold a Young Living starter kit. I have empowered people to trust their instinct when something is off. I've shown them to pay attention to the amount of chemicals in their home.

Never once have I sold a Young Living starter kit.

I issue the three cabinet challenge in my classes and tell them to go home, flip over the products in any three cabinets of their home and google the ingredients. If they don't know what it is, they shouldn't be slathering it on their body or cleaning with it. Then I encourage them to switch to chemical-free essential oils.

It's a journey. Some will go gung-ho and swap everything out as fast as they can, while others will take it one product at a time. Here's the way I look at it: neither way is wrong. Again, every oil they use is a chemical they're not using.

Never once since I started with Young Living have I felt salesy or that I'm pushing someone to do something they wouldn't do or can't afford. I am training them to pay attention to their bodies, to be aware of the chemicals in their cabinets, and to start living a less toxic life. It's empowering to see people get healthy. It's a calling, not an occupation. If they say they can't afford health, they will pay for it in other areas. Chemical use has a price, and the price is high. It's about creating an awareness so they start to take steps to swap chemicals out.

WHAT IT TAKES TO SHARE OILS SUCCESSFULLY

There are two things you need to do this business extremely well: passion and compassion. You need passion for the product, and if you have a Young Living starter kit in your home, you're likely in the process of developing the passion. Compassion is about meeting people where they are. It doesn't matter if they're a crunchy momma that does grass-fed pastured fermented organic everything or if they live on fast food five days a week. Meet them on their journey, without judgement, with passion, and walk them through.

Every person has a niche when it comes to oils. Perhaps the way to their heart is a diffuser for their new home. Some people put more into their pets than into their own health. Find that place where they can relate to the oils and share from that place. Be silent and listen to them, and then and you'll know where that place is.

YOU DON'T NEED TO BE AN EXPERT

What is one thing you don't need to market your classes? You don't need to be a certified aromatherapist. I have people come to me constantly saying they can't teach classes unless they are certified. They say they don't know enough.

I say it's not about what you know. It's about the resources you have from experts who have gone before you. It's about knowing where the tools are, and showing your team how to find them. There is a plethora of resources out there that will give them tips on how to oil up. You don't need to be the expert.

Let me repeat that: *you don't need to be an expert.*

This is actually a proven strategy in network marketing called "Third Party Validation." It's using a third party, a person or resource, to educate people instead of being the expert yourself. Connect your team with reliable outside sources. It gives credibility to what you are sharing and ensures that you have a duplicable system for them to follow. They don't need to be just like you. They don't need your gifts and talents.

They don't need to be experts in business or aromatherapy. They just need to know where to point people when questions arise. They can be successful with their own gifts and talents. It's not about what you know, it's about knowing where to point people.

Empower people to do their own research and lead them to the right resources.

It is a simple process: instead of trying to be everything to the people you are trying to educate, rely on experts to train your team. Lead people to the right resources and empower them to do their own research. That is the secret to growing a team: allow your leaders to see a clear, simple path to follow in your footsteps.

Here is what it looks like to use Third Party Validation when sharing oils:

"I don't know the answer to that, but here's where I'd begin my research. Check out pubmed.com. It's loaded with studies that will help you find what you're searching for."

"I am still learning how to run my own business, but I have a great resource in the Gameplan book. The book walks you through step by step. Let me hook you up."

"What makes Young Living such a good company? Well, I haven't been with them since they started. But there is a book filled with photos and primary source documents that chronicles the entire story of Young Living that will blow your mind. It's called "D. Gary Young: The World Leader in Essential Oils." I read that book and walked away with a complete appreciation of what it takes to do oils right. You have GOT to check it out if you think buying cheap oil is a good idea."

What happens when you use tools? You are training your new oilers and your new business builders that they don't need to have all the answers. You are training them that it will take a lifetime to amass the education to answer every question, but tools can point them to the answers.

If you wait a lifetime to start oiling, you lose the benefit and blessing of the daily application of the purest substances on the planet. If you wait until you know it all to start your business, you lose the release from poverty, stress, and exhaustion.

And there's the thing: you'll never get to a place where you actually know it all. I hold six aromatherapy certifications from aroma chemistry to Biblical aromatherapy to Vitaflex. I've worked with thousands of people in the past two years, either online or in person, in all 50 states, and several countries. Yet still, when I stand in the presence of Gary Young, who built the distilleries from the ground up and developed more than 140 oils, and who trudged through rain forests to find Copaiba oil; I feel like I know nothing at all.

Wishing you were the expert is a problem with pride. It's trying to be all things to all people. Don't do that. Just train them how to look things up for themselves. It's always better to teach an oiler to fish then to fish for them. It will save you stress, frustration and time.

The other day a member of my team said, "Sarah, I'm sure more people come to your classes because you throw the title 'certified aromatherapist' in your marketing material."

First of all, even as a Diamond, I still have classes of no-shows and low-shows so don't beat yourself up too hard if that happens. It happens to every single rank occasionally, regardless of title. You are no less of a distributor if you have a bum class. Just pick yourself up, dust yourself off, and do better marketing. Get more personal with your invites. Talk to them individually and build a relationship.

To answer the question of whether an aromatherapy degree is needed, I just look at the facts. I had ranked Gold before I completed my aromatherapy trainings. I have personally enrolled several hundred people, but my team consists of over 3,200 oilers, most of whom I don't know. I didn't sign them. My team did. People come to your classes and sign up because they trust you, not because you have a title. Or they come to your classes because they trust the friend who invited them, not because of what is printed next to your name.

The majority of the people I've enrolled come because they want to learn about oils. Your team is not built on titles, it's built on relationships. Relationships will open more doors than any title.

Why do you want to be the expert? Fear. You have fear that people won't accept you because you're not educated enough. Ask yourself this: do you trust the person at Panera because they are educated in the science of making bread? No. Do you expect the person selling books at Barnes and Noble to have a working knowledge of all books ever published? No. Do you refuse to order coffee at Starbucks because the barista doesn't know the ins and outs of where the coffee beans were sourced? (You still buy coffee. Coffee is not negotiable.)

Why then do you need to be an aromatherapist to sell oils? You're a Young Living distributor. Wear the title with pride, and without fear of having every answer.

Relationships will open more doors than any title.

Get good at locating third party tools and putting them in the hands of those asking the questions, and you'll grow like crazy without a title. You'll also build trust, which is far more important than any certification. Recommend reference guides (discoverlsp.com), pubmed.com, the Young Living blog (youngliving.com/blog), Fearless (oilabilityteam.com), the D. Gary Young World Leader of Essential Oils book for the Young Living story, and Gameplan for business training. If you can point to tools, you never need to be the expert. And your budding leaders won't think they have to be experts, either, which is the most important thing.

Release yourself from the pressure of having to be perfect. Release yourself from fear. And lean on what's already been written. If you get to a place where you're not sure where to point someone, ask your upline. Call the Young Living Member Service line and ask corporate directly. Every question you'll be hit with has likely already been asked. Don't miss the opportunity of a lifetime waiting on a certification.

You now know what you don't need to say and do to share the oils. The information and mindset from this chapter will make sure you're sharing the oils confidently and not turning people off. Next we'll discuss practical techniques to actually get people to come to your classes!

CHAPTER 8

THE OIL ABILITY MARKETING SYSTEM: HOW TO FILL CLASSES WITHOUT KNOWING PEOPLE

Some people will buy Gameplan solely for this chapter. This chapter has catapulted many a leader's business on our team. It's a strategy for overcoming one of the biggest challenges to sharing the oils: filling classes.

When I first began my business, I put a post on my Facebook page and 47 women showed up at my house. I did it again and got about 20. By the fifth class, I was out of friends and my classes were dwindling, so I asked a good friend who was a naturopath doctor to host a class for me. She had 60 women show up in a church gym. That worked out well for a while until that circle of people started to dwindle too. It was then when I realized that everyone has an end to their circle of friends.

Of all the questions I'm asked on the road or on Facebook, this is, hands down, at the top. "How do I get people to come to my classes? I post, but no one shows up. I don't know that many people."

73

Here's the thing—neither do I. Neither do the top leaders on my team. The trick isn't who you know. *It's who your friends know.* The trick to marketing isn't how many people you know. It's more about how many times you get outside your circle of friends!

Whether it's after your first class or your tenth, there will come a day when you will run out of people to fill classes unless you get out of your personal friend circle. You must tap into your friend's friends and that can happen from your very first class if you are strategic. Every person in that class knows someone outside your friend circle. In fact, the average person knows about a thousand people, if they were to sit down and write it all out. It's astounding.

Within my first 20 classes, different attendees had contacts in Germany, Italy, Thailand, Japan, Canada, and Mexico City. Guess where we now have teams? Did I know those people? Heck no. So take some pressure off yourself. It's going to take a lot more than just you to pull off a Young Living business. It takes a lot people doing the same thing you're doing. That is a network marketing company.

This is the formula that I follow for every single class that I hold. Each has the same pattern, and I still haven't run out of people to speak to.

THE OIL ABILITY EVENT MARKETING SYSTEM

1. Choose a date for your class

You should begin marketing a class at least two to three weeks in advance. People are busy. During the holidays or during wedding or graduation or vacation season, you may want to leave yourself even more lead time. If you give people three or four days' notice, you're going to have a low turnout. Most of the people who attend my classes are busy mommas. They have to know ahead of time if they're going to work it into their schedule.

2. Set up an event for your class on Facebook

It's free, and it reaches the widest swath of people. How do you set up an event? Go to your Facebook page. Look under your Facebook profile picture for a button that says "more." Click on that, then scroll down till you see "events." (Note: Not on Facebook? Get on it. Go to Youtube, go to the search bar, and type in "21st Century Social Media Trends" and watch a free 9-minute video on the power of social media that will blow your mind. One billion people are on Facebook. That's one in every nine people in the world. Social media is where the people are; if you're running a network marketing business, you should be there too. Our team has used just about every marketing tool out there: radio, newspaper, flyers, word of mouth, and texting. We've gotten the greatest return every time from Facebook events.)

Setting up an event is pretty simple. First you title the event, and then you decide if it will be a Private Event or Public. With a "Private Event" only those you invite and those your friends invite will see the event. This may be the option to choose if you are teaching a class for a member who is hosting in her home and inviting her friends. With a Public Event you will get more visibility and the event is easier for people to share. It's up to you and your host, if you have one. You'll fill in basic information, select a photo for the top of your event (google "Young Living banners" for some ideas), then put in the time, location, address, and an FDA compliant description of the class.

A note on writing: Wording matters on your events. Use power-packed action verbs that take them somewhere. For example, this is a snippet of an actual event invite that I saw online, before the English major and network journalist in me ran away, screaming in horror:

Bad: Please come to my essential oils class. I will have dessert. I will speak for 2 hours on oils. If you can bring someone, that would be good. We will have NingXia for an extra cost. If you can't come, I will teach another class.

Good: Do you want to learn how to kick toxic chemicals out of your home? I'll walk you through, step by step, and give *easy, simple, and affordable* tactics that anyone can use with the best essential oils on the planet. This class is totally FREE and will blow your mind! I come with an iced NingXia bar for weary mommas! Gear up for a fast-paced, ground-up lecture on everything oils, and have some fun and pampering in the process. I can't wait to see you! I'll have freebies at the door for those who invite 50 friends on the Facebook event. It's time to take control of the yuck in your home and kick it to the curb!

(Feel free to steal this if you can't write! It's all good! This book is full of resources for you at every turn.)

3. Invite three people to invite their friends

Once your event is live, here's the key to the whole thing; find three people on your Facebook friend list (any three who may have an interest in oils and live close enough to attend) invite them to the event and then ask *them* to go into the Facebook event and invite 50 people to the class.

Have them type a sentence in the event promoting you, for example, "This is my friend Sarah. She's a rock star! She made me a bottle of Thieves cleaner for a dollar and it did this to my sink in three minutes. It's chemical free. You can't get chemical free cleaning supplies that cheap in the store. Oils have so many other uses. You've GOT to come to this class!"

If you have three people each invite 50 people to the class, it means you'll have 150 people invited. Most people wig out at this point. Don't wig out. You *won't* be teaching a 150-person class, for sure! Standard network marketing numbers tell us that 20-25% will show. Of that, 20-25% will get the starter kits. So if you have 150 invited, with good marketing 20-30 will show, and five or six will get a kit.

4. Thank your hosts

When you have the event set up and three people have invited 50 people each to that event, make up a little basket to show your appreciation to your 'hosts.' Pop in some Thieves cleaner or lozenges or a peppermint roll-on. Add a couple of my oily education DVD's to the basket, and let them know you appreciate them. Keep the cost under five dollars, but hand deliver it with a thank you. If they aren't local to you, pop it in the mail. They will be surprised and delighted, and much more excited to help people get to your class!

5. Market the event

Once the event is set up on Facebook and people have been invited, market it. That means every single day you should be putting one to two posts up promoting the class. What does that look like? Pull FDA compliant photos off the Oil Ability with Sarah Facebook page and feel free to safely share those. Take a line out of the lecture and share that. Take a photo of the gift baskets you'll give away, the desserts that will be there, or how you're preparing for class. Let them know you're on your game and you're ready to rock their world. People's interest will be peaked. A word of advice: don't over post. Most of these people have never met you before. If you're putting six posts a day in that event, people are going to leave. Once or twice a day is more than enough.

6. Rinse and repeat

After the class, you'll have a few people purchase kits. Some may get it right at the class, and some may get them in the weeks after. Either is fine. To market your next class, dip into your downline. If you teach four classes a month, and four people get a kit at each class; in the first month alone, you have 16 people who can invite others to your classes. You literally never, ever run out of friend circles. It goes on and on forever. We still haven't run out of friend circles, and I'm meeting new people every single week.

Overview of the Oil Ability Event Marketing System:

1) Set up a Facebook event two to three weeks ahead of the class.

2) Ask three people to invite 50 people to the event and make them a thank you basket.

3) Grab photos and lines from the script and market it every single day.

4) After class, tap into your new downline and ask three of them to invite 50 people to the next class. Rinse and repeat. You have never-ending friend circles.

Encouragement from Silver In Six
Oil Ability leader Rachael DeValk:

I held 11 classes in the first three weeks of my distributorship. I was so excited to build a team like Sarah's after spending several days with her on her Gold Retreat at the Saint Maries farm in Idaho! Unfortunately, I was not very well networked in New York and didn't understand how to fill classes with people outside my circle.

Since moving here from Illinois seven years ago, I had either worked 70+ hours a week as a salaried manager at Walmart or I had been working 40 hours a week at the credit union, 30 hours a week at Walmart as a cake decorator and I was taking 2 to 8 cake orders a week. I had very little free time to build a personal network.

Of the first 11 classes I held, 2 had 5 attendees, 4 classes had 1 or 2 attendees, and 5 were no shows. Rather than giving up, I changed my tactics!

At the credit union where I worked, I began meeting with co-workers one on one during my lunch breaks to build my team. I did that from August until January when I used Sarah's method for filling classes.

I ranked as Executive in February and am working to reach Silver this month. I am teaching classes nearly every weekend now, because I ask previous attendees or leaders on my team to invite 50+ of their Facebook friends and I give them an oily gift basket or sign people under their sponsor number.

Network marketing is like any other business—if you stick with it and are adaptable, you will be successful.

Rachael with Young Living Founder D. Gary Young.

I STILL CAN'T FILL A CLASS—NOW WHAT?

I want to take a moment and speak directly to the people who say this marketing system doesn't work. I'll shoot straight with you—it is rare, but I have seen this system fail before, and it always comes down to one of two things: confidence or gifting. I wrote an entire chapter on confidence, and this next section will give you even more creative ways to share the oils!

Each of us have different strengths and weaknesses. You may need to try this from a different angle. Maybe you don't have the comfort level to approach people to ask them to invite 50 people. You may not have the writing ability to put together punchy FDA-compliant marketing posts. None of the people in the event may connect with you as you post. The good thing is that there are many ways of sharing. There were many, many millionaire-level network marketers long before Facebook.

LISTEN TO YOUR WARM MARKET

Go through your entire Facebook friends list. (In network marketing, we call that your warm market—the people who you know personally. They may be an acquaintance, and that's okay—they know your face.) Go through your Christmas card list. Keep a tally of the people around you at work, at play dates, homeschool groups, sports teams, and extra-curricular activities.

You can be more deliberate about the people you contact. Look through the lists of friends you know and write down the name of any person who would be blessed by the oils and the name of any person who would benefit from a chemical free lifestyle. One by one, contact them, offer to do a personalized intro class, mail them some samples, and show them the passion you have. *Keep the focus on them.* Listen to them. Pause—instead of you doing the talking, hear where they are at and meet them there.

One of my favorite stories to tell is of my brother, Aaron. For a good year, I sent him Young Living samples, but he didn't use them. They stockpiled in his house. When I'd bring up oils, he'd check out. When I went to visit him after he'd bought a new-to-him home and started in right away with Young Living, he asked me politely to stop. So I stopped.

As we toured his home, he expressed frustration that the basement, which was newly finished and gorgeous, had been the designated smoking room of the person who'd lived there before him. He couldn't get the smell out and was about to have it bombed, but that would mean leaving the house for three days so it could be sprayed with chemicals.

He asked if there was another way, and finally I had an open door! For stinky smells, I recommended Purification in the diffuser and the Thieves cleaner undiluted on every wall and rafter in the basement.

That weekend, the smell was gone, and without a $1,000 bombing fee. Eight weeks later, my brother had a starter kit and was texting me about how to buy fractionated coconut oil online so he could make his own blends. I jokingly told him he's not allowed to speak in oily acronyms until he's been using oils for at least six months.

The reason I was able to break through to Aaron was not because I was talking. It was because I stopped talking and listened to where he was. I listened for the need. If people see your heart and your desire to help them, it becomes a totally different ballgame. Suddenly it's not about sales, it's about people. That's what makes this a passion for most of the people doing this business. They are on the front lines to help people. So stop talking, and start listening.

HOST CLASSES IN A PUBLIC PLACE

Many people are uncomfortable about hosting their own friends in their home, much less a group of Facebook contacts their friends helped invite. Additionally, some guests might not want to come to the home of someone they don't know for an oils class. If you are having trouble finding people willing to book classes with you in their home, or with getting people to come to home classes, overcome this hurdle by scheduling classes in a room available to the public. People often feel more comfortable attending an event in a public place such as a room at a library, a conference room at a local restaurant, a community center, or a health food store. We've even had people on our team find that they could use the class room at the local craft store.

One word of caution: don't bite off more than you can chew financially. Don't book a $100 room for a 5-person class. There are many resources available locally that you can tap into a for a fraction of the cost: the YMCA, your VFW, churches, fire halls, etc.

If the class is in a public building, you can still use the same Oil Ability marketing system to invite people–create a Facebook event and ask three people from your warm market to invite 50 of their friends. You may find that those who were unwilling to host or attend an in-home class would be more than willing to invite and attend if it's at a public place in their home town.

BE WILLING TO TRAVEL

Another tidbit of advice I can give you is to go where the people are. Most people have moved several times and they have friend circles in other towns. If you live in New York, but grew up in Chicago, take the tax deduction on mileage, make a trip home, and teach a couple of different classes at friend's homes. It's worth it! Tap into home plate. It's the neatest feeling to visit your friends and family out of state and feel like you're at home, with Thieves soap in the bathrooms, Thieves laundry soap in the laundry room, Thieves dish soap on the kitchen sink and a diffuser running in the background. Chemical-free living creates bonds. If you have to save three months of your check to pull off a trip of that size, do it—but not till you have it saved. Make sure you're not living outside your income.

It's also been a joy and a blessing to see my closest friends and family doing what I do. I couldn't pay them enough to anchor news! No one would touch the 39 radio stations I've worked for. This is the first time I've had the honor of working closely with the people I love the most, so start there, build a team, and do it together. My strongest teams have a network of friends and family close by who they can lean on during the frustrating days, and rejoice with during the victories. Network marketing can be an emotional roller coaster, but the payoff far outweighs the ride.

TEACH ONLINE CLASSES

This one I learned from one of my Diamond friends, Joanna Malone, who got to Diamond in under two years using this protocol. Joanna is a sheer genius and knows how to rock the social media world. If you are tech savvy (I'll tell you I am NOT, but was able to figure this one out!), you'll like this. Here are some simple steps:

HOW TO HOLD AN ONLINE CLASS

1. Record the 101 Script

Grab the compliant 101 script in the back of this book, and break it into bite size 3-minute chunks. Record those chunks on your cell phone in a place with good lighting. Make sure your first video tells your oils story (compliantly) and that your last one has a strong close, with where to order.

2. Upload the videos

I recommend uploading the videos to vimeo.com because this allows you to password protect them all. I pay the yearly fee, (about $60) so that I can upload an hour of video in one sitting. You can skip the fee, but you'll have to upload the videos once a week for about a month until you hit your bandwidth limit.

3. Prepare your captions and photos

Write a little intro for each video and have it in a place where you can quickly copy and paste it into Facebook.

The trick to a successful online class is making sure you already have the content sealed and ready to go. I once did an online class with 22,000 people in it—and it took me three hours to do a one-hour class (that's bad, you'll lose people) because I got bombarded between generating the content and answering questions. Your content needs to be completely done before you head in, so all your time can go on answering questions and engaging with the class. Make sure you have taken and uploaded a few photos of the giveaways.

4. Market the class

Now you have all your content ready, and it's time to market your class. This is a class they can attend from their living room—in 30-45 minutes or less, so market it that way. It's easy for people to attend. Say you will be doing giveaways and keep the energy up. Use the same system as you would for a live class: set up a Facebook event, have three people invite 50 people, and market it once a day for two to three weeks ahead of time. If you have leaders, asking them to share it to their page will really give you a big boost, too. I popped an online class up this evening and had 150 people going within an hour—all by offering a free bottle of lime oil to one person who shares it on their Facebook page. That's $11 advertising. It's worth every penny.

5. Class day

Start on time and watch your clock, because the excitement of an online class can cause you to lose track of time. You want to hold them until the end so they know how to get the kit. If you can keep the class to 30 to 60 minutes, you'll retain the most people.

Pop up a little one-minute intro video so they know who you are, and you're off. Every couple of minutes post a new video with the password to unlock it, and stand by to answer questions under each video. You're just posting and answering questions. Keep the answers compliant, and don't forget your giveaways every few posts.

6. Close strong

When you end, your close is just as important as in a live class. Make sure you've shot a video telling them where to get the kit, how to get the kit, and which kit you recommend. Have them message you for more information. I like to post a link at the end of the class (Young Living has a link generator in the Virtual Office) which has your sponsor and enroller number already filled in. That makes it easy for people who are just starting to navigate the Young Living website.

7. Follow up

Leave the links up for a week or so for late-joiners. I like to leave my online classes up long enough to tease the next online class to the same crowd. You can really grow your audience size for the next class that way, because people will come to respect you and will come back for more.

Make sure you mail your giveaways out within a few days. I always use those as an opportunity to sell more kits, too. Inside, I put what I call my portable office: a 101 DVD, a Premium Starter Kit flyer with instructions on how to order, and an "oil revolution designs" booklet of the Premium Starter Kit to get their attention. As with regular face-to-face classes: rinse and repeat!

ATTEND VENDOR EVENTS

I'll be straight up with you on this one. I stink at vendor events. I'm way too ADHD. I can't make myself stand still for hours in one place. As a matter of fact, when I brought this book to convention I actually paid my 17-year-old son to stand at the table and sell it for me. I'm too interested meeting new friends, wandering the halls, connecting, and networking to stay put. In radio, they gave up putting me behind the table for meet and greets. I'd constantly disappear when I saw something bright and shiny. In oils, it's much of the same for me. But just because it's not my gift doesn't mean it's not yours! So let me give you a few tips and tricks I've picked up from Oil Ability members who have amassed quite a team using this method.

I'll tell you who is best at vendor events: the people who don't know anyone! This type of sharing works really well if you're new to an area or just have freakishly small friend circles (the kind where you don't know three people who can help invite to your class). Maybe you once had great friend circles, then you became a mom or dad, and all your friends dried up as you lived vicariously through your kids, shuttling them from activity to activity. You may have had an injury or illness that's kept you isolated for a while, or even a job that's so demanding you have no social life, and you really need a base starting point for your Young Living business. It also works if you're all tapped out and need new friend circles—and your business has plateaued. Whatever your reason, vendor events work. It just takes a bit longer then online or in person classes, so you have to be patient. But if you're committed and consistent, it will pay off. Oil Ability Team's Teresa Yeager built from 8,000 OGV to 35,000 OGV in 18 months simply with a weekly vendor event and a flip kit on the table. Here's her top tips!

TOP TIPS FOR VENDOR EVENTS

1. Make sure you have a starter kit on the table and the diffuser is running

The diffuser alone will draw people to your booth. (Bring an extension cord and make sure you ask for a site with electricity ahead of time.) The best reach-across-the-hall diffuser oil is peppermint. The starter kit should be the focal point of the entire table. It's where you want to drive their eyes. Don't lay out so many books or bottles that they miss the kit. It's the reason you are there.

2. Have a flip kit for sale

Outside of getting a drop of oil on their body, this is the secret to the greatest success at vendor events. People love to impulse buy, especially when it's right in front of them. If you have it right there, they are much more likely to order. This also works well if you are teaching 101 classes and have flip kits on the table that they can walk right out of the class with.

What is a flip kit? It's a Premium Starter Kit ordered right off Young Living's website, through the Quick Order button in your virtual office. It comes with everything you got in your first kit: NingXia Red, share it bottles, eleven bottles of oil, etc. Keep at least five kits on hand at every event. When a customer wants to purchase, they get online at young-living.com and click "become a member" just as they normally would. But when they check out, the shipping screen has a button that says "ship to this address". Uncheck that box. Then put your own address in as the shipping address. The order will ship to you that one time, and then orders will default to your new member's address in the future. It's completely legal in policies and procedures, and it works.

Theresa is a Gold on my team and this is the primary, consistent method she has used to build her team: vendor events with flip kits. On her best Saturdays, she sells six kits per event. On her worst, one or two. That equates to 15 to 20 kits a month on average! It's all because she has the kits on hand. Her OGV is currently over 42,000 because of successful vendor events with flip kits!

Send them off with the kit, a copy of Fearless, a Fearless calendar, and a date to touch base in a week.

3. Have a laptop on site with reliable internet

Just like an in-person classes, you want a place they can sign up for a kit on site. (Before the doors open, make sure you have a strong internet connection.)

4. Do a drawing for a door prize

Go for it. Create a big, beautiful, oily basket and do a giveaway. Make them leave their contact info to win it. Contact info equals leads for classes.

You should have a clipboard at the booth where people can sign up if they are interested in a class. Make it clear that it doesn't need to be at their home. Tell them it's free and short. Put the clipboard right next to that large, amazing gift basket they might win (if they fill out a form). On that clipboard, instead of one sheet, I have about a hundred. (See Appendix H for a sample vendor event form.)

5. Everyone leaves with something

I like to hand out a simple version of the Purple Follow Up Bags with a Starter Kit Flyer, a sheet with step-by-step instructions on how to order a starter kit, and a business card. If you can afford it, the audio 101 lecture at oilabilityteam.com is a great giveaway too. That gets the lecture in their ears on the drive home from the event. I only hand out the CD to people who check that they are willing to hold classes, not to every single attendee. That is expensive!

It's amazing how many people are interested in classes. One of my leaders walked away with 97 different leads from people checking the box that they'd love to host a class—from one 3-day vendor event. She also sold six kits because of the flip kits she had on hand. People move past the booth swiftly, often only spending a few seconds before you. Capture as much of their information as you can on the form.

6. Make it Eye-Catching

There are a couple of relatively inexpensive things you can do that will up your game when it comes to presentation.

> Get a Young Living tablecloth. They make you look sharp with minimal effort. Google "Young Living tablecloths" and pick one up at an online retailer. Expect to spend about $100 for a good one.
>
> Use height. Get your product off the table and at eye level. People are much more likely to stop if it's as tall as they are. I get wooden crates at Hobby Lobby for $9. They are a pain to haul, but they really look nice in a convention hall.
>
> If you can swing it, have a stand up or table-top banner. I get mine at www.crowndiamondtools.com.

For some incredible printables that will make your table look SHARP, check out www.theoilposse.com.

One word of caution: you still need to develop relationships from vendor events, and that can be a lot tougher if you're only seeing them for a few minutes in a booth. I'd recommend getting "Fearless:" in their hands right away to habit train them, and doing great follow up where you get to know the new member on your team. Invite them to local Young Living rallies, classes you're teaching, and stay in contact!

Do you need some examples of a good vendor event setup? These are shots from members of the Oil Ability team:

HOW TO TALK TO PEOPLE YOU DO NOT KNOW

One of the most frequent questions I have gotten since Gameplan's release is how to deal with your cold market. In network marketing lingo, that's the market of people you do not know. This includes people at the grocery store, your kid's soccer games, and the post office. How do you approach someone without having a connection to them?

Let me pause for a moment and take the fear out of it. It's about your mindset. If you can get your head wrapped around it, the fear disappears.

It's said that the most feared thing on earth is public speaking. It's feared even more than death. I am convinced that right behind that is a fear of talking to people we have never met. It's scary! Ditch the fear and instead focus on these two truths:

1)   Every drop of oil you use is a toxic chemical you are not using. And every person you meet needs less toxins in their life and would benefit from an oily lifestyle! Most of my fear evaporates when I realize that one conversation can truly change the direction a person thinks of how to care for themselves. You're helping people. That's always a good reason to get over fear.

2)   Anyone you meet could be a potential business builder. You never know who needs hope! You are out there changing lives. Go into it with that thought process. I am always, always surprised at who chooses to do the business. Always. It's never the person I would have thought. So go forth boldly, knowing you are a world-changer and a hope-bringer.

BUILDING CONNECTIONS

Cold market is about building connections. You need to practice the art of getting to know people. You never start a conversation with: "Hey, I am an essential oils distributor — want to buy a starter kit?" Get to know the person first. Find something that you have in common, and work from there. Let me do some role-playing to give you ideas on what to say. These are based on actual conversations I have had.

In Nordstrom

To the cashier: You look so tired today!

Cashier: Oh my goodness, it's been a long week! It's really stressful running back and forth between all these booths and trying to help women. But I do get to end each day knowing I made a difference in helping them feel beautiful.

Me: I completely get it! I used to work in retail for 11 years. I came home so tired. Do you have a way to unplug when you get off your shift?

Cashier: Yes, I actually design hats. I won an award at the Kentucky Derby for one! I also like themed parties. For my birthday, I did a 1920's themed party! (She shows me photos on her phone of the costumes.)

Me: WOW. You are really talented! That is incredible! The only way I got through my shifts was to build in "me" time. I love that you take time to regroup.

Cashier: I do, but I wish there was something I could do when I am at work.

Me: I actually have something that may really help you. (I share a stress away roll-on with her).

Within three minutes, this cashier is glowing and has showed the roll-on to every single Nordstrom employee within 30 feet of her. Four cashiers rush over — and all are interested in the starter kit. I left her my name and contact information—a "portable office" in a purple bag–and collected her information as well. (That's critical to signing kits. They need a way to you, and you need a way to them). BAM.

In Walmart

Cashier: How are you doing today?

Me: I have five kids. I have taken them to six stores in two hours. I have had better days!

Cashier: I wish I could even see my son.

Me: Why? Are you ok?

Cashier: Yes. I am only supposed to work one shift a week. This is my second shift, and I just got called in a third day this week, over my son's birthday.

Me: I remember what that felt like! At my job in Chicago, I used to get called in constantly to cover other shifts. That's SO hard. I had photos of my kids on the wall where I worked, and some days I felt like that was the closest I could get to them. One night, the fireworks were going off outside on the Fourth of July, and I knew I was missing my son's first Fourth.

Cashier: It's really hard. But it's a paycheck.

Me: Can I give you something that helped me so much? I used to be exactly where you are — but I found a way to dig out. The hard thing about being here is that you have no end date. There is no hope. No way to do better for yourself and no way out. I did this for years, and got out of it. I have a little book about what I did that will really give you some relief.

Cashier: Really? I'd totally read that.

That's when I hand her a portable office with "Your Gameplan" (the mini) and my business card inside, and COLLECT her contact info. How do I collect her contact info? Maybe it feels creepy to ask for someone's phone number that you have just met, but most are completely fine adding you on Facebook. There is a distance that makes it feel safer. I usually add them right while I am standing in line, then send them a message once I get outside saying, "This is Sarah, we met in the check-out. I hope you had a better shift after I left! I will check in with you in a couple of days to see if you enjoyed the book!" This short 2-minute conversation during checkout led to a thriving business builder on my team.

Post Office

Postal Worker: Wow. You mail a LOT of packages.

Me: Yes, I run a home-based business.

Postal Worker: I see you in here every week.

Me: It's the best financial choice I have ever made. So far, we have paid off $250,000 in debt, and paid for our home mortgage-free. I wish I'd done this in my 20's.

Postal Worker: Is this one of those network marketing things? Because I don't like talking to people.

Me: You just told me you're a single mom, you drive 50 minutes to this job every week at 5 a.m., and this job keeps you in survival mode. If I gave you something to read, would you read it? It's how I got out of where I was.

Postal Worker: Yes, I would read it. (One postal worker said she did not have time, so I offered her the "Sarah's Why" video on the oilabilityteam. com website [under Getting Started]. She listened on her phone and signed up that night.)

For the postal worker that would read, I gave her a portable office with a mini. When I saw her in a nail salon two weeks later, she joined my team.

Hardware Store (actual conversation)

Woman behind me in line: What are you buying all that organic gardening stuff for?

Me: I hate the chemicals in our food. Even the stuff at the grocery store isn't safe.

Woman behind me in line: Yeah, I have read some articles on sprayed crops. It's scary. What are you using?

Me: I do raised garden beds and essential oils.

Woman behind me in line: What? What are essential oils?

Me: I actually have an entire class on audio CD with me right now if you want to pop it in your CD player in your car and listen on the way home. It completely changed how I viewed yuck in my home.

Woman behind me in line: I would listen to that! (Grabs her friend) — this woman teaches on essential oils. It's about getting bad chemicals out of our house. We need to have her over to teach a class to our friends. (This was totally unprompted.)

Woman 2: I had heard about those and wanted to learn more.

This is where I hand out portable offices, collect their contact information, and book a class. There were 30 women at it. We had 80% kit sales and several business builders.

Woman at Convention serving food at the Diamond gala

Woman: (leans over to me, looking at the Diamonds on stage) Is this really real?

Sarah: Would you like to see how real this is for me?

Woman: Yes. (I show her my paycheck in the Virtual office)

Woman: How long did that take you?

Sarah: Two years.

Woman: Wow.

Sarah: Do you want to know how you can do this — and not work for a catering company?

Woman: YES.

I hand her a portable office — which has "Your Gameplan" inside with the income disclosure guide. I gather her contact information. She signs to my team.

TSA Agent as I am going through security following the Gold retreat in Spokane, Washington

Agent: The ice in your water bottle melted. You are going to have to go back through security a second time.

Agent: (after I come through the second time) What are all those yellow bags on your backs? (He is referring to the Young Living swag bag from the retreat).

Me: It's a swag bag I was given for attending an essential oils retreat.

Agent: Oh, I used some Frankincense once and it worked.

Me: Was it Young Living Frankincense?

Agent: No, I don't think so.

Me: Young Living is a pioneer in oils—the best of the best. Their distillation is copied all over the world. We are the first oils company to have OTC meds—approved by the FDA—that have no garbage in them.

Agent: Wow, really?

Me: Yes! I have a class on it online for free—mind if I text it to you? You can listen on your cell phone on the way home.

Agent: Yeah, I don't like the stuff I'm using right now.

Me: I didn't either. That's why I started with this. You are the only one that can protect your home.

Agent gives me his cell, I text him the 101 class on oilabilityteam.com, he listens on his lunch break and is signed to the team before I get home.

Woman I have never met at my son's basketball game

Woman: What is that smell?

Me: I just put on some essential oils. It stinks in here!

Woman: Oh my WORD yes. I have four teenage sons. Two play on this team.

Me: The best choice I ever made was purification in my 16 year old's shoes.

Woman: What is purification?

Me: An anti-stink oil. It works!

Woman: I need that in my life.

Me: The best way to get it is by become a wholesale member with a starter kit. The kit is half off. And it gets you 24% off purification for life.

Woman: I don't have much money right now.

Me: There are tons of uses of oils—far beyond smells. I used to get headaches constantly because of the cleaning supplies I was using. Young Living makes cleaning supplies with no toxins. My eight year old cleans the bathroom now and it doesn't tax his liver.

Woman: I just want to get my kids to CLEAN.

Me: (laughs) It works! If I give you something to listen to—and I promise oils won't break the bank (I can make Thieves cleaner for $1.50 a spray bottle)—would you listen?

Woman: I don't have a lot of time.

Me: Listen, your health matters. Your family matters. The stuff in your cabinets isn't safe. There is a better way. Just listen, and let me check in with you in a few days.

Woman: Ok.

I hand her a portable office with a Toxin Free Life audio cd inside and touch base three days later. The woman held a yard sale and got a kit that summer, and then later became a business builder.

Woman at an Essential Oils 101 Class I taught

(At the end of the class)

Woman: I'm not sure I'm can do this—the kit is pricey.

Me: If I send you home with some samples, will you try them out?

Woman: I don't know...

Me: Let's tailor it to exactly what's going on with you right now. If you knew there was a better way to take care of yourself with fewer toxic chemicals, would you choose that way?

Woman: Of course.

Me: What's something that is bothering you right now?

Woman: I have carpal tunnel syndrome, and I have to have my third surgery this fall on my hands.

Me: I have never had carpal tunnel syndrome, so I can't speak to that. But I love the way that my hands feel when I apply lavender. Would you like me to send you home with some lavender?

Woman: I guess I can try it.

Before the clock struck midnight, she had signed up for a kit. She is now the number one leader on my team, with an OGV of 120,000 a month, and runs a team called, "Changed By Lavender."

Do you see a pattern in these conversations? So many people ask me "for the exact words" of what to say to someone they have never met. It comes down to a few key principles.

Principle 1: Meet them where they are, do not hunt them down for a kit. With the cashier, I met her as she missed her son. With the Nordstrom worker, I met her in her place of stress. With the TSA agent, I met him in his experience with Frankincense. With the woman at the class, I met her in her physical need, without diagnosing disease — just by listening. Step one is to listen and ask the right questions. What do they do for a living? How do they spend their time? What do they do for fun? Who do they go home to every night? What matters to them? Sometimes the people around you will strike up a conversation, and sometimes you initiate. But the most important element is that the conversation is about them, and not about you. This is a business of serving.

But Sarah how do I start the conversation?? It can be anything. The smell of an oil. Something in their cart. Their cute baby. Their shirt. A snack in their hands. Anything. I sold a starter kit to a woman on an airplane, then starter kits to three of her kids — just by walking on with an oversized bag of popcorn. It was a conversation starter. Still afraid? Just remember, you are there to make a difference in their lives. Think about that place you were in pre-oils. It's where they are. Meet them there. Every time you step up, it leads to good change for an entire family. What if you are shy? Many of the conversations I started above began with two simple things: eye contact and a smile. Begin there, and you may find you're just responding to a conversation someone else has already started for you.

Principle 2: Always come prepared. You never know where the conversation will take you. Someone might walk out with a portable office, with your business card with a link to the Audio 101 class at oilabilityteam.com or the Toxin Free Life class at the same website. They might want information on the business, and you will need "Your Gameplan" books on hand. Why do I carry those with me? Because they are 40 pages long. In a 2-minute conversation, I can't possibly convey all the perks of a Young Living business, share my story, and show them the income disclosure guide that gives them hope. It is information overload. But I can gift them a book that they can read on lunch break, and touch base. The book sets the tone for the next conversation. It points them back to you to be trained. And it works.

Principle 3: Utilize Eric Worre's "If I Will You" statement. Always do a call-to-action. Always ask for something in return. They should expect you to check in. "If I give you this CD, will you listen to it — and can I check in with you in three days?" "If I give you this "Your Gameplan" book, will you read it — and may I Facebook friend you to see how you are doing?" Always expect something for what you are giving out. If there is no interest, kick the dust off your feet and move on. But remember, the average person can only say no seven times. No now does not mean no forever.

Principle 4: Never, ever walk away without getting their contact information. This is the biggest mistake I see when people are handing out "Your Gameplan" books. I picked up 13 business builders from those books tucked in purple bags in stores last month alone, and I have seen thousands of people rank up using them since we released them. I know they are an amazing prospecting tool — the only one in all of Young Living! They lay the groundwork for you to have a conversation about the business that isn't awkward, one where the person you are speaking to is waiting on you to contact them. But you have to do the follow up, or you will lose their interest. If it's someone I have never met, I rarely get their phone number because that falls into the category of stalker for me. Phone numbers are for people you're familiar with. But a Facebook friending is more distant, they can "unfriend" and "block" you if you bug them; and it feels safer. Stay in that place of relatability and you'll have a new friend. But don't ever walk away after handing out a portable office or a "Your Gameplan" book without collecting information, or you just gave that package away for free.

Principle 5: Follow up! This is where people go wonky on me. They say, "Sarah! Talking to a random stranger in line was hard enough on me, but now you want me to TALK TO THEM TWICE??" Yes, I do. And if you skip this step, you have just handed a potential oiler over to the next person that will do follow up with them. One of the biggest complaints I hear as a Diamond is that a leader had pursued someone, only to see them end up on someone else's team. 100% of the time that's because of poor follow up. If someone else had better follow up, they deserved the lead you initially pursued. Put down your frustrations, get over fear, and touch base. It can be as simple as a quick note on Facebook, a text, or an email message. It can be a phone call or a quick visit if it's someone you know. But don't put the time and effort into training on oils and handing out portable offices and "Your Gameplan" books, expending money and time, for the sake of handing them over to someone else. Your resources matter. So check in.

So are you clear on how to approach someone you have never met? Strike up a conversation, meeting them where they are, without any mention of oils. Come prepared with portable offices. I always carry at least five of them in my purse at all times. It takes the amount of information you have to pack into one small 2-minute meeting to almost nothing. All you need is a reason to touch base again. Go for that, and you have done a great job. Use "if I will you". They should expect to hear from you again. Never, ever walk away without getting their contact information. And follow up. Otherwise, all of your work was for naught.

On the oilabilityteam,com, I have put together an entire post on portable offices that's hyperlinked with all the supplies you need. It's under "share" and "purple follow up bags."

Also on the same site, TWO FREE audio classes. I have spent more than a decade and a half as a radio network news anchor, so putting together audio classes is something I love. These are totally free, and you can listen on your cell phone. We call them "textable classes" — because you can go to the website, copy the link for the class, and text it to people directly. And it works! Many have used this approach and put them on the back of their business cards to draw interest, too, like Judy:

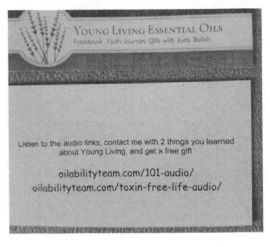

YOUNG LIVING ESSENTIAL OILS
Facebook: Faith Journey Oils with Judy Bafoh

Listen to the audio links, contact me with 2 things you learned about Young Living, and get a free gift

oilabilityteam.com/101-audio/
oilabilityteam.com/toxin-free-life-audio/

The last resource on the website is "Your Gameplan" book, which we have nicknamed "minis," that drive people to do the business. Get them in bulk and use them in your portable offices.

One of the things that drove me to write the mini was a Careerbuilder. com survey that came out in January 2017. It really convicted me to have eyes to see all the business builders around me. That survey showed, "More than one in five Americans will actively look for a new job in the next 12 months." One in five!

You already have eyes to find people who need oils. That's simple, because oils are used for just about everything. I encourage you to dig deeper, and find people who are poor. I'm not just talking about money poor. I'm talking about sleep poor. Time poor. Relationally poor. No-time-to-take-care-of-my-body poor. No dates with my husband poor. High-stressed, need-a-way-out poor. Dreaming-of-a-vacation poor. I-have-had-an-untouched-bucket-list-for-ten-years   poor.   I-have-given-up-hope poor. According to Careerbuilder, that's 1 in every 5 people around you. You just need eyes to see them. This book has given you hope. Now it's your job to spread it.

So how do you get that contact started as a business builder? Follow all the steps above. Strike up a conversation, drop tools in their lap and follow up. On the second conversation, it's time to take them through the seven steps of the Gameplan system.

The system is so crazy simple — so easy to follow — so duplicatable. It looks like this:

1) Get them a copy of the mini "Your Gameplan" if they don't already have one.

2) Hold a teacher training (in the Appendix of this book).

3) Coach them through teaching their first 101 class.

4) Get the Gameplan book and workbook in their hands.

5) Point them to the FREE bootcamp at oilabilityteam.com. Tell them to do one chapter of the book, one set of worksheets and one bootcamp video at their pace.

6) Train 2 to train 2. Once they have some interested builders on their team, guide them to pick two, train them on Gameplan, then have them train two, and do it again.

7) Rinse and repeat your way through one year of Gameplan bootcamps and through the power of duplication, and grow an organization of 531,000 in one year. That's a Royal Crown Diamond organization — if you duplicate.

Don't jump to the next system when you finish Gameplan. Don't reinvent the wheel. Those that rank aren't creating new systems; they are just crazy good at following directions and duplicating. I have seen it again and again and again and again — even on our own team. The ones that rank are the ones that use the Gameplan system. Your task is to get people to see where this goes. Once you do, you will have an on-fire builder.

What if you committed twelve months to the Gameplan system? What if you held one class a week, did follow up from those classes once a month, and did twelve bootcamps where you trained two to train two? What if you gifted Gameplan books to every person who finished training two of their own through bootcamp? Doing a bootcamp doesn't mean that you're re-watching all the videos. It means you're an accountability partner, posting something each day (even if it's a link to the videos) and checking in. We have created a bootcamp checklist chart in the Appendix to help you keep track. Do you know what would happen if you committed to those three income producing activities for a year? You'd explode your OGV, grow leaders, and equip lifelong oilers. You can do this!

WHAT TO SAY WHEN YOU INVITE

Remember, this isn't about selling, it's about educating people about the oils themselves. Why would they want to come to a free oils class?

I'll tell you first that a lot of it depends on your own passion. Passion is infectious. If you love the oils and you know that they work, it will be hard to turn you away. Speak with authority and excitement. Let's go through a little role playing exercise.

This is an actual conversation I had with a prospective oiler:

Sarah: Hey Jessie! It's so good to see you! I feel like we haven't talked in ages!

Jessie: What have you been up to lately?

Sarah: Well, I am teaching classes on essential oils. It's really blessed my family!

Jessie: I have never even heard of them before. What are they?

Sarah: (Note: you have 30 seconds to get her attention. Keep it tight!) Essential oils are a bit different than the oil you buy in the store. They have incredible effects on the human body. I use them all over my home; to get rid of chemical cleaning supplies; calm my kids down; for emotions, focus, and stress. I use them in my toothpaste, deodorant, and supplements. I have gotten really good at label reading, and I'll be straight up with you; I just don't like what I can't pronounce on the back of the bottles. I was poisoning my family with a lot of things that I thought were safe.

Essential oils are made of one thing: steam distilled or cold pressed plants. No yuck. The only ingredient in lemon oil is lemon. If you flip the bottle over and can't pronounce what's on the label, you really shouldn't be slathering it on your scalp, or putting it on your skin, eating it, or washing your dishes with it. Did you know the number one poison in the family home is fabric softener? Right behind that—air fresheners. I've replaced both of them with oils.

Jessie: That's crazy. I had no idea. I still have a plug-in air freshener in my living room.

Sarah: I have class Saturday that's free. I'd love to see you there! If you come, I'll have some peppermint for you to try and you can smell nearly a dozen oils in a starter kit. It's how I began. Will you come?

BAM. Done. Give them meat and potatoes. Tell them how they can use it. Tell them why they need it. I always carry samples with me (peppermint is my favorite "wow" oil) so they can take some right away. Then make sure you follow up and don't lose that contact.

I use the exact same approach when raising leaders. You just have to have an eye for the people who are dissatisfied at their job or the single mom who's trying to make ends meet at her second job. Look for the poor, the weary, and then show them that this way is better. Do the same among your family and friends. I want my top leaders to be my family and friends, and I want to see them financially blessed. Don't be timid.

Have the same conversation I just had above with potential business builders. Keep your "reason" for doing Young Living to 30 seconds or less and give practical information and substantial facts. If that doesn't seem to catch their attention, be quiet and listen! Listen to where they are. Then go from there, and based on what they are telling you, respond to their needs.

Here's a role play of a conversation with a potential business builder:

Grace: Hey Sarah! I don't usually run into you at the store at this time!

Sarah: I have switched jobs!

Grace: What are you doing?

Sarah: Network marketing.

Grace: Oh. You're selling stuff to people?

Sarah: I've never sold an essential oils starter kit in my life. What I do is teach people how to get chemicals out of their house and protect their families. Best. Job. Ever.

Grace: Yeah, I tried the oils thing, but it's really expensive.

Sarah: Not really. You can make Thieves cleaner for $1 a bottle. If you grab a starter kit and host a class, I will come teach under you, and you can work to get your oils for free. I don't pay for any of my oils.

Grace: It sounds interesting, but I'm really not interested in another job.

Sarah: So you like what you're doing right now?

Grace: Heck no. I work way too many hours and we barely make it.

Sarah: I worked 11 hours last week at my full time Young Living business. Maybe you should consider this.

Grace: But I don't like talking to people.

Sarah: It's as hard as grabbing a few people, sitting in your living room, and reading a 3-page script. Super crazy easy, and you're teaching people how to take care of their families.

Grace: It doesn't sound that hard.

Sarah: It's the best financial decision I've ever made. Do you have time next week for a Teacher Training?

Grace: Yes!

CONNECTIONS ARE ALL AROUND YOU

I actually had this exact same conversation, almost word for word, with a woman I met at the Young Living convention. I was sitting at the Diamond awards night and she was part of the catering company that was serving our food. She saw all the Diamonds going on the stage and turned to me and asked, "Is it real?" I said "Do you want to know how real this is?" Then I opened the Oily Tools on my cell phone and showed her my team stats. Her jaw was on the floor. I added her on Facebook immediately and made contact when I got home. That was someone I'd never met.

Be bold! I once sold a kit to a TSA agent on the way to my flight, another to the mail lady down at the post office, and two kits to some people who were on my zip lining tour for the Young Living Drive-to-Win Tour in Hawaii. You share because you love the oils, and you don't want people to be without them. Don't be afraid to speak to the everyday people around you. You come into contact with far more people than you realize!

Keep a running list of the people you run into during a week—and make sure you're not dropping the ball connecting, because connecting is key. You'll learn a thorough follow up system in Chapter 10. There are also follow up cards in the Gameplan Workbook. They are 3x5 cards that help you recall what you mailed out to whom, what oils they are interested in, and fills your new oilers with recipe ideas and resources. You can pick up the Gameplan Workbook at oilabilityteam.com.

I've now walked you through in-person connections and how to fill your classes, whether they are in person or online, big or small. It's time to get to the heart of what teaching a class looks like! Next I'll walk you through step-by-step, as if you're in one of my own classes. Let's go!

CHAPTER 9

ANATOMY OF A SUCCESSFUL CLASS

This is where the book gets interesting to write, because everyone has a different definition of what "class day" is. If you're primarily blogging or doing classes online, it will look quite different from someone who's meeting a person over lunch or someone who's teaching a class of 50 in a church gym. I will tell you this, whatever class style you prefer, try something new from this list. If you're a gifted blogger, try branching out with a bit of class time also. If you're doing it all in person, it's not a bad idea to add in a little social media. It's like diversifying your 401k portfolio. Don't put all your eggs in one basket.

CLASS STYLES AND SIZES

Our team has the best success with face-to-face, in-person classes. It's how we've grown so fast. Why? You're building relationships.

I held my first online class in November 2015, and we had 22,000 people on the class. It resulted in two kit sales and two new business builders.

Then I held a class in the nearby tiny town of Hornell, New York, which is in a very impoverished area. Eight people attended the class. We sold eight kits that night and picked up two business builders. We had 100% sales!

There's just something to be said for face-to-face relationships. It shows people you care, and that you're not just a line on a screen in front of them. You can do in-person classes one-on-one or you can do them in groups.

Large Classes

Very few people will actually stand in front of 40 or 50 people and teach; it's quite rare. But I'd encourage you to have classes of at least five to ten people. If you have a competitive personality, or just prefer to grow your business more quilckly, I recommend that you get your class size to at least 20 people. You'll grow *very* fast that way if you are effective at following up.

Small Classes

If you are not competitive—in fact, you're downright shy—but you *really* want this to work, we have a game plan for you, too. Some of the top sellers on my team are introverted and soft-spoken. You don't need to be loud to do this, you just need to be confident.

If you're really nervous about reading the 101 script in front of people, simply play hostess. Invite them to your home, share your story briefly on how you got your kit, and pop our Essential Oils 101 DVD (you can find it at oilabilityteam.com.) in your DVD player. End by passing the kit around and telling them how to get started with Young Living.

Speak for three or four minutes before the DVD and five minutes after, and you'll have a powerhouse class! No lecture experience needed! We've seen tremendous success with this model, even among people on my team who are very timid and shy. A few of my Silvers-In-Six have used this model with great results.

One-on-One Classes

You can teach one-on-one classes, but just recognize that your pace of growth will be much slower. If that's what you can handle, go for it! It doesn't matter whether it takes you ten or 20 years to get to Diamond. It's still the best job on the face of the earth. (And the best paid job, too!)

The only thing you need to watch for with this type of teaching model is getting burned out. Some people will give up because they don't see results fast enough. If you can stick with it—one or two one-on-ones a week, every week—you'll get where you want to go.

Speaking of getting burned out, don't make your classes such a production that the very act of doing one drains you for the rest of the week! Keep it simple. Do not spend a lot of money—that is not reproducible.

You need only a 3-page script and a starter kit to pull this off; not folders stuffed with 40 pages of photocopied material, not Peppermint Vitality brownies, not posterboards with science of oils taped to them when they walk in the door, not $200 worth of make-and-take supplies ordered from six different sites; not stickers for your glass bottles made with Cricut cutters. If you keep it simple, you don't scare away your incoming leaders. Always ask yourself if what you're doing will be intimidating to the person considering the business in the room. If that's the case, drop it. The most valuable thing you have in this business is leaders that duplicate. Make the system simple.

ANATOMY OF AN OIL ABILITY CLASS

Every class, big or small, should incorporate these ten elements:

1. Tell your story

Introduce yourself and share a bit about your oils story, how you got involved in oils, and why you're passionate to share them with others.

2. Introduce the chemical free lifestyle

Issue the three cabinet challenge. Ask people to take a look at three cabinets in their home and get familiar with what they're slathering on their bodies, or ingesting, or cleaning with. The rule of thumb is if you can't pronounce it—don't use it. The shorter the list of ingredients the better. If you're not sure if it's safe, type the word into Google with the words "dangers of" in front of it and do a little research. Why learn about oils? Every oil you use is a chemical you're not using.

3. Play the Oily Scavenger Hunt video

This is a 3-minute icebreaker video which shows people what a home infused with essential oils looks like. It features my five children, the Harnisch herd. (Heads up—we had a bit of fun with it.) You can find it at www.oilabilityteam.com.

4. Launch into the lecture

It's just three pages long when printed out and runs about 35 minutes. You have a free copy of that lecture in the appendix of this book. Why give a lecture? Because it's important that people know essential oil basics—safety, how they hit the body, what they're used for, and purity. Of these, purity is the most important, because you don't want someone leaving your class and to buy essential oils in the grocery store! Don't let the lecture run too long or you'll lose interest.

5. Pass around the Starter Kit

Get the caps off and let people smell the oils. Why is this so important? Because the magic is in the oil. When they get the smell of Peppermint or Frankincense in their nose for the very first time, that's when the oils will get their attention, more so then any lecture. It's like trying to teach someone to drive without putting them in a car. Book learning will only take them so far, they have to experience the oils. I have said many times in this book that you only need two things to teach a class: a 101 Script and a starter kit. This is the second half of that sentence and it's critical. Let them experience the oils in the kit. Don't forget there are compliant descriptions of each of the oils in the 101 Script for you to rely on as you share.

6. End with a strong close

You've given them a lot of information and they may be unsure what their response should be. Tell them exactly what their best next step is. Say something like, "This is the only essential oils company I trust. I began my journey with a Young Living premium starter kit, and that's where

I suggest you start your journey, too. It's as simple as going to 'YoungLiving.com,' clicking on 'Become a Member,' and entering my sponsor and enroller number. Thank you for blessing my family!" There are two strong closing scripts included in the Appendixes for you to work from.

7. Get their information

Make sure you grab their information on a clipboard so you can follow up with them after the class.

8. Give them resources

It is important that they have your information, too! I like to hand out purple bags with a one-page flyer of the starter kit, a paper explaining how to order with my distributor number on it, and my business card.

I also hand out free 101 DVD's or CD's. I tell them there was likely someone they know who should have heard the class, and I ask them to pass the DVD or CD along. That way, you have just doubled your class size. Feel free to point them to the Oil Ability Facebook page and website for more videos to continue their education. It doesn't matter if you're a crossline member. If they are on your team and they watch our 101 class, they'll order more oils, and it will bless your OGV. We put those together as a resource for all oilers to use as they learn to grow.

9. Find the business builders

If you're a genius and want to spark business builders, you'll pop in the "How to Get Your Oils For Free" DVD for ten minutes right at the close of your class. That's on our oilabilityteam.com website too. Or you can place a "Your Gameplan" mini book on their chair before they come in and say, "to learn how to get your oils for free, read this."

10. Don't let them leave without something oily

I love to have a few $1 spray bottles on a table and the new Thieves Cleaner sampler packs where they can make up a spray bottle to take home for $5. If that's not affordable for you right now, simply put a drop of Peppermint in the palm of their hand before they walk out the door. The goal is for your up and coming oiler to have an experience. If you get oils on their body or send them home with a wow moment (like Thieves Cleaner), you're much more likely to see them pop up in your organization.

DIFFERENT TYPES OF IN-PERSON CLASSES

The one-on-one

This is you and one person. Grab the 3-page 101 script and have at it. You will be slower to grow than someone with a larger class, but growing is better than staying still. You will get there. Just do not be discouraged by how quickly people are ranking around you. There is nothing wrong with your style or your gifting, it just takes longer. And that's completely okay. Don't ever rate yourself against other people's gifts. The end game is all that matters. A Diamond is a Diamond.

The lunch and learn

Grab the 101 script, contact a local business, and speak to their employees over their lunch hour. Keep it short.

The couch class

Before I started renting halls and speaking to lots of people, I started right in my living room. My first class had 12 people on my couch and my knees were a-knocking. Start small till you get your rhythm.

"But, I don't want people in my house." Then find a friend that will let you borrow their living room and have at it.

The big class

If you are expecting a crowd, you may need a larger space, a sound system, and a projector and screen. I have taught most of my larger classes in church gyms. Other ideas for venues: libraries, the "Y," community centers, senior centers, hotels, fire halls, churches, and public schools after hours. I have taught in them all.

The connection class

This is a one-on-one I hold with the owner of a bulk food store, a dentist, a chiropractor, a massage therapist, or anyone I want to host classes for me in their business. I am leaning on their friend circles and business connections to fill classes. If they are willing, it's always wise to leave portable offices in their office: an organza bag with a DVD or CD, a flyer, a sheet on how to order and your contact info. I also ask if someone is willing to run the diffuser each morning, and I put up new banners in the office each month with topics I'll be speaking on. The diffuser alone is usually enough to generate interest in the class.

Gotta eat

This is a class I do with three to ten friends over lunch or dinner. We pick a restaurant, I give my intro, we eat, I read the 101 Script. It's a great way to gain some weight! But it sells oils kits! I train a lot of leaders in this environment. It's different from a lunch and learn in that I usually do these with leaders.

Speed oiling

This is a type of class where you set up stations, usually with several of your leaders, who teach a 5-minute topical oils class like Oils for Fall and Winter, or Oils of the Bible. As long as you sneak a 101 in there somewhere, I'm down with it. Always push to the starter kit—and don't forget your close. Rotate every five minutes.

Make and Takes

In this type of class, you give a condensed (10-15 minute) 101 class, then create something. Themes I have done in the past: Spa, Chemical Free Home, It's All About That Base, Oil Your Man, and Make Your Own Diffuser Necklace, etc...

The downside to this, it doesn't sell oils. If you want to build dedicated oilers, give them a reason to order on Young Living's site, rather than collecting supplies on their own.

The smart way to do make and takes is using the new DIY Kit from Young Living (item number 21861) and only using starter kit oils for the class, or by teaching a Toxin Free Life class with the Thieves Home Cleaning Kit (item number 20421). The small red pouch comes with a recipe book that would work for a make and take class. Then the people coming to your class can experience making their own cutsom Thieves Cleaner spray, and will be more likely to restock ingredients through Young Living . You can also use the DIY kit class to funnel to the starter kit, and the Thieves Home Cleaning Kit to funnel to the Thieves starter kit.

TEACH WITH THE PROPER RATIOS

Teach three 101 classes for every specialty class you teach. (Specialty classes include Beauty School, Make-and-Takes, Oil Affordability, Biblical Oils, etc.). Why? Because the 101 Class is the class that sells the starter kit. You'll be inclined to focus on all the people you have brought in by teaching them all the aromatherapy classes you possibly can so they have an oils hunger and ideas for Essential Rewards. But that truly isn't the fastest way to grow. The reality is that Oils and Emotions doesn't sell starter kits. And 80% of your time must be spent prospecting, or bringing new people in. So put your time in the most efficient place, and you will grow. Unless Young Living develops an Oils and Emotions starter kit, that's not the class (or any non-PSK class) you should be spending most of your time on.

You also don't get the same kind of results from make-and-take classes. At make-and-take classes, 70% of the people who attend never order the oils and never make the product again. That is not the shortest path from point A to point B. If your goal is to sell starter kits and raise leaders, focus on the class that funnels to the starter kit. If your potential leaders show up to your make-and-take and see that you spent $200 on supplies from three online stores and put 90 hours into setup, you're going to scare them off. They can't commit to that kind of time. Make-and-takes scare away leaders. They are not duplicatable. Even if we are not talking about potential business builders, these kinds of classes encourage the people in the class to buy product (bases, jars, labels) that are not on Young Living's website. It will not boost your OGV. That's not the quickest way to build your business.

END YOUR CLASSES STRONG

Whatever your class style, you must not neglect a strong close. Remember the beginning of this book, where I gave you five mistakes that all stagnant business builders make? This is one of the most common mistakes I see.

I once had a woman teach a dozen classes and didn't sell a single kit at any class. I finally went to one of her classes and sat in the back of the room. She gave this beautiful 101 lecture, and then ended by saying, "You have just survived Essential Oils 101!" And that was it. No starter kit explanation, no laptop in the back of the room for people to sign, no instructions, no paper with her number as sponsor and enroller. Nothing. Those people left and got kits under someone else. One woman told me she didn't even realize that the lecturer was selling oils. Oy.

Why do we get so skittish over our close? That's easy to explain. This is the part where we think we're selling something. It's the part where we feel like we're imposing on someone. We're forcing them to spend money they do not have. We are the solicitor at the door. Oh, and they might say "no."

Here's the thing we don't realize: these people gave up their time to come to this class! They wanted to learn about oils, they have a desire to swap out the chemicals in their home, and you failed to open the door to the start of that journey. They walked away from their families or their other obligations to attend your class. But, you failed them because they have no knowledge on where to start and they left your class with absolutely nothing.

In the Appendix of this book, I have included closing scripts that lay out word for word what to say. But the gist of it is this: tell them that this is the company you trust, that this is where you began your oils journey, that this kit is the only thing on Young Living's site that's half off, so it's truly a bargain. Explain what comes in the kit and pass it around (11 oils, a diffuser, literature, NingXia samples, a Theives cleaner sample, and 24% off your oils for life!)

Essential oils are the bridge to natural living.

As you close, tell them that you have a laptop in the back of the room and that anyone who needs help navigating the website can get assistance at a station in the room. Let them walk out with a purple bag that includes information on how to order at home. Make sure your contact information is in it. Go through that sheet. Tell them it's as hard as going to "youngliving.com," clicking on "Become a Member," and using your sponsor and enroller number. Select the premium starter kit with Desert Mist diffuser, and they're off.

Then you get the blessing of seeing where that goes. You get to field the texts of glee coming from them as they open the box. You get the updates as they discover the kits for themselves. You get to walk that journey alongside them and experience it all over again, as if it were your first week with the oils.

I tell people that if they're nervous about the close, imagine what you felt like when you knew absolutely nothing about oils. You were in darkness. You really didn't realize what a wonderful tool the Lord had given us. As you discovered them one by one, fear melted away and was replaced with confidence, joy, and the satisfaction of knowing that yet another chemical had been banned from your home.

They're so easy to use, easier than a tincture or an herb. I like to say essential oils are the bridge to natural living. Instead of having to learn about tincturing and fermenting for six weeks to begin their journey toward health, they can literally just grab a drop out of a bottle that's been expertly distilled. No prep required. The oils are powerful, they're accessible, and they have millions of uses. Find a way to share what you know with someone who was in the same place you were before you had the kit in your hands. Remember that place so you can communicate effectively with them.

If you can pull that off, you have had a very successful class. If you can connect, educate, and train people how to research the uses of the oils for themselves and catch the vision of where Young Living goes, you will have lifelong oilers!

PART THREE

AFTER THE CLASS: HOW
TO FOLLOW UP

Gameplan helped me increase my ER percentages from 38% to 46%!!!

Michelle Wipper

Last January my OGV was zero. In April I read Gameplan and was on fire for this business! I began praying over my business and implementing Gameplan tactics. I went from Distributor to Silver in seven months! My ER % consistently runs over 40%.

Alisha Palmer

I did Gameplan with my team in March and we had 90,000 OGV growth in one month and got to Diamond!

Chelsa Bruno

CHAPTER 10

THE OIL ABILITY FOLLOW UP SYSTEM

One of my team members approached me last week and said the last four people she's tried to sign to her team ended up on other people's teams. Do you know what causes that? *A lack of follow up.* You planted the seed, you got them interested in oils, and then *you walked away.*

You never touched base.

You never made the call to see why they weren't at class.

You never checked in to see how that Peppermint oil worked.

Consistent follow up is key to a successful business and the residual income that will bring true financial freedom to you! You've got a system for filling classes and sharing the oils, and now I'm gonna give you...

THE OIL ABILITY FOLLOW UP SYSTEM

I'd love to say this concept was my idea, but it really wasn't. I first learned about 3-10-30 from Royal Crown Diamond Teri Secrest's materials. I had the opportunity to connect with her in person on the Global Leadership cruise to Venice, and to pray with her and her incredible daughter Elizabeth Rose, my whitewater rafting buddy, at the Gold retreat. Their family is just wonderful. That's what I've found of all the Diamonds, though, is that they're just real people, like you and me, who have trudged through life, been poor, and found a better way. Teri's advice was fantastic and so is her book, "How Big Is Your Wave." Check it out!

This is a shot of Elizabeth (in the center) and me (on the left) rafting. (Whoever gave Young Living Corporate water guns to spray us as we came off the rapids, payback hurts!)

At about the time of this picture, I was frustrated trying to get people on Essential Rewards. That's where your residual income is, the income you don't have to hunt down in new starter kits month after month after month. It means that instead of starting from zero every month, you're starting from 300 PV when three people sign up for Essential Rewards. After you get ten people on Essential Rewards, you're starting with 500 to 1,000 or more OGV. The groundwork is already laid to kick off the next month.

But how do you get people to follow through on their desire for a kit or to get Essential Rewards? You touch base with people. It's called follow up. Teri uses a fool proof system called 3-10-30. She checks in with attendees 3 days, 10 days, and 30 days after a class.

As you begin to follow up, you'll run into three types of people:

1) The first type of person who wants nothing to do with you and asks you to leave them alone. This is the reason we all fear doing follow up after a class; we believe in our minds that 100% of the people we speak to will respond in this way, but this is extremely rare. These people came to a class to learn and they were grateful for the information. In the rare event that they react negatively, drop them and move on. Never call again.

2) The second type of people are those that say, "Oh man! I meant to get a kit when I was at class but I had to get Junior to

soccer practice and have been running like crazy since then! Can you walk me through it?" Bam! You just sold a starter kit.

3) The third type of person is the one you're most likely to encounter. "Yes, I want to get a starter kit, but I just can't afford it right now."

What they're actually telling you is, "I don't know whether I need this." So it's your task to show them they need it. However, my first question isn't, "When can you afford it? When do you get paid?" That's rude and it's also counter-productive.

My first question is, "If you could wake up without one thing tomorrow—a feeling of frustration, stiffness, anything—what would that one thing be?" Write down that one thing and bring them an oil. Have them put it on and see how they feel. Most of my kit sales aren't from being pushy, they're from loving the people who came to the class and having a heart for them, wherever they are.

Follow up takes many forms. It can be a text message, a phone call, or a message on Facebook. It may be a face-to-face meeting or a Skype training to go through the kit for someone who lives far away or who has a busy schedule. I spend more time doing follow up and mailings than I do in the classroom, and follow up is one of the reasons why we have so many people on Essential Rewards.

So when you're making these calls, what do you say? There are two different types of calls. The first is for people who haven't got the kit and the second is for people who have. Let's start with the newbies.

FOLLOW UP FOR THOSE WHO DON'T HAVE A KIT

I'd tell them I'm calling to see how they liked the class and what stood out for them. I'd listen for a while in order to determine what they are interested in--perhaps they'd like oils for their pets. I'd ask if they'd like to get a kit. Then I'd talk them through how to order.

If they say not now, I'd ask if I can mail them some more resources. If they say yes to that, I'd slip a sample, a handwritten note, and one of my other lectures on DVD in the mail. But if they have said yes to getting a starter kit, I walk them through it and slip a similar package in the mail.

FOLLOW UP FOR THOSE WHO GOT A KIT

If they have already purchased the kit, the goal is to get them on Essential Rewards as a regular oiler. Then my first question is, "Did your kit arrive?" I'll ask them which oils they've used and which ones they haven't used. I'll ask if they know how to set up their diffuser. We'll talk about the NingXia samples. I'll explain Essential Rewards and discuss the other products Young Living has on their site. Did they know they can swap out their laundry soap, dish soap, and cleaning supplies as well? Do they know about the supplements? (Nitro. Oh. My. Word. It's a saving grace for tired moms!) Then I'll explain the Essential Rewards freebies for that month and give them the lowdown on Essential Rewards.

On our website at oilabilityteam.com, there are graphics of sample ER orders at 50, 190, and 300 PV that you can use to email, text, or print and mail. You can find them under "Share."

Follow up takes a lot of time, at least an hour a week, depending on the size of your team. But, if you are committed to it and train your leaders to follow your example, you'll see slow and steady growth. Another thing I do is to offer contests on my leadership page specifically for people who sign others on Essential Rewards.

The rise in numbers of people on Essential Rewards is rewarding in multiple ways. First, it's your ticket for periods of rest. Second, you get the joy of seeing more people on your team using the oils. And third, you get to see your leaders breathe a little easier, too, as their paychecks increase. It's a triple blessing. Best of all, you're developing relationships with the people who came to your classes—relationships which are built

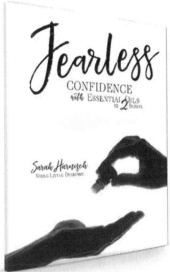

out of a love for oils and a passion to educate. You can't top that!

Essential Rewards your base, your cornerstone in this business. It keeps you from having to start back at zero the next month as everything resets. Imagine you're a farmer that plants a field at the beginning of the month, and when the calendar flips, all the seeds and sprouts you sowed get plowed under! That's what happens to you when help someone get a starter kit and they never get on ER. You are planting a seed without cultivating a lifestyle.

What is my favorite tool to train an oils lifestyle? Fearless. It's a tiny book I wrote after Gameplan, because I realized that there was no resource out there that trained in the little habits that create an oily lifestyle. Fearless takes them through the science of a clean living lifestyle so they understand the "why", gives them basic aromatherapy training, explains the Premium Starter kit, drives hard to Essential Rewards, and ends with ten challenges to get them oiling with confidence every single day.

When someone first joins my team, I give them a copy of Fearless and a Fearless calendar, available at oilabilityteam.com. It keeps them on track as they complete the challenges. They're not time consuming—like making body butter or bath salts—they are practical, hands-on knowledge that every new oiler should know, like how to make carrier roll-ons and strategically place them around the house.

Once they accept the challenges and fill out the calendar, they send me a screenshot or photo. Then I connect with them to tell them that if they get on Essential Rewards, I will gift them $25 toward their order. You can do that with an account credit or simply a check. I don't mail it until I see their first ER order process. Now they have been habit trained to use their oils, do their own research, and they have had their diffuser going for 30 straight days! They have navigated the Virtual Office and they understand why they oil. They are standing on their own two feet and they're ready for all the other great follow-up books out there.

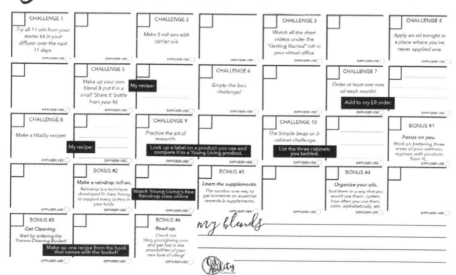

Does Fearless work? Before I wrote it, my own Essential Rewards percentage was 28%. After I implemented it, and trained my leaders to use it, it's now at 42% six months later. It absolutely works. This is always the first thing I hand new oilers. Train them from the beginning, and you'll have an oiler for life. One of the biggest mistakes I see with oils users is they don't oil often enough or use enough oil when they do. Fearless nips that in the bud

PLAN TO FOLLOW UP!

There's one more tip on follow up that our Oil Ability team members, Joy and Hans Hinterkopf, Young Living Golds, came up with. They were really struggling actually getting a hold of people after they'd purchased a kit. They'd call and call, and because the person on the other end didn't recognize their number, they would not respond. They'd email or text and get no response.

They found a simple way to fix that. When new people are signing up for their starter kit, *right then and there* set a date to go through the kit with them. Tell them you want to show them how to use their diffuser without frying it, how to utilize the oils in their kit in their home, the benefits of NingXia, and how it will blow their mind to break out that Thieves Cleaner sample and do a good mop of their kitchen floor. They will never look at cleaning the same way again! Tell them you'll train them how to look stuff up when they have questions and how to log into their Virtual Office to order more oils. Offer 30 minutes of time and set a date. Write down the date and time you'll be at their home (or if they're a distance away, will meet them on Skype) and put it in your Gameplanner. Then they are expecting that call.

There's one more critical thing to tell you about follow up. It can be summed up in one word:

CONSISTENCY

Consistency is essential to every part of your business but it's especially crucial with follow up. You need to be consistently following up after each class, or you won't see the rewards of all your other efforts.

I've found that I spend more time behind the scenes touching base with people than I do teaching. If you are aiming for Elite Express and teaching four to six classes a month, you will see growth, because you are consistent.

Consistency will make or break your business. If you teach one class a month, you'll earn enough to get a free oil. If you want a sustainable, livable income, then the reality is that you must teach more than once a month. Would you expect to get paid $40,000 a year for a 40-hour-a-week job that you don't show up to? Then why would you expect to make $10,000 a month for a Young Living business that you only work two hours a month, by teaching only one class?

If you want to grow, you have to be consistent! Let me show you what that looks like. On the next page are two snapshots, used with permission, of different members of the Oil Ability team.

The first held just one class, in the month of December. Every other month since then, they have privately added one or two people a month. What you'll see in the mapping of their business from the dashboard on their Virtual Offices is that they are all over the place. It's because there is no consistency to the way that they run their business. There's no game plan. And with no game plan, there's no solid execution. That means no steady income and no reliable business.

The second person regularly holds classes four to six times a month and follows up. That's 90 minutes a week of class time and a couple hours of follow up.

Person 1:

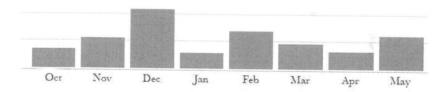

Person 2:

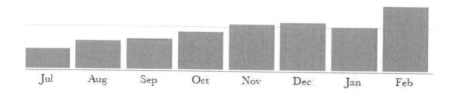

What I found to be most telling was the month of January. That was a low month for my whole team. But, can you see how hard it hit the first person versus the second? The second didn't take such a hard hit because they had consistently been signing people up on Essential Rewards. It wasn't as painful. This is how you build a multi-million-dollar home business—no excuses. Get out there and do it, and do it regularly, consistently, and with a game plan.

You have survived follow up 101. It's truly not painful! It's actually the fruit of your work because it's the place where you get to hear their stories and feel their excitement. Drop the fear and run for the relationship! It's the part of this that makes it all worth it.

CHAPTER 11

DEALING WITH DIFFICULT PEOPLE

As you follow up with people who have attended your oils classes, expect some opposition. In this chapter I want to equip you for what to say when people want just one oil, when they don't want to commit to a wholesale account, or when they are just plain negative.

PEOPLE WHO WANT JUST ONE OIL

Why would someone need just one oil? Because they don't know what the oils do. That's the only reason.

Every single person should be funneled through the premium starter kit wholesale option, because this kit trains them with 11 oils how to become oilers. You're going to get great at using lavender if that's the only oil you own, but I can't imagine a winter without Raven™ for respiratory support, or Thieves® for immune support. When you allow people to order only individual oils, you are training them to be needy and they will have a lack of commitment.

If those in your friend circle just order a single oil off of you every few months, it's not their fault. You have not equipped them to buy, you have been enabling them. You drop things off at their door for them to try. You add oils to your order so they don't have to get on Essential Rewards. They pawn Thieves cleaner off of you when they are low. They are the "just watching from the sidelines" oiler, the "lack of commitment" oiler. But there is an easy solution.

Don't Enable—Educate!

Have a gentle conversation with them about all of the products they should be using daily and should order themselves: NingXia, Pure Protein Complete, Thieves cleaning products (dish soap, dishwasher soap, and Thieves cleaner), personal care products, etc. They are either serious about wanting a chemical free life, or they are not serious. If they are not serious, kick the dust off your feet and move to the line of people that are.

The one exception I'll make—and I only do it once for them. If they really want to try an oil but aren't sure they want the kit yet, I'll add one oil, or one other product, to my order and let them try it out. But I always encourage them to purchase the starter kit. I make sure they've heard the 101 class, either on audio CD or on DVD. I lay the groundwork for a chemical-free home. They get one freebie from me, and then they have to set up their own account. I have had, at one time, over 20 people wanting to place orders through me. I don't have the time to drop off all those orders! Stop enabling them to leech off your account and have them set up their own.

PEOPLE WHO DON'T WANT A WHOLESALE ACCOUNT

If you have gone through the process of enrolling someone with a starter kit, then you've seen the options they can choose when they enroll. They can be either a retail customer or a wholesale customer. Some people will shy away from the commitment of becoming a wholesale customer and want to just buy a few oils as a retail customer. This is simply lack of education, as we discussed above.

I tell you that to this day, I have never enrolled a single retail customer. I just don't believe in it. I am thankful Young Living has made the option for us, but I believe it's a cop-out for people who are trying to save cash. (There. I said it!) By saving cash on oils, they are inadvertently spending it in much more dangerous chemical-laden places. I never feel like I am pushing people to buy product they can't afford. I am far too passionate about getting the garbage out of their homes, the chemicals that are poisoning their families. It's all about showing them a better way.

Sometimes you have the people who ask about professional accounts. Those are accounts that you can set up if you're a small business with a storefront. It allows someone to purchase the oils at wholesale and sell them at retail in order to make a profit. However, people with professional accounts forfeit any right to a downline, which makes no sense, because your true money-making ability is in your downline. You never know who will come into their store and turn out to be a Diamond!

I would never, ever encourage someone to throw away the opportunity to have a successful business. I'd recommend skipping the professional account and just going with a regular wholesale account. Even if the store owner doesn't want to do the business side, they'll be blessed by those under them who do. Always leave that door open.

NEGATIVE PEOPLE

Now we'll talk about facing negative people. You will encounter them. Goodness, Christ encountered negative people. There are two types out there: the type that bashes your family business, and the type that bashes oils.

This is where one of my life verses comes in. "If anyone will not welcome you or listen to your words, leave that home or town and shake the dust off your feet." (Matthew 10:14)

There are so many people out there who need oils. In fact, every single person you come into contact with needs them, whether they're at the post office, Walmart, or Panera. (I have sold kits in line at each of those places! I even sold a kit to the TSA agent in Spokane, Washington when we were flying home from the Gold retreat!) There are more than enough people to keep you busy, so stop focusing on the ones who you want to be oilers, and speak to the people who are ready.

I know that some of the people you desperately want on your teams are your mothers, your best friends, and your sisters, but recognize one thing; just because they say no now, it does not mean the answer will always be no. It's impossible to be around an oiler and not have a positive oils experience at some point, especially if you're in regular contact with them. Let the oils and the success of your business speak for itself. They will see it when they are ready. Forcing it is one of the worst things you can do. It took some of my family members two years to warm up to oils (and a few of them I'm still working on!) Do not be discouraged. The field is wide and you have more time then you think you do.

If you waste all your time trying to convince everyone that oils are a great option, you're losing time with the people who are already eager to learn and sick of the chemicals in their home. So follow Biblical principles, kick the dust off your feet, move to the next person, and don't look back. Don't let it wear on you. It's better to be out there collecting no's then not moving and having a stagnant business. The trick is to prevent their response from hitting you emotionally. They're just not ready yet. Did you catch that? Because it's a critical principle if you want to have a successful business.

Emotionally detach yourself from the sale of the starter kit

If you're so busy holding classes and doing follow up, you have little time to notice those out there that gave you a resounding no. Move on, stay focused, and work with the scores of people attending classes. It sounds difficult to do if the person telling you no is a close friend, but it's truly not. You just need to refocus yourself. Let it sting for a second and then remember that the answer may not always be no, it's just no at this moment, and likely because they need to have an oils experience. They need to see them work. It may take a while. And in that time, redirect yourself, stay positive, and put one foot in front of the other.

"There is precious treasure and oil in the dwelling of the wise."

While I'm at it, let me throw another Bible verse at you, one I have on my wall at home: Proverbs 21:20: "There is precious treasure and oil in the dwelling of the wise." Oils in your house. Be wise. Oil up. And according to Scripture, have backup oils, too. When I am down about the loss of a kit, some of my favorite emotional oils are "Magnify Your Purpose™," "Highest Potential™," and "Forgiveness™." Put a little of them on the back of your neck or in the diffuser for a few minutes and see how you feel. It's a great pick-me-up.

What about the family members that don't believe in multi-level marketing? Well, that's just ignorance. You can work 40 hours a week and survive or work ten to 20 hours a week and make $10,000 a month or more in your Young Living business. If they are willing, I'd point them to Eric Worre's Rise Of The Entrepreneur DVD. For 50 minutes, it will throw out all sorts of facts and statistics for the non-believer. If they don't want to waste another second on your business, keep this in mind: you don't need their approval.

A year after getting my starter kit, I really struggled with coming off my anchoring shift, but I chose to retire. It was an emotional hit to me. All of my radio friends wrote and asked, "What are you doing!??! You have a morning drive position on a powerful network that broadcasts to five million people, and you're walking away??!? You waited 11 years for that job! Are you insane? No one gets morning drive jobs at 29 years old. Why would you leave radio to sell oils kits???!!!?"

I got it good and I got it from all angles. I got it from people I had worked with in Chicago and in New York. I got it from family members and some of my closest friends.

The secret to handling negativity

Here's the deal: my identity isn't as a news anchor. My identity isn't as a mom. My identity isn't even as a Young Living Diamond. My identity is in Christ, and if my eyes stay focused on Him, all else fades away. It really doesn't matter. I don't have to search for hope and meaning. I already have it through Jesus's death on the cross.

So if my identity isn't in speaking to five million people every morning, did it matter if I walked away? Nope.

I have a hope and future far beyond the whisperings of this world. The Lord has taken care of us. That one decision allowed me to multiply my income by five after I stepped off my full time anchoring job and now, two years out from my starter kit, my husband is retiring as well. We are blessed, despite the naysayers.

CHAPTER 12

No One is Coming to Classes—Now What?

Network marketing is an amazing business, if you can get past the psychology of it. In most of what we do, we expect the answer to be "yes." It's rare to have someone tell us "no" three quarters of the time. But in this business, that is the norm. Three in every four people you meet likely won't be interested in oils immediately. Those are standard network marketing numbers across the board, in any company that you take part in.

There are a few things to ask yourself when someone says no:
        Did you have a strong enough close?
        Do they understand why they need oils?
        Were you salesy, or did you build a relationship first?
        Was it good timing for them?
        What was the reason for their no?

If you are doing the same motions again and again with no results, it's time to take a look at where you might be going wrong. Do you feel like you've exhausted your friend circles and you have no one who wants to host a class? There are three reasons people avoid you. Only three:

1) You are hunting them.

2) They are missing what oils can do for them.

3) You spew negativity and are not a person they want to follow.

There is the possibility they truly have zero interest in oils, but because of their ten billion uses, that's likely not the case. It's more likely they are turned off by your approach, they truly don't understand why they need the oils, or you've let a negative attitude spill into your business and relationships. Let's face each one of these pitfalls head on and focus on the actions that will get you out of this slump!

1. DON'T BE A HUNTER!

Running out of people to share oils with can happen to every leader at every rank, and it's not so much that friend circles are exhausted, it's that we are exhausted. We're trying too hard. We are becoming a hunter, focused too much on the next sale. You're desperate and this comes from a scarcity mindset.

The reality is, every person you know has a friend circle of 2,000 by the time they are 20, whether they realize it or not. It only takes a team of about 100 to hit a Silvership, depending on how many of them are on Essential Rewards. So if you know one person, you have enough potential in that one relationship to be a Silver 20 times over! When you remember that the odds are FOR you, it helps your mindset.

People feel hunted if you are going into every conversation with the eye on the prize of selling a Starter Kit. Don't give every person you pass your "pitch." Your focus needs to be on relationship and meeting people where they are at.

This is true in a class setting as well. I have much more success teaching small classes (fewer than ten people) than large ones, because I can connect better relationally in a smaller setting. If you can emotionally detach yourself from the sale of the starter kit, you'll have much better results in this business, because each lost sale won't be a personal affront.

Do you remember the story of my brother Aaron, from Chapter 8? I really wanted him to be a Young Living distributor. He had worked in sales for nearly 20 years, and I knew he had the blood of a Royal Crown Diamond. I wanted him on my team, but more than anything, I genuinely wanted him to succeed. He had a toddler and another baby on the way and was working 12-15 hour shifts. I did not want to see my brother so depleted.

I reached out to him multiple times. I tried the chemical free home angle, telling him that he was poisoning his family with the cleaning supplies in his house. I sent him sample after sample after sample, but 18 months later, it was all in a cabinet, untouched, and he still didn't have a kit.

He didn't respond because he felt hunted. He knew my passion for the oils, but had no desire to join me. Why? Because I came across as coming in for the sale instead of building a trust relationship, even with my own brother.

It was not until I was visiting him in his home and he complained to me about his basement smelling like smoke, that I saw where I could met his need. He had a stench he couldn't get rid of in his house. I showed him what purification and a diffuser could do; and he made the purchase. The oils worked, and now he is a die-hard oiler.

You need to stay so busy scheduling 101 classes; and so busy talking to everyone you meet about oils and getting them to classes; that you don't have the time to focus on the people who are naysayers. Make sure you have good follow up, for sure, and don't leave people in the dust. But also don't take the time to dwell on those who say no. If your focus is always on educating people and teaching them to live a chemical-free life, your heart is always for the person. It's never for the sale. They will feel it. They'll feel your passion and your compassion for them, and over time that will build a relationship of trust.

The Skill of "Relationship First"

When you share oils with people, you will have those who are into oils from the start, they'll get the kit and run with it; or those who get the kit and need a little help (you can show them the resources to get started in the oily lifestyle like Fearless!). But there will be others who you so desperately want to help, but they just aren't buying it.

For that last group of people, there are two options. If you truly desire to see them on your team, then engage in a gentle pursuit. Eric Worre has some wonderful training in one of my favorite network marketing books, "Go Pro." He uses the "If I, would you?" question.

"If I give you this 101 lecture on DVD or audio CD, would you listen to it? If so, when? May I call you on Saturday to touch base afterward?"

"If I invite you to a free class, would you come?"

"If I set up a coffee break, would you have an hour to meet with me to talk oils?"

I love that concept. You're not pushing something on someone, and you're never just freely giving something away. You're giving them a choice, and you're always asking something in return. It's a give and take. It's a dance. You're not a hunter, you're in a relationship. Don't take it personally when people say, "no," and don't take it personally when they say, "not yet." The average person can only say no seven times—keep pursuing! But do so with the focus on relationship.

"If I, would you?"

For the others who are constantly saying "no," I'd move on. There may be a time when they will listen, but it's not now. You can't control the timeline of their journey. If you have engaged in a way that's genuine and real, and have built a relationship of trust with them, most of them will follow. Some will do it right away and some will do it after they have processed the conversation (or many conversations.) That's okay. Just make sure that your heart is always to educate, not to go in for the sale.

If you switch your focus from selling a kit to building relationship, suddenly there's no pressure to perform! You're out there helping people. Do it more frequently and you'll grow more quickly.

What About No-Show Classes?

If you have a no-show class, there's only one reason for it: you did not build relationships first. That relationship might be built through a mutual friend if you're using the Gameplan marketing system of asking three to invite 50, then having them edify you on the event page. It might be from the trickle of a conversation at a vendor event or in a line at a grocery store. But if you try again and again to have classes, and are not having results, it's time to change your tactics.

Review why people are saying no to you. It's nearly always a lack of relationship. They will give you many reasons: "I don't have time," "I don't have the money for a kit right now," "It's too much to learn," but it always comes down to the fact that you have not taken the time to develop trust with them by pouring into them.

When I am picking up the phone to ask someone to come to a class, or to do follow up, my first question is never, "Hey, are you going to order your starter kit that I asked you about LAST WEEK?" I always lead with the relationship first. Start with asking how their son's arm is after his little league injury, if they got their date night in this week with their spouse, or how they are sleeping at night.

Once the door is opened, I will offer to loan out my diffuser or will put a drop of oil on the palm of their hand, just to meet them where they are. Many, many kit sales on the Oil Ability team were from a single drop of peppermint in the middle of someone's hand. Make sure they are experiencing oils, and not just listening to you talk about it. Meet them in that place where they are standing, without judgement of their lifestyle or how long it takes for them to move. If you get one on-fire oiler, you can tap into that friend circle and they will get people to come to the class. But it all starts with relationship building. That is the missing element.

2. MEET THEM WHERE THEY'RE AT

When someone doesn't understand why they need the oils, it all boils down to education.

I want you to walk back in time with me for a second. Do you remember the place you were the moment you were in your first oils class? You didn't have the oodles of experiences that you have now that has made you so passionate. You hadn't heard all the amazing stories of what the oils have done for people!

That is the place where your almost-oiler is. You have to walk back into that place, connect with them, find what they need right now, and connect them with the experience or story they need. It may be emotions. Or chemicals. Or supplements. Or pets. Or so many other places. Young Living now has a pain cream—and that little ditty alone has sold many a kit for me.

Start where they are. Meet them there. Don't give up on them because they don't understand at first. Don't walk away too soon. Drop it at their feet and wait. Then do it again. Some will pick it up right away, others will take longer. But if you walk into the blackness of a total lack of oils knowledge and pluck them from that place, by meeting them where their needs are, you will have won trust and developed an oiler. Educate them with what they need to hear for where they are at.

The Skill of Storytelling

One of the biggest traps in network marketing is believing that if you just shove enough facts at people, they will eventually change their minds and buy in to whatever your selling. But scientists have proven that we as humans make decisions based on emotion, not information (yes, even the most analytical of us!) So, how do you lead people past whatever blocks they have to the right emotional place to make a decision that's best for them and their family's future?

With stories. Stories draw people in and connect with the emotional part of their brain. A story about how an oil touched your family, or how you felt when you were able to finally get your bathroom clean without your child or your dog gagging at the fumes of chemical cleaners, or how your aunt felt when she started drinking NingXia Red®—this will help them FEEL the difference Young Living can make. You will move more people with stories than with facts because you will help them imagine the hope, confidence, and excitement of finding chemical-free solutions to every area of their life.

Make it your goal to have as story for every oil in your starter kit, and then put a new product on your Essential Rewards order to build your next story with. Collect stories from your team, your upline, your crossline friends, and use these stories to effectively educate your friends to join you on this amazing journey!

3. DITCH THE NEGATIVITY

This is a hard one, because there are SO many reasons why it happens.

You may have been disappointed so many times you won't allow yourself the pleasure of believing that financial miracles can happen in your life.

You may have been hurt over and over and over again. You may have had your trust crushed.

You may have been abused, and have built terrific walls that no one can break through. (If that's your story, I'd encourage you to get plugged into a church and a Christian counselor that can speak life and hope into you, and pray with you, and start to break down some of the barriers. A wonderful place to start is the ministry familylife.org. Do a search for a Healing Journey group on their website. The groups are incredible!)

Whatever your reason for spewing negativity or sarcasm, you're going to struggle building a business, because people do not want to follow that.

People are looking at you and asking themselves if you have something in your life that they want. If all your posts online are negative or your conversations are divisive, they won't be attracted to you or anything you have to offer.

Consider every word out of your mouth, every conversation with those around you, every post on any social media platform as an arena where you are studied. If you're not emulating the Young Living values of abundance, purpose, and wellness, people will run the other way. They have no reason to follow something they don't want in their life.

Usually when you are not filling classes or people won't return your calls, it's your mindset. People are not attracted to you because you are down and out. You have to be a leader that attracts people to you! If you're teaching from a place of frustration that no one has gotten kits, you'll portray that. Focus on the positives and say them over and over again until you believe them—you CAN share oils effectively, people WILL be excited about the kits, and you WILL rise to Diamond. Speak life. You'll generate excitement and passion that will carry you to the kit. That's something people will follow.

I mentioned at the start of this section that network marketing success relies heavily on your mindset. Sometimes, you're just not in a place to have a powerful positive mindset. You may have had your dreams crushed over and over again. It may be hard for you to trust. You may be caught in a place of exhaustion and stress that's so overbearing that it's hard for you to see beyond the next hour of your day.

The Skill of Speaking Life

Let me share the secret of getting out of that pit in your mind: *act and speak as if it's already happened.*

One of the tips I try on myself when I find my tongue slipping into negativity is something I do with my homeschoolers. We call it "opposite day." When we face a block in learning a new skill, we say the opposite of what we feel. "I am GOOD at division!" It plays wonderful tricks on your mind — tricks that will get your feet moving in the right direction. If your words are uplifting, your mind will focus up, your feet will follow, and you will rank.

I want you to flip to the Gameplan workbook and find the section on mindset. Make a list of all the beliefs that you have right now and be completely honest and frank about it.

Beliefs such as:

I can't fill classes.

I can't find leaders.

I can't seem to get my OGV to move.

No one will sign up for essential rewards.

All my leaders move SLOW.

No one will come to my rallies or events.

I will never hit Diamond.

Then I want you to write the exact opposite beside it. Speak words of life over yourself:

I CAN fill classes.

I CAN find leaders.

I CAN explode my OGV.

I WILL sign people up on ER THIS WEEK.

My leaders are amazing, powerful, focused, and driven!

My events will be full!

I AM A DIAMOND RISING!

Take that list, photocopy it, and put it somewhere where you see it daily. It might be taped to your bathroom mirror or inside your Gameplanner. Speak those words of positive affirmation every single day, until you believe what they say.

Another mindset boost is the vision board. I want you to see exactly where you want to go! Fill out a check, sign Mary Young's name to it, and put the dollar amount of the paycheck you'd like to see with Young Living in six months. Go to the recognition page on Young Living's website, print off one of the rank up pin emblems, and paste it to your vision board. It sounds wonky, but every single thing I put on my vision board in 2017 has already happened: we purchased a new home, we are debt free (including our home), I am able to travel with my teenagers, and I get to sleep eight hours at night. It's incredible what happens when you visualize your dreams and goals and put them in a tangible form so you can lay your eyes on them every single day.

Focused on Diamond

In February, 2017, it was a longshot for me to hit Diamond. Our highest OGV ever was 220,000, and that was four months earlier. We had been in a plateau for eight months. But the October before, I'd heard the Lord tell me that February was our month. I knew it in my gut, even though the math didn't add up. I started to tell my team that this month was our Diamond month. I had my children draw diamonds every single day before midnight, just to keep my eyes focused on where we were going. They took it as an honor to be the diamond drawer that night! My husband even drew one!

I got online every single day that month and wrote down how far our OGV was from Diamond. I wrote out each leg's totals, and how far they had to go. I encouraged, edified, and spoke life. We had just completed a bootcamp, and the team was on fire. We saw a 70,000 OGV spike last February, in the shortest month of the year, simply because of words of life. I spoke it over the team, they believed it, I believed it, and all of our feet followed.

We hit Diamond on the 27th that month, a day and a half before the end of the month. And we didn't get the 250,000 required—we ended at 274,000 OGV—and have never looked back! More than half a year later, we've not lost rank, we have exploded and are on pace for Crown Diamond. It's all in the power of the tongue.

What comes off your tongue when you wake up in the morning until your head hits your pillow at night is profoundly powerful. It can be a course correction for you. You either bring joy into your business, or you burden it with doubt. Don't let doubt creep in. Stand firm, speak life even when you don't believe it—until you DO believe it, and watch miracles happen.

If you can master these three skills: building relationships, telling stories, and speaking life; and have a genuine heart as you do them; being real and raw, you'll attract and motivate people in all walks of life. It's about your growth as a person. It's about filling yourself with good things and then pouring that out to the people around you. The harvest will be guaranteed.

CHAPTER 13

KEYS TO CONFIDENCE

It would be a disservice to tell you how to launch a Young Living business without giving you a chapter on confidence. Why? Because there are two things you really need to know to do this well. First, you need to understand the ins and outs of Young Living: the Virtual Office, the 101 script, and strategy. This book walks you through just about every question you may have on launching a business, in depth.

But there is another element to pulling this off: confidence. That's heart training. If you do not have confidence, no one will trust what you are saying. They definitely won't follow someone who doesn't have what they want. It's one of the top reasons I see people unable to fill classes. There is no passion to their invite or passion to their story. There is no passion in their close. It's just rote memorization or reading.

We have a saying in the newsroom: "fake it 'till you make it." If you don't know an answer, give them an honest response and either teach them how to look it up themselves (the better option) or tell them you'll ask your upline or call Young Living Member Services for guidance. There's nothing wrong with not knowing an answer. But I've seen people take a lack of confidence to extremes.

I had a woman on my team who held class after class after class—with zero attendees. Finally, I took a look at the wording she used for her events, and it went something like this: "If you want to learn more about essential oils, PLEASE come to my class. If not, it's ok. I will be holding other classes in the future, if you are busy."

Wuh?!? Who will follow leadership like that??

That's like saying, "If you want to douse yourself in chemicals for another two weeks until my next class, I'm totally okay with that. I don't have the confidence to tell you that you're poisoning yourself and your family." The people you do not speak to, because of your lack of confidence, will be hurt. There are people that have been placed in your path specifically for you to speak into their life. Do not be so timid that you steal their lifeline when they most need you.

A lack of confidence can come from a lot of places. Setting goals and not hitting them repeatedly can end up with you telling yourself you can't win. Losing hope. Being abused. Here's the thing: God didn't make you that way. I've never met a toddler who wasn't confident. It's a learned behavior. There was a point in your life when you weren't afraid, and that's who you really are.

There was a point in your life when you weren't afraid, and that's who you really are.

I believe a lot of our fears are fear of rejection and fear of what people think of us. None of that matters when you do a mental shift and focus on the person, not the sale. It's all about education. Then it's all about being so busy selling starter kits that you don't notice the no's. Remember that you are not hunting. You are building relationships and educating. Always go in with the goal of education and not kit sales. That takes the pressure off a sale mentality, and it makes it easier to teach. Emotionally detach yourself from the sale of the starter kit.

BUILD CONFIDENCE

Sometimes our confidence needs more than a pep talk, we need to do some deep work in our own hearts and minds to be able to focus on others' needs effectively. That deeper work is not something that can be done inside a book. But I can tell you where to go to learn it, with a system that works, because I've put dozens of my team members through this training. I put myself through this training. The month I went, my OGV had been stuck at 46,000 for five months. Five months later, it was at 152,000 and I was a solid Platinum, because I was no longer afraid.

My favorite resource to get over emotional blocks in your business is from a gifted network marketer named Dani Johnson. She does a 3-day weekend seminar called, "First Steps To Success" that will blow your mind. It addresses blocks you may have, and she also teaches how to understand personality types on your teams, how to connect with your leaders, how to stop emulating a person who is afraid, how to stop making excuses, how to get out there, and take action. Check it out here: www.danijohnson.com.

DITCH THE EXCUSES

One of the things Dani speaks a lot about is excuse making. In fact, she spends her entire first day speaking about it. Early on in this book, we covered the typical excuses I hear from my team:

- I don't have time
- I don't have money
- I don't have the right personality
- I can't talk to people
- I don't know anyone
- I live in the middle of nowhere
- I am too tired
- I have no resources
- My upline stinks
- I can't find a place to teach
- I can't find anyone to watch my kids
- I'm not you
- I don't like "selling" stuff

Here's the deal. Do you like where you are? Do you have enough income? Do you have enough time with your spouse and your children? Are you able to bless other people and pour into their lives with your time and finances? Are you crossing things off your bucket list every single year, or are you waiting five more years for your dreams to happen? Those aren't just dreams—they are your heart's desires that God put there! You're supposed to be pursuing them!

If the answer is no to any of those—get over your excuses and fix it. My team includes software developers who are making $70,000 a month, a surgeon, a doctor, several dentists, chiropractors, a university researcher well respected in the field, and many other professionals; some with extremely high paying jobs. Just because your job pays well doesn't mean you have time economy or freedom. It also doesn't mean you have your retirement said and done. If you don't like where you are, change it! It's as simple as that. Get over the confidence issues, stop making excuses, and do what you need to do to succeed, without distraction.

Another word I absolutely hate is "try." I'll "try" to do my business, but I can't make any promises. You're either in or you're not. I will work with people who show me they are serious and will work the business. If you're not serious about digging out of where you are, I shake that dust off my feet and move to the next person. I have a passion to raise people from poverty, but only those that want to be raised.

At the Young Living International Grand Convention in Salt Lake City in 2016, there was a wonderful demonstration with 22,000 people in the crowd. We were all asked to stand. Then we were asked to sit. Then we were asked if we "tried to stand" or "tried to sit." We didn't try, we did it. You don't try to do things. You either accomplish or you don't. Trying is an excuse as you look for a way out. If you want this, fight for it!

TRAIN YOUR BRAIN

The most important thing that you can get trained on is not products or tools, it's your mindset. We all have the same oils, the same tools, and the same 24 hours in a day. The tools and the quality of Young Living are not the issue. The number of friends you have—the size of your town, your aromatherapy knowledge or the money in your bank account; it's all a non-issue when starting a Young Living business. The difference between you and a Young Living Diamond is mindset.

In November of 2017, more than 20 new people hit Diamond in Young Living in a single month. Twenty new families were running multi-million-dollar organizations. Something must work in this business!

The biggest obstacle in your climb to Diamond is yourself. It's your thoughts, your speech, and your belief. You get past that by getting to events like Young Living rallies, International Grand Convention, events hosted by your upline, or network marketing training events. You get past it by surrounding yourself with people that are heading in the same direction. You get past it by crowding out the naysayers in your life with the ones that will SPEAK LIFE over you. And the family members and friends and co-workers that still don't support your decisions, you just show them the check. Facts speak for themselves. Your decision for freedom does not need to be supported by everyone in your life. But it's time for you to choose your inner circle carefully. Who you allow inside it will have an impact on your life.

Proverbs 13:20: "Whoever walks with the wise becomes wise, but the companion of fools will suffer harm."

Who do you want in your circle? Choose hope.

It's important that in between events and trainings you continue to pour into yourself with mindset training. Get your head in the right place, either with a book, with a Youtube video, or an audio or video recording. It's one of the reasons I sat in a professional studio and recorded the Gameplan book for iTunes and Audible—so you could train your brain by listening. Get your head out of places of doubt by surrounding yourself with focus, hope, and intention.

Any Diamond you speak with will have their own lists of resources that inspired their journey. The list below is absolutely not comprehensive, but it's a good place to start. Chase results. If you want to be a Young Living Diamond, look at what the Diamonds are doing, because they have results. If you're getting recommendations from someone who has not walked the path of Diamond, consider the source and ask yourself if it's where you want to go.

Here are some of the Diamonds favorite mindset teachers:

- Jim Rohn (many of his audio recordings are free on Youtube)
- Royal Crown Diamond Vicki Opfer's Essential Sharing at discoverlsp.com
- Dale Carnegie's How To Win Friends and Influence People
- Ted Talks
- Brendon Burchard's YouTube channel (or books)
- Go Pro with Eric Worre
- Richard Bliss Brooke's 4-Year Career
- Hal Elrod's Miracle Morning
- Success.com
- Darren Hardy
- Shawn Achor
- Robert Kiyosaki
- Crown Diamond Oli Wenker's Essential Oils Symposium (Google "biocodeacademy")
- "12 Days of Diamonds" is a Facebook group that features over 100 Young Living Diamonds sharing their stories and best tips for success.

Find something you resonate with. Fill your head with it. And get inspired. Surround yourself with hope. Get to events. Get your head in this business, because you have what it takes to go all the way, if only you believe. That is the key to confidence.

PART FOUR

STRATEGIES FOR GROWTH: STAR AND BEYOND

Gameplan gave me simple directions to motivate and put into action what I need to do to propel my Young Living business. It has created a fire on my team as each member goes through the book and workbook and puts it into action. A fire can't burn with one piece of wood alone!

Dawn Harvey

Gameplan is AMAZING!! I have been in Young Living for over five years trying to build a business and have hit several plateaus. Right now this book is blowing my business out of the water! I have more motivated business builders than ever before and all I'm using is Your Gameplan mini and the free videos on her website to get people started. Then I have them buy this book and the workbook and they're off and running!!

We started our group training in February and there were more classes scheduled and being taught in the month of March than ever before on my team!! Absolutely crazy!!

Jenna Culleyon

CHAPTER 14

YOUR BUSINESS TOOLKIT: OILY TOOLS, TAXBOT, AND MORE

At this point, you've walked through one full cycle of a Young Living business. You have practiced the 101 lecture diligently and you have set a date. You marketed the class heavily, invited 100 people and 15 showed. After that class you did great follow up, and four people got kits. Congratulations!

If you continue with that model, you're following in the footsteps of the Diamonds, Crown Diamonds, and Royal Crown Diamonds before you. If you're tenacious and don't give up, you will get there, and it won't take as long as you think! Rinse and repeat. If you rinse and repeat four to six times a month, most of my leaders reach Silver within six months. That's usually $2,000 to $3,000 in monthly income.

In my house, that was a game changer. That was me stepping off my job full time. It was letting a second job go. It meant paying off some serious debt. I love to see everyone reach the rank of Silver, because this sets the stage for Gold, Platinum, and Diamond!

I'd like to take a chapter and put some strategic resources in your hands. Hopefully you're fairly comfortable at this point with marketing and filling classes—you've checked out the appendixes and collected some scripts to help you with follow up and your close. And you're getting a bit more confident. Let's make you super confident. I promised you a meat and potatoes book. Here's the second helping.

RESOURCE NUMBER 1: OILY TOOLS AND OTHER YOUNG LIVING THEMED CELL PHONE APPS

There are many gifted people involved with Young Living and they have created some pretty incredible things. Take Jake Dempsey, for example. Jake is a software developer like my husband. He's pretty amazing at it. When his wife had a tough time calculating her Young Living paycheck, he made her a software app to do the math. It was so wildly successful that he made a cell phone version, and now thousands of us can accurately calculate our checks because of Jake. Jake is now a Young Living Crown Diamond, so the app was a pretty good motivator for his wife. That app has now been purchased by Young Living and is run by them. It's my

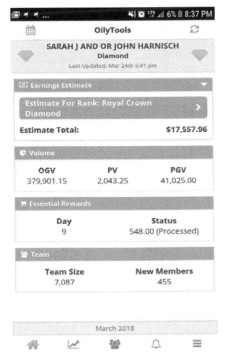

favorite motivator to show people what happens when they hit the next rank.

The neat thing is that you can use this app without a lot of effort. It's called Oily Tools. Download it from the Google play store or the Apple store. It's seriously awesome.

You can see your projected paycheck by rank, what your pace OGV is set to hit, how many people are ranking up, how much you have in Essential Rewards, and a money misser report for those that haven't spent their 100PV and won't get paid. It's awesome! If you're an English person like me, this man has incalculable worth to you. (That guy with the curly hair is Jake. Those other people in the picture are a couple of my kids. They are pretty amazing too).

Other apps I like designed by Jake Dempsey are Oily Manager and Project Broadcast. Oily Manager helps you track your oils inventory, your oils recipes, personal supplements regimen, and wish lists. Project Broadcast allows you to mass text certain groups (like new members, or leaders, or your entire organization) with Essential Rewards promos, Young Living sales, etc. I also use it for the newly enrolled on my team each month. I text them the 101 class or the Toxin Free Life class (free on my website at oilabilityteam.com.)

The EO bar, run by Jen O'Sullivan, is an app loaded with aromatherapy training, usage guides, system flushing, and so much more.

RESOURCE #2: TAXBOT

Are you afraid of doing your taxes? It's not bad. Here are some simple rules: for every penny you make, save 20% and put it in a savings account and forget it's there.

Also, every time you get a receipt for absolutely anything, upload it to a program called Taxbot. It costs $5 a month for Young Living users. I spoke with the creator Stanley Botkin (who by the way does the taxes for Bill Gates) and he's a genius. He says the program makes you virtually audit proof. You type out the "who, what, when, where, why" on each receipt; who you were with, what it was for, etc. Taxbot also syncs with your smart phone and tracks all the miles for your business automatically—by satellite. It's pretty awesome, and completely worth the $5/month.

They created their own page specifically for Young Living users that gives you free 14 day trial and 50% off retail. You can find it here: https://taxbot.com/z/yl/

What are some items you can deduct? Here's a brief list.

- The room where you do you Young Living business (not your whole house, but a percentage of your home. For example, one room is your office. That room is 8x10 and takes up 10% of the square footage of your home. You can deduct 10% of your utilities, 10% of your taxes, etc.)
- The same percentage for each utility
- Your mileage. Check with the IRS to see what the current mileage rate is
- Your business expenses. That would include things like Taxbot, Oily Tools, Gameplan books, purple bag supplies, etc.
- Business trips, for example, costs of hotel rooms for business related events, including CONVENTION!
- Half of all business-related meals
- Awards for your team, up to $25 per person
- Oils and other Young Living products you are using for your business
- Any employees you pay to help with bookkeeping, mailings, follow up, and events

The Taxbot website has some wonderful videos to explain the ins and outs of running a small business. Take an afternoon and check some of them out. Whether or not you choose to use this resource, make sure that the accountant you are working with has knowledge of network marketing businesses, and can help you with the maximum allowable deductions.

RESOURCE #3: THE GAMEPLANNER

This planner was put together after over a year of research and study of hundreds of other planning systems. It's the first revolving planner designed for network marketing. Every three months, it's pulled down off the website and new months are added, so if you have a leader explode in June, they can still get a full year of accountability. This is the glue that makes the entire Gameplan system stick for your budding leaders. It keeps them laser focused on teaching classes, getting people on Essential Rewards, and training their leaders.

What's inside? Rank mapping to help you plot out how far you are from your next rank. Stat tracking so you know your weaknesses in your organization. Are your ER percentages dropping? You can see them side by side for eight months. Places to track your classes, your leaders, and your follow up. Track bootcamp with your leaders so you know what days you are on. There is a list of every important Young Living date: qualification periods for retreats, convention, rallies, etc. 250 Gameplan quotes for inspiration. And SO much more. You can see pages from inside the planner here: https://oilabilityteam.com/product/gameplanner/

RESOURCE #4: OILABILITYTEAM.COM

The Oil Ability team has put together some incredible DVD's, CD's, bootcamps, and books. They will take you through, step by step, how to grow your business or how to train your new members to use the oils. They're even more comprehensive than this book. There are scripts and videos to train your team. See "Resources to Catapult Your Team" on page 291 for a full list of what is available.

We also have a knockout Facebook page thousands strong--just search for the "Oil Ability with Sarah" page!

RESOURCE #5: BRAIN FOOD

Personal development is huge. A lot of the time, I find that people don't advance in rank because their mindset isn't ready for it.

It's said that you should commit one hour a day of your work day to stretching your brain, growing it, and thinking outside the box. With five children, I'll be straight up—it's about one hour a week for me. (Hey, it's more when they go to summer camp!) But even with that commitment, these resources have really made a big difference in how I lead my team, the negative talk over my business, how I pray for my distributors, how I spend my time, and what types of goals I set.

As a leader, it's important that you're being fed good food. Changing your brain is the first step toward digging out of the places you don't want to be. You have to believe you can make it, and if you believe and you speak life over yourself and your business, it's amazing the places you will go! Your feet will start to follow your mouth. You may go 37 years of your life without a single vacation, and then 18 months into your business find yourself in Hawaii with Young Living. It's happened before, so speak life!

CHAPTER 15

GROWING YOUR BUSINESS ONLINE

Okay, you've got me here. Although John and I were able to catapult to Diamond less than three years after our starter kit arrived on our door, I'll be the first to admit that I'm not tech savvy. I did not build my business online; I did it through in-person relationships developed at classes.

But that's the neat thing about Young Living. There's no "wrong way" of sharing—online or in person. The trick is to be genuine and to use your gift set. This is a good place to pause for a moment and talk about a quality that's critical to lead a team—knowing your weak spots and being willing to delegate them to others and defer to their strengths. I recognize that technology is an anomaly to me; but thankfully, I married a software developer, so I get a leg up occasionally. Unfortunately, said software developer isn't available for my every whim, so I had to hit up one of my friends to help me write this techie-geek chapter.

Mary Souther Clendenin is the author of "The Encouraging Home," a blog with over 100,000 followers. She is also a homeschool mom of two boys and a treasured friend who loves the Lord. Because she has grown the bulk of her business online, reaching Gold rank primarily through her massive blog, (which she wrote while living in the boondocks in North

Carolina and surrounded by 800 cows. She commands an audience out of her sheer genius. Mary is going to share the nitty gritty of growing your business online, and then I'll wrap up the chapter with my tips for Facebook Lives.

GROWING YOUR BUSINESS ONLINE
BY MARY SOUTHER CLENDENIN

Word-of-mouth marketing is one of the most powerful ways to promote your products. But today, with the Internet, creativity, and planning, you can get the word out on a larger scale and at a faster pace!

It is about building relationships, gaining trust, and caring about people. It is about letting them know that you are not just selling products to get a paycheck, but that you have a passion for helping others improve their lives.

It might take a little longer to get that across online as people are getting to know you, but it is possible and sometimes goes much faster than you think! That is the way I have grown my business, while still doing some local classes, but focusing mainly online.

Share your heart and your passions. Be cautious about what you post or share because this is all they know about you. They look at everything you share, not just what you post about essential oils. Be honorable and be the best you can be. People are watching what you say and do—often more closely than you think!

You want to brand yourself, not your company. Don't build your social media or blog around a company or a product. Build relationships. Compel people to ask what you do. Let people get to know you and it will take you far.

Always remember to stay compliant online. Watch your words, pictures, and the links you post. Keep up to date with policies and procedures. You can check under Member Resources in your Virtual Office for a hot word list and more.

SHARING VIA SOCIAL MEDIA

One of the fastest ways to start sharing is on social media. Facebook is the most popular. It is all about creating culture and sharing your stories. People aren't buying the product. They are connecting with you.

You will want to have a business Facebook Page with your blog or business name. Make sure you follow current Young Living policies about social media pages.

Your posts should be positive, encouraging, and motivational. People will be curious about you and want to get in on whatever makes you this happy person who is spreading joy, light, and encouragement. You should be building relationships, just like in person. You create a culture. You post things that encourage, such as favorite quotes, simple recipes, asking questions, throwing in some product education and every now and then, real life pictures of your oils and diffuser, or a sale that is going on.

Provide value every day.

While people follow you on social media to learn more about you, they also want to know how you can help them. They aren't just coming to see what you wore, what you ate, etc.—they want to know what's in it for them. Besides personal, real life posts, you should also be encouraging and helping people. You just have a few seconds to capture their attention before they click away, unless they are friends or have become faithful followers. Make sure you provide value for your followers every day.

There are other forms of social media that are great ways to share. I recommend getting proficient on one platform before adding another. Instagram can be more personal and helps to connect you. Twitter is like text messages. It is great for business and getting your point across in 140 characters or less.

Don't get overwhelmed posting on all platforms. Choose one or two and get really good on those before adding more, if you choose to do so.

A word of caution, don't be on social media all the time. It can take over your life. Literally. And you will lose productivity and momentum, as well as precious family time. Use a scheduling platform like Hootsuite.com to schedule posts. It will simplify your life.

Get on social media several times a day to answer questions and monitor for trolls and rudeness. Use the delete and ban button if needed. Your social media platforms and blog are like your home. Would you allow people to enter your home and be rude or say ugly things? No, you would protect your family. The same is true for your online presence. You are protecting your name and your community that has put their trust in you.

SHARING WITH A BLOG

Another good way to grow your business online is with a blog or website. Creating one from scratch can take a little time, so if you want to start quickly, get a YLDist.com website. It is a nice, clean site that you can link to different pages on social media or when you email people. You can also add in the blog function when you are having classes and events. This can connect to your other social media platforms and is how people can get in touch with you. I have a blog at TheEncouragingHome.com, but I also have one of these sites that I love.

Do you want your blog just to be about essential oils? Do you want to expand to other natural health areas? I recommend blogging about other things, not just one focus. My blog is about inspiring hope, health, and happiness at home. My target audience is moms who need encouragement in life, family, marriage, parenting, self-care, have a natural health interest, and may be looking for work at home. Essential oils pair well with this and complements the other content.

Ask yourself some questions: What are you an expert at? What do you love? Decide on your niche and what you can talk about every day, or a couple times a week, besides essential oils. Who is your target audience that you are able to help? Having a wider variety of content will draw more people to your site, where they can find other things you have to offer. Focus on providing quality content that can touch lives and that people will want to share with others.

6 STEPS TO STARTING A BLOG

1. Choose a name

Some people use their own name. My blog is The Encouraging Home. Either way, your name or a business name, will work. You are branding yourself and you can be successful with either. Don't build your blog around what you are selling. This is about connection and relationship, not a specific product! Be a resource and provide great content that can change lives.

2. Choose a blog platform

A blog platform is the software or service you use to publish your content on the internet. I recommend a wordpress.org site, where you own your blog and can also sell on it. There are many free Wordpress.org templates you can use to set up your blog and a lot of training videos to learn how to use it. The beautiful thing about a blog is that it can lead in many directions and become income-producing in a number of different ways. So make sure you start out with the right platform.

3. Choose a hosting company

A hosting company is a site that holds all your blog files. I use Bluehost. com, Sarah uses Siteground. You can begin with a free option like Wordpress.com, but it's better to start off like you intend to continue and get a professional hosting site using Wordpress.org. You want one that provides excellent customer service and is available to help you anytime you need it. Other companies also provide this service, so do your research.

4. Choose a domain name

A domain name is the address typed in the browser to get to your site (ie. www.oilabilityteam.com). This points the browser to your hosting site and pulls up your blog for everyone to read. Check to see if the name you prefer is available. Try to use one that ends in ".com," since that is the most popular. You can check this through your hosting company, or just google to see if it comes up. You will need to renew this each year. Whether you use your name or not for your blog, I recommend purchasing it as well and holding on to it. You never know how big you might grow, and you might want to use that sometime, too.

5. Choose a logo

Your logo should be something that shows what your blog is all about. Check on your team to see if there are any graphic designers who can help you. Otherwise, there are many graphic designers out there who provide this service.

6. Create great content

I recommend writing several posts before you launch your blog so you have content ready to go. Try to blog at least once or twice a week. Perhaps one post can be about essential oils, practical ways to use oils, or DIY projects, etc. The other weekly post can be something that adds value and encouragement to your readers on another topic.

A blog is also a great place to create resource pages for your team. You can upload files, images, and videos for education and support. You can password protect these pages so only your team can access this (check the Wordpress.org help section).

Your blog can grow quickly, or it can grow slowly and steadily, just like your Young Living business. Be careful not to allow your blog and social media to overtake your life. It is easy to get caught up in how many followers you have, or how many comments there are on your blog. It is easy to become distracted and take time away from your family and income-producing activities for your business.

While you want to blog regularly, life can happen. You can take some time off from blogging and just post on social media, if needed for a little while. Or you can recirculate some great content from past posts when you need a break. Just like your Young Living business, it can continue to grow if you need a few weeks to breathe, but if you take your hands off for too long, it will slow down. Be careful not to get burned out in the online world and work at a steady pace.

THE IMPORTANCE OF AN EMAIL LIST

While social media platforms are the quickest way to start sharing, you don't own the platform you are posting on. Your posts or the community you are building could disappear at any time, or get lost in a new algorithm. If you are blogging at wordpress.org, you own your platform, but people come and go on your blog at their whim—you have no control.

Which is why you need an email list. You own your list, people choose to subscribe to your blog and email list, and then you have a guaranteed way to connect with them on your schedule. There are several great email providers to choose from, but carefully read their Terms of Service to see if they allow work at home or MLMs. Contact their customer service with questions. Aweber is what I currently use. It is a paid program and people can opt into your emails/newsletter and give you permission to email them.

People must choose to be added to your email list. You can create a list in your email service and place a box on your blog. Don't randomly add emails to your list, but remember, when people purchase a kit from you, they have given permission to be emailed.

You can encourage sign ups to your list by creating a free opt-in, a gift in exchange for their giving you their email address. This can be a one-page report or cheat sheet, an eBook, a phone consult with you, or password protected video. Be creative and make it something valuable that is a taste of what your blog offers.

Remember to always stay compliant in everything you write, post, and share. You are responsible for your content as well as where links lead to once they click through. Be safe and always check before posting. If in doubt, delete for your protection and for Young Living.

SUPPORTING YOUR TEAM ONLINE

Facebook groups provide an excellent place to support your customers and members. You can create secret or closed groups and post product education, team news, company news, host contests, giveaways, and provide a place of community for your team. It is a great place to build relationships and support each other. You will most likely find that this helps your team become like a family and that it provides a venue in which they can encourage each other in many areas of their lives, not just Young Living.

You can create learning groups for product education, as well as business groups for those wanting to do the business and learn how to share. Use these groups to encourage, educate, support, and lead your team. Live video is great for building connections—announce the time you'll go live and use them for team trainings, too!

Help your team become a family

It can be hard to keep things organized in Facebook groups due to the fast pace of questions, comments, and new posts. To help with the organization, go to "Files" and "Create Doc." Fill out this document with links to popular or key posts within your group. Or you can create different topics, like "Essential Rewards," or "Team Calls." To grab the permalink to include in the document, click the date and time under the name of the person who posted. Then grab the URL and put that in the document. You can "Pin" this document to the top of your group. This will help with organization and making things easier to find, especially for new members.

Remind members to use the search function in your group and help them be independent. You do not want the support groups to become dependent on you to answer all their questions. Encourage leaders and team members to help answer questions and point people in the direction to find answers themselves. Create learners and researchers.

Set the rules that you want for your group and highlight them in your pinned post. Yes, you will need rules, and "no drama" is one of them. No bashing the company or others.

As with everything we do, be sure to stay compliant online in social media, your blog, even in your private groups. Set a good example for your team and let them know where they can find their own answers and that you will have to delete non-compliant questions and answers.

The world is a huge place and building online allows you the opportunity to reach more of it than you think possible. This can open many new doors for you. Have fun and be creative while you are helping your family and others.

These are just a few tips to help you grow your business online. If you would like more information on growing your business online, visit: www.theencouraginghome.com/ylbiz.

TRAINING AND GROWING ON FACEBOOK
FROM SARAH HARNISCH

As Mary said, social media is not just a way to share the Young Living opportunity, it's also an excellent platform for connecting with your team! The reality is, you will be outside your friend circle almost immediately once you begin sharing, even sometimes with the first class. Your team will grow far beyond your ability to host them all in your livingroom for team trainings—and that's a good thing! Facebook is an amazing tool that keeps you connected, and Facebook Live video is how many Young Living Leaders are efficiently and effectively training and building culture on their teams.

Does the idea of going live, even in a private group terrify you? Can I be honest with you? Doing Young Living as a business was a total stretching experience for me—I didn't start out wanting to build a business. God is always stretching us to do things outside our comfort zone, because when we are stretched, we rely on Him more. I was convicted to step outside my comfort zone by an intern at my radio job when I'd been in Young Living just 6 months.

We had minutes until I had to go live in front of five million people, I had a blank sheet of paper in front of me, and I had writer's block. My intern's face went ghost white as she watched the clock ticking away. Finally, I started writing, punching it out. Three minutes later, I had penned seven stories and pulled five soundbites. The stinger went off; telling me it was go time. I was still finishing the last sentence. I pulled the mic close to my face, turned it on, and anchored the newscast top down without a prior read-through, and without a single mistake; editing with my eyes as I went. I was in my zone.

As I turned the mic off with a victorious look on my face, I looked over at the intern sitting next to me. She had a completely different look on her face. She said, "Sarah, you're not doing what you were called and created to do." My jaw hit the floor. "How do you know that??" I asked. She replied: "Because I just watched you put a newscast together in three minutes. It would have taken me three hours to do that, and I still would have made mistakes. You are way too comfortable. God always calls us to be stretched outside our comfort zones. You're in the wrong place."

I could not get her words out of my head. They were like a knife in my back! For two weeks I mulled and mulled and mulled over them. And I realized she was right. I was working my dream job—that I had prayed, worked toward, and relocated across the country for, but it wasn't stretching me anymore. It was time to step out into the faith zone again.

You may be doing a job you love. You may be in your zone. You may have a comfort level because your routine is set. Standing in front of people, even a few, may be terrifying. Doing a Facebook live may be terrifying. But what if God is using Young Living as a tool to mold you into the person you're created to be? Be willing to step outside your comfort zone and into the God zone!

THE BASICS OF GOING LIVE ON FACEBOOK

There are only three essentials you need to know to do a good Facebook live:

- have good lighting
- look at the camera on your phone and not the picture of your face
- begin and end the video smiling

Those three things will carry you very, very far. Not sure on the lighting aspect? It's simple. Grab a $7 desk lamp from the store and put it on a tray table next to you. That's enough to brighten your face. Your setup need not be pricey, your content need not be expert level. It's about connecting with your leaders, your team, and your up-and-coming team; and if you're doing that, you're doing great.

TRAINING YOUR TEAM USING FACEBOOK LIVE

For those of you who plan to maximize Facebook Live to train your team, here are some more tips and deeper strategy to make the most of this tool.

1) Appointment listening. It's a term we use in the radio world. Tell people what you are doing and when you are going to do it, tell them again—then tell them a third time. It builds anticipation. "Tonight at 7:00 I'm going to be doing a giveaway of the BRAND NEW SAVVY MINERALS BRUSHES! Do not miss it!" BAM. You will have a larger Facebook audience when you go live.

2) Go live when you have a strong connection. In other words, do a dry run first from where you will be shooting, even if it's just for 60 seconds (You can delete this video immediately after testing). You want to make sure you won't embarrass yourself by going live and then losing your audience mid-stream. I shot many of my Gameplan bootcamp videos (which are FREE and online at oilability team.com) from my van near a cell tower, because I used to live in a place with poor reception.

3) Write a catchy description. Don't just say, "Today's Video 8-16." Make it more like, "Psycho Savvy Brushes Giveaway". The description will be on your video forever, it's how people will find it. Write it before you go live on a piece of paper, not as you are going live and are up against the clock.

4) Before you go live, chart what you want to say. It may be a 3-sentence bullet point on a sheet of paper, but write it out. You'll have much better content if you know where you are going. Also, always write out your close. Then you have a way out of those videos and you come off sharp at the end. People watching will remember the close of your video more than the beginning, so end strong.

5) When you are live, ask viewers to subscribe to you. Then they will get updates when you're about to go live, and you'll build your audience much faster. After four months of this, I now have a live audience of 40,000 people on the Oil Ability with Sarah Facebook page.

6) You choose whether or not you want to respond to people who are chatting while you are live. If you have a large audience, that can be tricky. If it's small, it can be welcoming. One word of caution—don't respond to every comment, it can derail the purpose for your video, and don't wait three minutes to start on your content. Say hello, and get to your topic. Average online stats show

that you have seven seconds to catch someone's attention. For a Facebook live, it's closer to 60 seconds. But based on Facebook statistics, if you start your video and walk away for three minutes, or chit chat to wait for more people to join, you will lose the people that first hopped on.

7) Go live often! One leader once said to me, "I went live, but no one gets on. So I just stopped doing it." It's because you have to build trust in two areas.

    a) First, you have to show them that you're consistent. I train my leaders every single Tuesday. They know after three years of trainings that I will be there, even if I am on the farm with Gary Young in Ecuador; or live from convention in Utah. It's consistent. So they show up. When I first started going live, I had eight leaders who actually got on and watched! Within two months, it was up to 40. Now, every week we average 800, about 400 live and 400 who watch the replay in the days following.

    a) The second reason you go live often is to build trust that you'll generate good content. Not sure what to talk about with your team? Go through your Gameplan book and look at all the things you highlighted or wrote notes next to. That's a great place to start. Pick one thing a week and have at it. If you make a bullet list of what you're going to talk about first, you'll be more concise, and more people will stick around.

8) Keep your content concise. Three bullet points, interact, then make sure you have a solid close—a way out of what you have started. You can even use a canned response that you do the same every time you are on—"thanks for hopping on with me! I'll see you again next..."

9) Unless you are doing a training, keep your videos short— under ten minutes. Trainings with your leaders or on product should not go over 30 minutes. It's the same with online classes—the shorter the better, 30-45 minutes max or you will lose your audience. If you can do a 15-20 minute class, you will hold more people.

BUILDING A PUBLIC PLATFORM ON FACEBOOK

What about talking to people who aren't on your team yet? Want to use Facebook to expand your reach and grow your business? You will have to build a public platform, which is a whole 'nother set of skills that requires understanding the best way to get content seen on a public page.

I built my public Facebook page, Oil Ability with Sarah Harnisch, from a handful of followers in 2014 to now reaching over 100,000 people each week. It's the main way we funnel traffic to our Gameplan website, which has 40,000 visits a month. This is because I have studied facebook and learned what works and what doesn't. Facebook has many algorithims that affect visibility of your posts. Ignore this and your posts will be lost in the mix. Play by the rules and Facebook will help you be seen by new people every day!

Things to avoid

There are certain words that decrease viewer count because of the way Facebook sets up its algorithms. This is even if it's in your live video — it's not just posts. Words like kit, free, giveaway, contest, or sale can get you flagged and they will block the number of views.

If you want to post a giveaway, post it like this: G*I*V*E*A*W*A*Y because the algorithm can't read graphics, and you're less likely to get capped on viewers.

Facebook is targeting promotional posts — so if you're using words like discount, winner, sale or giveaway, you're going to get blocked. "PM me for prices" is another phrase they look for. It will limit the amount of people that see that post to 1.2% of the people active on your group. So if you have a group of 800, only 33 people will see it. Also, the algorithm is punitive. So if you continually post promotional posts, it will get choked down more. Facebook is also targeting outside links, like your yldist page or the youngliving.com page. They are trying to herd online sellers.

Popular content

Facebook loves Facebook live. They will boost that live far more than a video that you upload.

Facebook loves "loves." Ask people to love your post. It's shown to more viewers than likes. They didn't roll out emoticons just to make us happy — but to track how people react, and then tailor Facebook to the reaction. It helps them organize the newsfeed.

Interaction

Respond to your own posts after you make them and always leave a reaction, like a heart. Every time you do that, it boosts the post on people's newsfeeds.

If you watch your own videos and give reactions, Facebook does not recognize who is reacting. It will count to boost your post and help make it more visible.

Go back and respond to comments and questions on your live feed. Again, this boosts the post back up on people's live feeds. Make sure you're posting when people are on so you get the most impact.

Hashtags

Sorry hashtag lovers, but hashtags kill your views. If you use them, Facebook will limit who sees your posts. Leave them off posts you think will go viral.

Post frequency

Watch your volume of posts. If you're posting five to six times a day, you'll get censored. If you're posting two to three times, people are more likely to see them. That means you need quality content and your posts need to be good. Be concise and plot out what you want if you want visibility.

Facebook watches for "over-posters." You're aware of the friend that shares every joke and every image? They don't have visibility because Facebook blocks it out. Don't be one of those people if you're running a home-based business.

Content

Watch what you post. People want to follow strong, positive people. If all your business posts are knockout good, then you put up political posts or controversial posts on issues, you're far less likely to get good engagement on your business posts and when you are marketing your classes. What you say ALL day long matters.

Post timing

When's the best to post on Facebook? This one is REALLY interesting. There have been over 20 studies done on social media engagement, and according to the researchers (Neil Patel, MarketProf, Elle and Co, Fast Company, Track Maven, etc.) the best times for a Facebook post are 9 a.m., 1 p.m., and 3 p.m. The days with the most engagement are

Thursday, Friday, Saturday, and Sunday; with Sunday being almost 32% higher.

Now I'm going to tell you to ignore all the statistics. Young Living, with its millions of active distributors, defies the odds. Seventy-eight percent of Americans define themselves as Christians, and I see it on my team; because when I post on a Sunday, the "high engagement" day, my posts flop. Everyone is out enjoying their families and the Sabbath. There are very few responses, likes, and comments. When I post on Friday and Saturdays, posts flop. Why? Because statistically, more of our teams teach on the weekends than the weekdays. Therefore, I always do my trainings on Tuesday nights when everyone is around.

My most engaging posts on the main Oil Ability page are done either early morning — 7-9 a.m., noontime (12-1), and evenings, 7-9 p.m.; and we get the best response on Mondays, Tuesdays, Wednesdays, and Thursdays, hands down. What about a Facebook Live? For those, I prefer the evenings when people are home and can watch, or over lunch. In the morning, most are too rushed to watch anything. So pick your times well and you'll get a larger audience. After 7 or 8 p.m. is best. What about factoring in time zones? Eighty percent of the U.S. population lives in either the Eastern or Central time zones, so base your Facebook Lives off that.

SAY GOODBYE TO YOUR COMFORT ZONE

Facebook is a powerful tool. Don't be intimidated by it! I had a leader say, "I can do anything but go Live. I have no desire to do it. I don't like the way I look on camera."

This is not about you. It's about the people you will bless with the opportunity to build wellness for their family, and a legacy income for the future. Do things that scare you. Step outside your zone. Step outside the places your feet go every day. Do a Facebook live on your personal page. Teach a class. Pick up a phone and call someone you don't know. You will be stronger for it on the other side. You'll wake up one day and say, "this was one of the best decisions of my life."

Of all those places the Lord will take your feet in this Young Living adventure my friend, all I can say is, "it's worth it." The woman I am today is not the woman I was three years ago. And I am so very thankful that I said yes.

For me personally, the best perk of being a Diamond isn't the paycheck—though that's tremendous peace of mind. It's the joy of seeing my leaders rank. It's seeing the freedom they experience and the lives they get to lead forever because they were willing to do the hard things that made their business grow. So be brave. You can do it! Is it intimidating? Yes. But the payoff in personal growth is something you can't put into words.

CHAPTER 16

STAYING LEGAL:
COMPREHENSIVE FDA TRAINING

I can't write a book for business builders without a chapter on how to protect your businesses. By protection, I'm referring to the Food and Drug Administration and what you're legally allowed and not allowed to say about essential oils.

First off, I want you to know I wrote this because I'm really good at screwing it up. I've made just about every mistake you can possibly make. My business was flagged twice in 2015 for non-compliance. Because of that I've had about 50 hours of training directly from corporate either on the phone with the Conduct and Education department, or in person at trainings and retreats. I'm passing along what I've learned in order to save you stress.

Why is the FDA going after Young Living? That's not really accurate. They're not going after anyone. The rules that are being broken have been broken since they were written back in the 1930's. They are not new rules. They are in place for our protection because unfortunately, there are a lot of companies out there that sell vitamins filled with wood chips instead of actual vitamins and weight loss supplement gimmicks.

We want the FDA, because they are there for our benefit. Unfortunately, this means good companies like Young Living are restricted in what they say about their oils.

Why doesn't Young Living just become FDA certified? It's because then oils would be considered a drug; and to get a drug, you have to go to the doctor, get a prescription, and have it filled at the drug store. Young Living wants oils to be for everyone—every home in the world—regardless of how good your health insurance is. But unfortunately without that approval, we can't speak about the oils as drugs. Oils are not about curing disease, they're about supporting systems. Respiratory support. Immune support. Don't live in the land of sickness, live in the land of health. You need to learn a new language!

Young Living wants oils to be for everyone

I shared my migraine story with you for more than one reason. I wanted you to trace my path to oils, but also one of my greatest frustrations with the medical world: it's always chasing symptoms. When I spoke with my final neurologist, I asked him why he didn't look for the source of the migraines. He said it was too complicated and instead gave me pills for swelling, pills for pain, pills for vomiting, and pills to counteract the side effects of the other pills.

One of the things that makes Young Living so amazing is that it's a wellness company. Wellness is exactly what I was searching for with that neurologist. It's about preventative maintenance. It's the first time I've seen a company go after the root causes: full system support. Oils don't cure disease. They set the stage for your body to do its own fighting. Always keep the dialogue in that place. Don't talk about the illness, talk about the organ. Talk about where you put an oil, not why.

Still unsure? Check your wording against Young Living's website. That language has been through a team of lawyers. One of my favorite lines is "gosh, I don't know about that. I've never had to deal with that before. Why don't you take this oil home and see how you feel?" Or you can say "Here's a place where you can start your own research." When you are not the expert, and you are not pointing to cures, you make it a lot easier for your leaders to copy you—because they also don't need to be the expert. And you stay compliant.

Don't slap the word "support" behind a disease and think the wording is OK. "Eczema support" doesn't fly, because you're still talking about disease.

If you are recommending an oil to support a body system, it must be an oil labeled for internal use. This means that you cannot say, "R.C. oil supports the respiratory system" because it is not a Vitality oil. Only Vitality oils are approved for use inside the body and your respiratory system is inside the body. You can say that "R.C. oil gives a soothing aroma when placed in a diffuser."

Here's a simple guideline: if you can buy a product that treats a symptom at the drug store, you probably can't say an oil works for that same symptom. The product in the drug store is most likely FDA approved, and comparing oils to it will get you into trouble, because oils are not FDA approved for treating diseases. Only if Young Living has created a product that's FDA approved, like Insect Repellant or Mineral Sunscreen, is it OK to make product claims. But if you say a single oil can achieve the same purpose, even if that oil is an ingredient in the sunscreen, you fall out of compliance.

Let's get more specific.

HOW TO STAY COMPLIANT WHEREVER YOU ARE

We'll start with online posts, because that's where marketing for your classes begins. When you're online, everything is out there forever, so here are some tips to make sure you're following the rules.

Facebook

1) Only pull graphics from Young Living's Virtual Office or the Young Living Blog. Both have been run past a team of lawyers for compliance.

2) If you are running a Facebook page, do not post any links that people can click on. The article you're posting might be compliant, but the FDA doesn't just look at that one article. They click through the entire website, so any article on that site that isn't compliant can get you in trouble. It's not safe to post links that take you other places—to other blogs, websites, or even other Facebook pages.

3) Don't "Like" or react to someone else's post if it's not compliant. By liking it you're affirming the comment, you're agreeing with it, and it's going to get you in trouble.

4) If someone else posts a non-compliant comment on your page; delete the comment, contact the person who posted it, let them know that you appreciate them, tell them you had to delete the comment and why.

5) When you're writing posts: don't imply anything. Talking about fibromyalgia without using the word fibromyalgia is still not compliant. The FDA is looking for your intent. Are you intending that people use the oils as a drug? The rule of thumb is, if it's something you can buy at Walgreens, it's probably FDA approved. Sunscreen, bug spray, and the more obvious—asthma inhalers, eczema cream—all of that can be bought at the store. Don't talk about the oils as drugs or even make implications.

6) Don't ask leading questions that can get you into trouble. What are you using your diffuser for today? What's your favorite use of PanAway? You will end up having to delete a lot of comments.

Other forms of social media

Twitter, Instagram, Periscope, blogging—the rule of thumb is to talk about how you are using the oils, but not what you're using the oils for. For example, "today I'm diffusing R.C. It smells great! I love eucalyptus!" is a better post than, "Upper respiratory infection, broke out my oils." One is completely compliant, the other—you're dead meat. Carefully look at photos, I snapped a picture at the lavender farm that I thought was totally okay, until I looked back at it and realized it had non-compliant speech on a sign; so I didn't post it. If you have a Pinterest oils folder, delete the entire thing. That's the safest advice I can give you. Unless you know with confidence that every button on every page is compliant, you are not safe. Pull from Young Living's blog or shareable graphics under the Member Resources button in the Virtual Office, and you'll always be compliant.

Oil Application

There is one more trick to sharing correctly, and it's the hardest one to master, so I recommend you lean on the experts by using the documents in the Virtual Office. We know that there are three ways to apply oils to the body—topical, aromatic, and internal—and sometimes we use one oil in multiple ways. But that doesn't make sense to the pharmaceutical world. You can't take an antibiotic capsule and smear it on your skin, so the FDA says that you can only talk about one use for each oil. It's either topical, aromatic, or digestive. A handful of the oils can be talked about in two ways. If you talk about taking lavender internally, you fall out of compliance because that's listed as a topical oil by the FDA. Young Living has made it easy for you to know how to speak compliantly and one way is with a new chart under the Member Resources tab in your Virtual Office. Click on "Member Resources > Product Education > Suggested Product Uses Chart." Stick to the chart and you're safe! Stick to the language on the Young Living website and you're safe. It's not something to fear and it should not hold you back. Tens of thousands are sharing and ranking up every single month. It's just a matter of learning to use the tools that this amazing company has put together.

Don't talk about the oils to treat disease

Classes

These rules apply no matter what type of class you're doing—webinars, in a restaurant with one person, or before a class of 100. We have written an FDA-compliant 101 class that you can use in your classes, and it's in the appendixes. Read from the script and you're safe. Do not share personal testimonies that talk about the oils as a drug, and do not use testimony photos.

If you hold a make-and-take class, the safest way to do it is simply to put the names of the oils on the containers. Lavender. Peppermint. Lemon. Don't write Young Living's name on it, and don't name blends. Just write the oils in the blend, for example, Cinnamon, Clove, Rosemary and Eucalyptus for Thieves®. When you are talking about cleaning supplies, all "anti-" and "dis-" words are banned; for example, antibiotic, antiseptic, disinfectant, anti-viral, anti-bacterial, etc. But you can pop a picture of your sink up before and after you cleaned it, and just say that you wiped it down with Thieves® cleaner, and you're totally compliant.

Books

A lot of people ask me how you're supposed to educate your team on the oils. The FDA does allow you to have a table of books for sale at your classes, but there are two rules. First, keep them on a table separate from the oils and outside the room you're teaching in. Two, have more than one book for sale, because otherwise you're promoting only one author. It breaks the law to give books away as an incentive for buying the starter kit, but you can absolutely have them for sale.

Teach people to fish instead of giving them fish. I've found this is a lot more freeing than answering non-compliant texts at 10:00 p.m. Point them to PubMed (a website featuring studies on oils) or a selection of reference guides. There is a ton of information out there on how to use them. They just have to do their own research. The minute you open a book and issue a recommendation, you have crossed the line!

A WORD OF ENCOURAGEMENT

Now, some encouragement. In March of 2015, my OGV was 46,000, and five months later, in August, it was 67,000. A few months after that, it was 153,000 and I was a Platinum! A year and a half later, it climbed to over 500,00 OGV. That happened even though I'm teaching compliant classes. I teach the exact same script that is in this book, with no bells and whistles. I want you to know that you, too, can teach compliant classes and still grow.

In three months, right after the FDA crackdown in 2014, I made it to the top 1% of income earners in the company as a Silver. It's all about getting out there and sharing...the right way. Share correctly to protect Young Living, to protect your family, and keep the purest oils in the world available to everyone.

PART FIVE

Strategies for Building Your Team

In January 2017, I participated in The Gameplan Bootcamp. My mindset changed from selling the oils as a hobby, to owning my own business. I overcame my fear of hosting classes and I started implementing the strategies from this awesome book. I set a goal of ranking to Executive by December 2017. Through the implementation of the Gameplan Strategies, I surpassed my goal and hit Executive in October 2017. I am now hustling toward Silver!

Becky Hixson

I went from Silver to Gold after my upline sent me Gameplan on Audible this last spring. I have listened to it on repeat, over and over. I have found my voice and finally learned how to train two to train two. Platinum bound now!

Sarah Duval

CHAPTER 17

THE YOUNG LIVING COMPENSATION PLAN IN LAYMAN'S TERMS

There have been *lots* of books written on this subject. As with anything I write, I'll read what's out there first, and I have a half dozen of these books next to me right now. I recommended several of them in the resources chapter earlier on. But I owe it to you in a business book on Young Living to at least not shove you to another book, so let me give the simplest, easiest way to understand the compensation plan. Because I'm an English major, not a math major, this is the best you're going to get from a girl who's paid to talk for a living.

HOW YOU GET PAID

This is the fastest compensation plan training you'll ever receive. You can make it hairy and complicated, or you can boil it down to four simple concepts.

Your check is mailed out or direct deposited on the 20th of the month and it represents your labor from the previous month. For example, your March 20th check will be from your work in the month of February. By the way, you can enable direct deposit anytime by going to "Member Resources" and "Direct Deposit Instructions For U.S. Members".

The four parts of your check are as follows:

1) Starter kit Bonus: $25 per kit

2) Fast Start Bonus: 25% of all purchases for the first three months after enrolling (including $25 for the starter kit)

3) Unilevel: You are paid 8% on your level 1's, 5% on your level 2's, and 4% on your level 3's, 4's, and 5's.

4) Other Bonuses: At the beginning, the Rising Star bonus is paid by shares on a qualifying number of legs with a minimum OGV each. (You can earn up to 6 share which average $40 to $50 per share. See Chapter 18 on page 181for more information on Rising Star). As you rank higher, Generation Leadership Bonuses (paid on either your leaders ranked Silver and above, or a percentage of your OGV from Silver to Silver—generations deep) kick in. A Gold is paid on volume three generations deep or three Silvers deep.

A bit more detail:

Starter kit bonuses

For every kit you sell as the enroller, you receive $50. That's pretty sweet, since the kit is already half price and you're getting a third of Young Living's profit. Of that $50, $25 is the Starter Kit Bonus and $25 is the Fast Start Bonus. When you sign people for kits, one person is the sponsor and one person is the enroller. The enroller is usaully the one who is working directly with the new person, helping them get signed up, and is the one who gets the bonuses. The sponsor is where the new person is placed on your team (more about placing in the chapter on strategy on page 181). Everyone seems to get the two mixed up. Here's an easy way to remember it: "E" comes before "S." The enroller can be higher in your organization. You can be enroller and someone below you can be sponsor, but not vice versa. If you try to switch them out, it won't work. Can you teach classes and sign one of your leaders as sponsor and enroller? Yes, but you won't get the Starter Kit or Fast Start bonuses. Can you teach for a crossline member and share the sponsor and enroller numbers? No, they must be on your team.

Fast Start

When you first start with the company, most of your check will be Fast Start and Starter Kit bonuses. As you rank up, it'll be more Unilevel and Generation Leadership bonuses. Fast Start is an incentive to motivate people to order right away and not sit on their kit for six months before they place another order. For the first three months, you will get 25% of everything they order, including their kit, up to $200 each. You also will get a 10% bonus on your second level enrollers (anyone enrolled by your personally enrolled) for their first three months up to $80. So when someone you have enrolled sells a kit, you will get $10 on that kit sale and 10% on every purchase for the first three months. Beginning in the forth month, you only get paid in the Unilevel system.

Unilevel

A "level 1" is a person you have signed who is directly under you, for example, your mom. If your mom were to go and enroll her coworker, that person would be a "level 2." If that coworker signed someone, they'd be a "level 3." You're paid on your first five levels. The only way to make more than that is to be paid on your generations, which don't kick in until you're a Silver. As you rank up, this will become a large part of your check.

Generations

Once you reach the rank of Silver, you qualify for generations. These are nice, because they allow you to get paid on more than just the first five levels. You're paid a percentage of the OGV from Silver to Silver. If you have a Silver who is three levels deep and the next Silver is 100 levels deep, you're paid a percentage on all of that volume. Generations are a HUGE part of my check, about half of it. It's how Diamonds make $30,000/month.

The second part of generations is the Leadership Bonus. For that, you're paid based on shares for your own rank, as well as on your leaders ranking Silver and above. I make about $130 per Silver (it varies month to month slightly). I know of some Golds who are paid more than Platinums because they have so many Silvers on their team. As soon as you reach Silver, definitely be developing your Platinum leg, but also be working hard to raise more Silvers on your team. The fastest way to spike your paycheck is to collect Silvers. If you have hit Silver, spend your time collecting as many Silvers as you can en route to Gold. That's where your check is—more so than Unilevel pay, Starter kit bonuses or Fast Start.

If you had a single Silver under you, you'd make $1560 in one year simply from them holding rank. If you had them under you for 20 years, that one business builder would result in an additional $31,200 in your account. Now imagine if you grew 100 Silvers, or a 1,000!

If you want to take a closer look at the compensation plan, you can find it in the Virtual Office under, "Member Resources" and, "Compensation Plan."

In my future book for Silvers and above, I'll include strategies on how to help more people achieve Silver rank on your team. If you added just five Silvers to your team by the end of the year, your paycheck would go up by about $800/month, solely for them holding rank. You're paid even more on your Golds and Platinums (as long as they haven't outranked you. You can only get bonuses for the rank that you are, i.e., you can't be paid on a Diamond downline if you are a Platinum. If you have a Diamond under you, and you are a Platinum yourself, you'll be paid on them as though they were Platinum rank until you hit Diamond). What I love about Young Living is that you benefit when others are blessed financially by this business. There is a vested interest for you financially to help other people out. Network marketing is the best business model there is!! My bosses in any other field were never paid a higher check if I was better compensated. If I stayed later to anchor a newscast for another reporter, I did not make more. But if you work with a leader and invest in them, and they rank up, it blesses you right back in your check. If you are looking for a career where you get to help people, this is about the best that there is. You are blessed as you are blessing others.

ELITE EXPRESS BONUSES

Now that you get the paycheck, let's talk about rank for a few more moments. If you're a person who likes goals, and LOVES incentives—check out the "Elite Express" plan (you can find a detailed explanation of it under "Member Benefits" at YoungLiving.com). Not only does Young Living reward you with a free flight and hotel stay to the farms for holding Silver, Gold, or Platinum rank for three consecutive months, you can also earn points if you rank within a certain time period. If you need a tangible goal with a deadline, this is a good place to start.

These are the benchmarks, so you can keep them in front of you:

Executive in 2 (E2)
Reach Executive or higher within two months of first obtaining Senior Star

Silver in 4 (S4)

Reach Silver or higher within four months of first obtaining Executive

Gold in 8 (G8)

Reach Gold or higher within eight months of first obtaining Silver

Platinum in 8 (P8)

Reach Platinum or higher within eight months of first obtaining Gold

Diamond in 8 (D8)

Reach Diamond or higher within eight months of first obtaining Platinum

BONUS: Elite in 30 (E30)

Obtain Diamond or higher within 30 months of first reaching Senior Star

If you miss one gift, you can still catch the next one. If you don't make Executive in two, but you do make Silver in four months from ranking Executive. You will lose the E2 gift, but can still earn S4.

I will tell you that if you don't hit these benchmarks, you can still earn your trip to the farm. There is no deadline for that prize. You must simply hold rank for three consecutive months. Three months at Silver gets you the Silver retreat, three months at Gold gets you the Gold retreat, etc..

John and I ranked before this program was in place, but had it been around when we started, we would have hit every benchmark. I love how generous Young Living is! Not only do they make it priority to fly you to the farms to see the purity of the oils and understand the process it takes to make them, but they also have a plan in place to reward you as you rank with considerable prizes. It felt like Christmas when our buttons appeared in the mail with a recognition letter. Young Living has so much love for their distributors.

CHAPTER 18

A YOUNG LIVING STRATEGY GUIDE ON WHERE TO SIGN NEW OILERS

Let's dig a little deeper on where to place people as you sign them onto your team. There are many, many schools of thought on how to do this — and honestly, there is only one way that is wrong, and that is to build too wide. One of the things I love so much about Gameplan is it's not a book that tells you, "this is the only way." It's a book that shows you that, "these are the ways it's been done, find your style." You can be successful at anything you put your mind to. If you are successful, it's not because of Gameplan, it's because of you! You found the system that resonated with you and fought for your rank. And I am so very proud of you! What I can do is show you the pitfalls so you don't get stuck. Then you find the method in this book that resonates best with your gifts.

To give you a starting point, let me tell you how I have laid out this section. First, I'll explain the biggest pitfall, then I'll show you how I build, as well as one other strong strategy placement based on Young Living's Rising Star bonus. How you assemble your team simply depends on your personality and pace. Many, many Diamonds have done it many, many ways. The strategies you read in this book on placement are absolutely not the only way, the best way, or the smartest way. It does not mean other systems are incorrect. It's just a starting place, a focal point, and two plans that works if you need a system.

THE BIGGEST PITFALL

The most successful way to mess up placement is to build very, very wide. You only need six legs to build to Royal Crown Diamond. If you have more than six legs, you have more than you need to rank. What's a leg? It's a person with another person beneath them. It's different than just having individual people on your front line, your level 1's (the people signed directly under your name, with you as enroller and sponsor). I never want you to get ten or 12 legs going, because you'll be spread so wide it will take forever to rank. You'll have the volume (the OGV), but never the legs to qualify. That leads to discouragement and quitting. My job is to show you the shortest point from A to B. Too many legs is not the shortest point.

I see wide placement all the time with strategy, and it usually boils down to two major mistakes: the gravest is that you give up on your leaders too fast. If they don't teach classes at your pace, if they get discouraged and temporarily give up, you walk away and start a new leg. Instead, let me put something new in your mind. Always assume a leader is there for life, and continue to encourage them. I have had leaders walk away for three solid years only to return and rank. No now may not be no forever. It doesn't mean you're doing the work for them, but you are always there to give them hope.

The second reason people build very wide is for the paycheck. They build many level 1's because they are paid the most on them—8% versus 3% or 4%. Getting 8% on all those level 1's feels great, until you don't have the depth to rank Silver and lose a check that's a hundred-fold greater. Always keep your eyes on the goal. The goal is to fly far past Star, Senior Star, Executive, and beyond. Don't think shallowly about 8% per person in your check. Instead, set up a legacy business by structuring correctly so you can rank and, ultimately, will that income to your heirs.

TWO STRATEGIES FOR GROWTH

If you have studied color personalities (Jacob Adamo's book, "Full Spectrum Success" is wonderful for this), you know that people are motivated differently and can take widely different paths toward the same eventual goal. My path to Silver was fast and furious and my strategy fits those who are red or blue. They like to move fast. The downfall to this method is that you may forgo some bonuses along the way. The positive is that your Silver check (which averages $2,200/month, is significantly more than the $50 to $300 you may make in Rising Star bonuses.)

To make sure this chapter speaks equally to all personality types, I've detailed a second strategy that will equip you to make the most of the Rising Star bonus. This will likely appeal to the yellow or green personalities. Neither way is wrong.Find what works for you and soar with it.

A benefit to Strategy 1 is speed. Because you are not building so wide from the start, generally this tends to lead to a "Silvership" more swiftly. Psychology is really important in network marketing. One of the top deal-breakers I see in this business is people feeling they are not moving quickly enough. Most people quit because they think they can't do it. But the reality is they can, they just haven't given themselves enough time to succeed. If you get discouraged easily, this may be a better method for you, because the rank will come faster. I'd also encourage personal development training, because you're going to need it to grow into your ranks as a leader. Getting your mind around discouragement is one of the hardest things in this business. If you can pick yourself up and keep fighting, you have the spirit of a Diamond.

Let's dive in. This section is one of the most intense of the entire book, so you'll want a shot of NingXia Red, an entire Nitro packet, and at least two capfuls of MindWise before you start to take notes. A little Northern Lights Black Spruce in your diffuser isn't a bad choice either to encourage you and keep you on task. (I am not kidding. Go get these things. You'll also want a note pad handy, as you'll likely read this chapter at least half a dozen times before it clicks!) I had to write it a dozen times before it clicked for me! I will tell you this was quite a labor of love—I consulted with many, many Diamonds before piecing this together to make sure I had it right.

Here we go.

Strategy 1. Focused On Silver
Sarah's Method (designed for red and blue personalities)

Step 1: Sign everyone directly under you on your first level. Every class you teach, you are the enroller and the sponsor. Hand out "Your Game-plan" books at every class and promote the business. The first goal is to get ten people under you on Essential Rewards (these are all level 1's, not legs). You are going for 1,000 PGV, volume outside your two Silver legs. If you have ten people spending 100 PV a month, that will give you 1,000 PGV. So the "ten" number is a bit loose—it depends on what you need to hit your 1,000 PGV goal. You may have three at 300 PV, one at 100 PV, or 20 at 50 PV. Just get them on Essential Rewards to build your PGV base.

Step 2: Wait for someone to "pop" (or sign someone). This usually happens in four to six classes, depending on how much promotion of the business you're doing and how much follow up you do to get people excited about Essential Rewards. (I have developed tools for both of those things, by the way. I used the "Why Do Young Living as a Business" DVD and showed it after every class I taught. I picked up 800 business builders in two years with a 10-minute DVD that we have at oilabilityteam. com. As soon as the class was over, I asked them if they wanted to get their oils for free, and popped in the DVD. I was always amazed at who stuck around to watch it, and even more amazed at who said yes to the business! The second tool is the second mini, "Fearless: Confidence with Essential Oils in 2 Hours." It's a powerhouse! I use these little buggers in my follow up mailings to explain ER and get people breaking out their kits.)

Let's talk more about popping. (This has nothing to do with popcorn!) A leader "pops" when they sign someone up underneath them—it could be their mom, friend, or a co-worker. You'll see it in your Virtual Office under "My Organization," they will have a small plus sign next to their name, and you know there are people on that team. You can click the plus sign to see the whole team. Once someone "pops," I immediately reach out and start the 7-steps of the Gameplan system.

Step 3: What do you do once they pop? I divide my time. If I teach four classes in a month, I sign the people from two classes directly under me, and the people from the other two classes under my new business builder to encourage them. (Note: I *only* do this if they meet a few qualifications. They must show a pattern of spending 100 PV, they must be coachable, and they need to be willing to teach classes on their own. Ideally, they would schedule at least four classes a month, too, but if they are just starting out that may not be the case. Give grace and let them take it at their pace. Once I see that pattern established, it shows they are willing to work for this and not have it handed to them). If you have two people that "pop," build under them equally once your PGV of 1,000 is established.

You are now set to shoot to Silver. Pace doesn't matter, tenacity does. I am not going to give you a timeframe on how long this takes, because it varies by each person. Just know that if you're committed and out there teaching, you will grow. If you are not out there teaching, you will not rank, no matter what strategy you are using.

After you hit Executive, go ahead and start your Gold leg and work with a third person that has "popped." If you don't have one, hand out mini's at classes until you find one. Remember, only work two legs ahead—never more.

Strategy 1 in simple terms: Build 1,000 PGV by signing ten people as level 1's. Then focus on your two Silver legs and build them to 4,000 OGV.

Now it's time to take another swig of NingXia Red, Nitro, and MindWise. Because that is the simpler strategy of the two. This next strategy is more complex, but it gets you a better paycheck earlier in the game.

Strategy 2: The Rising Star Method
(designed for greens and yellows)

This method takes a bit longer because your OGV is spread wider. With width, you don't have the volume in your legs to rank to Silver as swiftly. For Silver, you need 1,000 PGV outside your two legs, two legs at 4,000 OGV each, and an overall volume of 10,000 OGV.

However, this method works very well for green or yellow personalities, or those that would rather work methodically and cash in on all the bonuses. One of the downsides of building with Strategy 1 is that you'll most likely lose out on Rising Star bonuses. For me, it did not matter, because I was a Silver twelve weeks after I got my starter kit. You lose the Rising Star bonus once you hit Silver, and it shifts to Generations instead. (It's ok, that paycheck is nicer!)

Let's delve in to the second method to build your team.

Step 1: Start exactly the way you did with Strategy 1. Teach four to six classes this month, and sign everyone directly under you. You're still going for PGV, but it's set up slightly differently. You'll be building clusters of volume to get the bonuses instead of signing them all as level 1's immediately.

Let me explain.

Rising Star bonuses are paid out in shares. One share varies each month, but it averages about $40 to $50. You get shares for meeting certain qualifications. If you have three legs at 300 OGV under you, that counts as one share. If you add two additional legs at 500 OGV under you, that counts as two additional shares. And if you add two more legs at 1,000 OGV under you, that's worth three additional shares. Shares are added to your paycheck as a bonus every month you qualify, until you hit Silver, and then you get generation bonuses instead.

Your very first goal is to get three people on your first level on Essential Rewards that are spending 100 PV each, and have an OGV of 300 each (that means they are either spending the 300 PV on their own, or spending 100 PV and have others ordering under them). Once you have those three, sign four more level 1's that are spending 100 PV each on Essential Rewards.

Step 2: Build each of the seven to an OGV of 300 each.

Step 3: Build the two with the highest OGV to 500. (I would sign each new member under them on your second level so you get the most in your check. Don't sign people too deep.) Once you have two legs at 500 OGV, and three at 300 OGV, you get an extra three shares in your check—or around another $150!

Step 4: Build two more legs to 500 OGV then two with the highest OGV to 1,000 for the maximum shares.

Step 5: Continue building your two largest legs to 4,000 OGV for Silver!

Rising Star Bonus Structure at a Glance:

Sign seven people at 100 PV on Essential Rewards. Build all seven equally to 300 OGV by placing people under them. Pick two of those legs and build them to 500 OGV. Pick two more legs and build them to 1,000 OGV. Then take the largest legs and build them to Silver.

One word of caution with Rising Star bonuses: you have to fill three legs at 300 OGV before two at 500 OGV and two at 1,000 OGV. It's done in a certain order. If you have two legs at 500 OGV, you may still miss out the bonus if you don't have your three at 300 OGV. Sign a third and get 300 OGV under them to get the full first set of shares.

Rising Star Method

Simple explanation:
> Step 1: three legs at 300 OGV (worth one share)
> Step 2: three legs at 300 OGV + two legs at 500 OGV (worth two additional shares, or three total)
> Step 3: three legs at 300 OGV + two legs at 500 OGV + two legs at 1,000 OGV (worth three additional shares, or six total)

The Perks to This Method

You energize your leaders by placing people under them. They get a bigger paycheck at the get-go and start to do the business on their own. You cash in on bonuses, and you have all six legs in place (plus one additional leg for PGV) for your Royal Crown Diamond rank. There's no need to build wider.

So how deep? Not too deep. Always keep in mind that you're only paid on the top five levels of your organization for Unilevel pay. Every person you sell a kit to should never be more than five levels deep. As you're working on Rising Star bonuses, and placing people under your Level 1's and Level 2's to get to clusters of 300, 500, and 1,000, don't sign them more than 5 levels deep. That carries no matter how high your rank.

Is that as clear as mud? Here's a quick recap of the entire section. In Strategy 1, you build PGV, then two solid legs. In Strategy 2, you build PGV and go no more than seven wide to get the most out of your Rising

Star bonus (you can build all seven legs simultaneously if you wish). But remember, never go wider than seven legs.

Remember, it's not about the time that it takes for you to rank. It's about tenacity and consistency. Schedule four to six classes a month, don't build too wide or go beyond five levels deep (or you are giving away your paycheck), and you'll be well on your way to an amazing future, one that pays far beyond this lifetime.

GROWING YOUR TEAM

So many come to me and say, "Sarah, I can't find anyone who wants to be a leader. No one is interested." I tell them I can't find anyone who *doesn't* want to share the oils!

When I look over my list of friends and see what they're doing for a living, how they're investing their time, and what they'd rather be doing; I truly don't see a single person who wouldn't be blessed by Young Living. Instead of looking at who isn't out there, look at who *is* out there. We think no one has interest, but if we really knew how our friends felt about what they did 40 hours a week, I think we'd be far less timid in approaching them. Even people who absolutely love their jobs, just like I did, have moments when they come home, look in their children's eyes, and wish they had a bit more of themselves to give. That's where Young Living comes in.

The only people who wouldn't be blessed by a Young Living business are those who are already millionaires in another MLM. The thing I've noticed from working this is that we never really know who will show an interest. It depends on the place they are in their life and what their desires are, and all of that constantly changes. Some people I'd never, ever imagine doing the business have completely blown me away. For example, people who are very timid are some of my top sellers and that's because it doesn't have much to do with personality. It has to do with drive and how much you want it. If they can catch the vision and see where this goes, you'll have an impassioned leader.

What's the benefit of Young Living over other MLM's? A consumable product that works. Instead of selling clothes, or a diet fad, or a pan, or a book; oils are something that people use every single day, multiple times a day, for everything from cleaning to personal body care to emotions. These always needs to be replenished, and that makes it extremely easy to share with people. Educate and empower and you'll have a lifelong oiler! No one uses Thieves cleaner and then goes back to their $3 cleaner loaded with chemicals. They just don't. The passion is easy to ignite because moms and dads care about what they have in their home.

Nonetheless, it can be a bit daunting trying to raise leaders. Where do you start without coming off pushy or awkward? Our team planned for that, and we have a simple system. I've recorded a 10-minute DVD that we play right after every single 101 class, every make-and-take, and every Beauty School class. It's called, "Why Do a Young Living as a Business." It goes through every benefit we've already discussed, such as no income ceiling, you are your own boss, you set your own hours, etc. When we play that DVD, it's amazing how many people will sit there and watch it after the lecture. I believe it's one reason we've grown as fast as we have.

One more thing: pray for leaders. I remember in 2014, before we made the DVD, I'd had a three month dry spell where not a single leader had contacted me. So I contacted a friend in desperation. She asked me if I'd prayed for leaders. I told her no, not specifically, but I'd prayed to grow. She said that I needed to pray specifically over my business if I wanted specific answers. I did, and within two hours, seven different people contacted me. Right now, four of them are top leaders in my organization. Prayer works!

A WARNING AGAINST POACHING

Poaching is when someone is already signed to another Young Living team, and you actively try to recruit them for your own team. I don't care if they were signed at a vendor event and they have never met their sponsor in their life, God has a reason for where each person ends up.

It is unethical to poach from other teams. It's the same as stealing. I know that you would not walk into a store and walk out with product you have not paid for. Yet leaders seem to have no issue trying to convince someone to be on their team "because they are local," "because they have no upline support system," or "because they would blossom if they were working with a friend."

Please hear my heart. When you poach from another team, you are taking someone's hard work. Perhaps they poured time into that person. Time is the most precious thing they have! They may have financially invested in them with educational material. When you walk off with that member, you have stolen something precious from that team. And it's wrong.

If you want the Lord's blessing on your business, it's important that you are ethical when no one is watching what you are doing. It's what you do in those still quiet places, when you are alone with a leader, when you are instant messaging someone at night, when you are at a class and a leader on someone else's team shows show up looking for support, when they send you the random email message about switching to your team, it's in those places that the Lord is watching how you run your business. What choice will you make? Will you run it with integrity?

If they say they need local support, remind them that their team will grow to an international multi-million dollar business. Thinking local is thinking too small. Within my first class, a friend of a friend signed someone in Mexico. They can bloom even from Mexico, without me standing right there. Because it doesn't take me for them to build. It takes them.

What is crossline recruiting? It's when you actively hunt out distributors and leaders on other people's teams with leading questions or tactics to get them to switch teams. For example, telling someone they can only attend your event if they switch to your team. That is UNETHICAL. I've seen it done at in-person classes and events and at online events. I've had leaders copy me on messages when they have been contacted by a crossline recruiter. There are many fish in the sea. There is no reason to pull from another person's team. Get skilled in the art of building the relationship with those that are not yet members and stop approaching people that are already on other teams.

Never instruct someone to create a duplicate account. Husbands and wives cannot have simultaneous accounts unless the second account was created before they were married. If a wife is signed to a different team, don't sign her husband under you and tell her to let her account go inactive. In the same vein, don't instruct someone to let their current account go inactive just so they can join your team. Don't encourage distributors with retail accounts to let their retail accounts go and sign up wholesale under you. Those are the markers of a predatory business builder.

I believe with my full heart that what you do will be returned to you ten-fold when you let a leader go who is already signed elsewhere. They can bloom on their own two feet. It only takes a starter kit and a 3-page script, not an upline pouring gifts down on you and recognizing you. That's not what builds Diamonds. It's rolling up your sleeves and teaching, in the way that you have been uniquely gifted to share. And that can be done on any team, anywhere. If you are taking a leader for your team, you are doing it for yourself, not for them. Choose to run your business with honor.

What do I do when someone contacts me and wants to be on my team? I ask them to look in their Virtual Office under "My Account" and give me the name of their Diamond. Then I connect them with their Diamond so they have "support." I give them the number for Member Services if they have more questions. I point them to Gameplan as a resource. And I gently let them know that they can bloom anywhere they are planted, because the Lord makes no mistakes on where He put them. They have a personal responsibility to grow their own business. It is not on your shoulders. Point them to tools and contacts, and stand down.

No Diamond grew five legs on someone else's labor. If they want it, they must fight for it. It's not your job to build their team or to move them to a place where they feel they can build "better." It's your job to run your team ethically. And let them grow, ethically, where they are.

A WORD ON UPLINE SUPPORT

While I'm on the topic of uplines (the members signed above you), there's one more thing I want to include in this chapter, since we're talking about strategy. Don't blame your upline if you don't feel you have support. That's another excuse. We bloom where the Lord has planted us.

All of the materials in this book I've written myself. My upline didn't compile it for me and I wouldn't have expected them to. Each of them are wonderfully gifted people trying to manage their own organizations and grow their own business; it's not their job to manage mine. If my business is faltering, it's my responsibility.

My upline does not need to provide me with resources, or money, or time, or gifts, or even training. There's so much training out there from many other Young Living teams, that if you can't get your hands on something your upline has developed, you'll blossom by purchasing another team's material. We all work for the same company—we're all Young Living cousins. Roll up your sleeves, do your homework, study, and grow!

Expecting gifts or encouragement from your upline puts a lot of pressure on someone else. If you don't feel that you have support, be so busy looking down at what you do have, (down into your team), that you don't have time to look up at what you don't think you have. You don't need leaders above you teaching nearby or gifts in the mail to do this thing. You just need a three-page script, a starter kit, a passion bigger than your excuses. Focus on having a grateful heart. That is half the battle. The Lord will do some pretty amazing things when you're depending on Him instead of the team above you.

STRATEGIC PLACEMENT

This is a completely different thing than poaching, and totally legal. Strategic placement is putting people on specific legs on your team to make the most of the Rising Star Bonuses or to achieve rank. The people you are placing are people who are not currently on another Young Living team. It's not poaching to purposefully place people in your organization or to move them around—it's smart strategy. Here's the nitty gritty details on placement and moving:

When you enroll a new member, you have three options for how to place them.

1) You can be both the enroller and the sponsor, which places them directly on your first level.

2) You can be the enroller and make one of your leaders the sponsor, placing that new member further down in your organization to help a leg grow.

3) You can assign both the enroller and sponsor number to the leader you are building under, to further encourage and support them.

You have up to 20 days after enrolling someone to reassign their enroller and/or sponsor number. After that you will have to go through the sponsor transfer protocol and pay to have them moved, and you will not be able to change who the enroller is. So it's a good idea to wrap your mind around this part of the business so you know what strategy you are going to use as you build your team.

If this person has been on your team for more than three weeks, you can still move them as long as they have not signed any members underneath them. You cannot move whole legs around on your team, only individual members with no downline attached to them.

Investing in your leaders

So, how do you decide who is sponsor and who is enroller when strategically placing? There's many schools of thought on this, but I recommend that if the person you are placing them under wants to grow a business, and is on ER (so they qualify to get the check!), let them be both the enroller and sponsor. They will see a much bigger difference in their check and be more likely to catch the vision for where this could go.

Here's the paycheck breakdown so you can see what this means to you and your leader:

Paycheck breakdown when you are enroller and sponsor:
    Starter Kit Bonus: goes to you
    Fast Start Bonus: goes to you
    Unilevel: goes to you

If you assign your leader as both the enroller and sponsor, they will receive all above compensation just as if they had signed that member themselves.

When you are enroller and your downline leader is sponsor:
    Starter Kit Bonus: goes to you
    Fast Start Bonus: goes to you for the first three calendar months
    Unilevel: goes to your leader after three calendar months

They'll show up under that leg, instead of directly under you.

You may be questioning why you would do the work of selling a kit and your leader getting all the bonuses. But when your leader sees the check and catches the vision, the $50 you lose immediately on the sale of the kit is far less than what you gain by the classes they will teach, the leaders they will raise, the generations pay you will receive as they rank to Silver and beyond, and the Essential Rewards base they will build under you.

If you understand strategic placement, you can see the amazing opportunity to build a strong organization with loyal leaders by investing in them from the start.

CHAPTER 19

THE KEY TO REACHING AND MAINTAINING RANK

I have touched on this lightly in a few areas of the book, but for the leader that keeps starting at zero OGV every month, this may be the part of the Gameplan book that saves your business. Let's go into deep detail on the importance of educating your team onto Essential Rewards, and why it's critical for you to rank.

THE KEY TO RANKING UP

It's terribly important that you don't let someone walk out of class and never touch base with them again. It is equally important that you don't help them through their starter kit purchase, shoot them a text or email on why they should be on Essential Rewards when their kit arrives, and move on impatiently when they don't respond.

The fact is, you could conceivably get to Silver completely on your own. You could find two friends, or sign your mom, and sell 40 kits on each leg and a few outside those legs and you could make it. Your pin will show up in the mail, you'll enjoy every moment of the Silver retreat gifted to you by Young Living knowing you literally earned every single drop of that rank single-handedly (which is not a good thing). Your two "leaders" spend their 100pv and you're off and running.

But that tactic will never work to hit Gold or even to maintain your rank as Silver. For that you need groundwork, and you need a team. I don't want you or the hard working leaders on your team to be unable to rank because your distributors are only ordering the one product they know about and spending 50PV a month. Or they ordered a kit and dropped off the planet.

After a year, because of my lack of follow up, I was losing 130 people a month. If your distributor orders a kit and then never orders again, they will go inactive and will disappear from your team after 12 months. It's incredibly difficult to maintain rank as that happens! John and I never lost Platinum, but it will take more than a year to get to Diamond—and my plateau was not necessary. The entire secret to the thing holding me back was Essential Rewards.

If you wait until Silver to start getting people on Essential Rewards, you will sit at that rank for a very long time. Or you'll get Gold and lose it over and over and over again. (You can lose Silver over and over and over again, or Star as well). It's because your path there was not solid and organic, based on relationships and trust. It was based on quick sales, and moving onto the next person.

Don't be so timid to touch base that you lose your business. Those people came to your class for a reason—they wanted to know about oils. So talk to them. A strong team will have at least 30% of their people on Essential Rewards. As you are growing from Star to Silver, I like to see that number closer to 50% or higher. You can check to see where it's at by logging into the Oily Tools app and clicking on "stats."

EDUCATING ONTO ESSENTIAL REWARDS

Here's the reality—if they didn't respond to your email about Essential Rewards, they didn't drop off the planet, you did. You'll never be able to hold rank without people placing orders regularly. It takes an OGV of 10,000 each and every month to maintain a Silvership!

Some of it will happen organically as your team flips through the catalog and their eyes land on Thieves laundry soap, but most will need your nudge. And they need ideas. They have the kit, they believe in oils because you have passion and you passed it to them, but they really don't know what the next step is.

It's just as critical that you touch base with these people as it is for you to hold classes. Build time for follow up into your week just as you build a calendar of classes, and just as you build time to train your new leaders. My monthly calendar looks something like this:

Last week of the month: schedule all my classes for the next month

First week of the month: do mailings and follow up (I have found I tend to be more consistent with them if I do them in one batch, rather than try to dribble them in throughout the month. People get missed.)

Rest of the month: Schedule trainings with leaders and hold classes

Let's dive into the Oil Ability Strategy for getting people on Essential Rewards. When my new oiler gets their kit, I immediately gift them a copy of Fearless and a Fearless calendar (it's free at oilabilityteam.com). My first goal is to train them to research, to read labels, to find yuck in their homes, and start the simple swap with Young Living room by room. The Fearless Tools and Resources (look under Share in the menu) on my website is outstanding for helping with that. There are printable graphics, a Fearless class, media, oils checklists, Simple Swap checklists, and even a letter to include in your mailings.

When I have them in front of me, I also set a date to explain the new kit to them—to show them how to use their diffuser, and point them to more resources. If they accept the ten Fearless challenges and fill out their calendar, I gift them $25 toward their Essential Rewards order (after it is placed). It is against Policies and Procedures to gift more than $25 before they have their kit, so make sure the nature of your gift is ethical.

Once they are Fearless trained, the world is wide open for you. There are a number of resources you can use for oils education. Some of my favorites are:

- Any of the Life Science Publishing reference guides (discoverlsp.com)

- Pubmed.com

- The "Look Book" (hello-essentials.com/lookbook/)

- Royal Crown Diamond Jordan Schrandt's beautiful "Welcome book" (discoverlsp.com)

- The "Now What" book (discoverlsp.com)

- Royal Crown Diamond Connie McDanel's amazing Aroma series on discoverlsp.com (like Aroma Clean, Aroma Breathe, etc.)

- Oil Revolution design books are outstanding (oilrevolutiondesigns.com)

- Jen O'Sullivan's books, like French Aromatherapy or Live Well (jenessentials.com)

- A Lucy Libido book (lucylibido.com)

- suggest a number of the cell phone apps I suggested in Chapter 14 on oils tools (Oily Manager, the EO bar, etc.)

More great ways to encourage an oily lifestyle:

- Get them to Young Living rallies

- Text them free classes off the oilabilityteam.com site

- Invite them to your classes, classes of local leaders, or online classes you are teaching

- Encourage them to get to the Young Living International Grand Convention

The first week of the month when you do follow up, your going to pull from the list of names of people that got kits the previous month. Every person that I sign gets a follow up package in the mail. (Refer to "Follow Up For Those Who Got a Kit" on page 116)

For those who have ordered a kit, the follow up package I send them looks something like this:

1) A resource listed above

2) A sample of something not in their kit like a Thieves cough drop or some Cool Azul pain cream in a little container

3) One of my lectures on audio CD or DVD

4) A brochure or graphic that explains Essential Rewards

I love to keep them excited about learning. I will also tell them about upcoming classes. If they don't respond to that, I mail out something that looks a little bit like this:

1) A hand written note explaining how it's wise to get 10% off their cleaning supplies and personal care products, like toothpaste. I also mention that after four months they get 20% back!

2) A different sample (more ideas: a Thieves cleaner "stain stick" in a roller bottle, a Vitality oil, a packet of NingXia or

Nitro, Thieves mints, Thieves hand sanitizer or spray, a small sample of the Satin Mint Facial scrub, a small sample of any oil that is not in the kit)

3) A visual idea of what three months of Essential Rewards would look like (we have many more of these graphics available—look for them at oilabilityteam.com)

4) A snapshot of the Essential Rewards program and what the freebies are for that month from Young Living

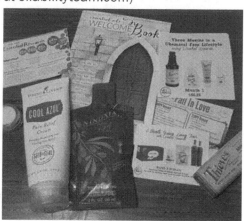

Here's a photo of what one of my bundles looks like. (Just add a handwritten note explaining the little care package!)

GETTING OVERWHELMED WITH MAILINGS

There are a LOT of mailings options. What if I can't afford to do all that?

Here's the thing. When I first started, and my paycheck was just enough to cover my Essential Rewards order and put gas in my car to get to classes, I was not doing massive Essential Rewards mailings. I send out a couple of roll ons or a textable class, or a sweet note by email. And I still grew a Diamondship. Even now, I focus only on my personally enrolled, those about to go inactive, or legs I am growing. My team is far too big to do these kinds of mailings to everyone. If you try to be all things to all people or cover your entire team, it will turn into a project that is unmanageable.

Set a goal. Set a budget. And work within those parameters. Never spend more than you make. Never go into debt for your business. The Lord will bless the fruit of your hands if you are faithful with the income coming in.

OVERCOMING OBJECTIONS TO ESSENTIAL REWARDS

What if that doesn't work, Sarah?

Then I'd encourage you to call them and touch base. Find out what their reservation is. Maybe they can't afford a $300 a month commitment. Show them how they can make a difference in their home with just $50 a month. Fifty is enough to keep them on Essential Rewards, and still swap chemicals out of their home.

Maybe they just don't really understand how autoship works. I've had people drop out because they didn't realize that the same stuff in their cart will ship out if they don't change it every month. Help them understand how and why of it.

Why does Young Living ship what went out the month before? Many people order the same supplements each month, and it's a beast to add NingXia, Nitro, Master Formula and Life 9 to your cart every single month—over and over again. So instead you leave it in, and Young Living will send you an email notice two days before it will ship just to remind you to update your cart.

Most of the time, I've found the reason people are hesitant to get on ER is truly just a lack of knowledge. If they understand how Essential Rewards works: that they can cancel it at any time with a single phone call without penalty, that they can change the date if they are on vacation, that it's completely customizable to their family's needs—it's usually enough for them to get on board.

Make sure you are communicating all the details of the program with them: 10% back the first 3 months, 20% back on month 4, 25% back after 25 months. Young Living has the most generous, gracious rewards program of any company that I've ever seen. If your distributors love the oils, they will love getting them every single month. It truly is Christmas in a box, just for you.

Here is an idea of what a 50pv order looks like:

Three Months to a
Chemical Free Lifestyle
using Essential Rewards

Month 1
$50.25

Three Months to a
Chemical Free Lifestyle
using Essential Rewards

Month 2
$51.50

Three Months to a
Chemical Free Lifestyle
using Essential Rewards

Month 3
$55.00

Here is an idea of what a 190pv order would look like:

3 Month Young Living Tour
with Essential Rewards

Month 1 $192.25

Essential Rewards Points Earned $19.23
Plus all the free oils on the 190PV Level of Essential Rewards freebies

3 Month Young Living Tour
with Essential Rewards

Month 2 $200.00

Essential Rewards Points Earned $20.00
Plus all the free oils on the 190PV Level of Essential Rewards freebies

3 Month Young Living Tour
with Essential Rewards

Month 3 $195.25

Essential Rewards Points Earned $19.53
Plus all the free oils on the 190PV Level of Essential Rewards freebies

WHY ER IS CRITICAL

Why is it so important that you and your team understand Essential Rewards? There are two reasons.

First, because you'll have a lifelong oiler. This is how they learn to incorporate the oils into their homes. This is how they learn to get rid of the junk. It's through simple, tiny steps. It doesn't all happen at once. I made an icebreaker video for classes called "Scavenger Hunt DVD" that's three minutes long, that shows what an oil-infused home looks like. It showcases dozens of Young Living products in a silly way, with my 5 kids bounding through rooms and opening cabinets (and even on the roof!) Find it at oilabilityteam.com. Share it with prospective oilers, in your classes, and with your leaders. This is why we do what we do.

The second reason that it's so critical that they get on ER is because that's one of the key secrets to going from Star to Senior Star to Executive to Silver and beyond. If you cry each month on the first of the month when your Virtual Office dashboard is reset to zero, this is your way out. Lay the groundwork that will help you rank. If two people on your team get on ER, the next month you may be starting at 300 or 4000GV instead of 0. It's much easier to rank up.

Train your leaders to do the same things with their own teams, and you have learned one of the key secrets to growing very quickly (and not getting burned out by trying to manage all your leader's legs). Show them how incredibly important it is. Make sure you show them what a follow up mailing looks like when you train them with the Teacher Training in the Appendix of this book.

I truly believe that alongside raising leaders, this is the one thing that people never understand about network marketing. It's one of the main reasons that they jump from MLM to MLM, saying the business model doesn't work. They have never laid an organic groundwork for their business, and every single month, they start from scratch. Could you imagine working on a project at your current job, and every month that you came in, it was as if the last month never existed? Then why do you do it to yourself with Young Living? Lay your groundwork. Touch base with your team. They WANT to hear from you.

They are looking for a chemical free life. And you have the answer for them. You have been given such a gift in all that you have learned already in the simple changes you have made in your own home. Remember—it's not sales, it's education. Drop ideas in their lap and stand back and see where they go. What have you already swapped in your house? Start there. Many of my "non" business builders, who swear they only wanted oils, ended up building businesses because they developed a passion from their monthly Essential Rewards order.

Essential rewards has many rewards. Be bold and talk about it like you talk about the oils. You'll develop deep friendships, get to know your team better, and will learn some cool things along the way on how others have used the oils in their own homes. And you'll explode your business. It's worth it.

PART SIX

EXPAND YOUR INFLUENCE: SECRETS TO GREAT LEADERSHIP

Crazy story—you told us to pray specifically and I did: for someone on my team to have the faith to step out and go for it and start building their business.

I prayed specifically for two of my team members to have their heart open to sharing their love of YL. Less than 24 hours later (and thanks to Your Gameplan Mini) one of them has taken the plunge AND has her first team member. The other called me out of the blue (I was actually free to talk, another miracle with six-year-old triplet boys at home) and God provided the words and the opportunity for me to share Your Gameplan Mini with her. BAM!

Thank you for encouraging me to pray for specifics and not just for "my business to grow." Gameplan, combined with giving God control of my business, has given me a peace and confidence that is in itself another answer to prayer!

Julie Martin Cole

Gameplan book helped me to recognize and conquer distractions. Through the system I was able to increase my team's percentage on ER each month and ranked up to Executive.

Lisa Ammerman

CHAPTER 20

BALANCE, BOUNDARIES AND TREATING YOUR BUSINESS AS A BUSINESS

I must confess, I wrote this chapter for myself. Every distributor has an Achilles heel, and I know mine well. I have no boundaries. For example, I repeatedly tell my leaders, "Anything you need, anything at all, tell me, and I'll bend over backwards to make it happen." Then I realize that I've over scheduled my classes, yet again filled my calendar to the brim, and spent another night away from my littlest Harnisches. That's when mommy guilt overtakes me.

When I retired from anchoring news in August of last year, I was determined to get the balance back into my life. I didn't want the hours of my anchoring shift to get replaced by other things and filled for no reason. If I was going to give up something I loved as much as putting together a newscast and

performing before millions of people every day, I wanted that time in my day to have purpose.

I wanted to wake up holding my husband's hand and seeing him off to work. I wanted to see the sun rise—something I'd missed for 16 years. I wanted to go on a run each day. I wanted to do devotions with my teens before the little ones rose, and get an early start on our homeschool day so I could work my business each afternoon.

Let me tell you what actually happened.

- The first week I slept. It felt SO good to sleep past 3 a.m.

- The second week, I woke up and made my husband an amazing breakfast a few times.

- The third week I started homeschool—with the hopes of finishing by 1:00 each afternoon and then pouring into my Young Living business. Well, we're on week 18 of school now, and I have yet to set hours each afternoon. Instead, I find that school runs until 4:00 or 5:00, then I become mom taxi and shuttle kids to sports, then run home and get dinner. Before I know it, it's bedtime and yet another Young Living day has escaped me.

So I let my full time job go—but I never made room for my business. Now what?

A few months ago, Jay Carter, a member of my Diamond upline, said something very convincing to me, and it was about over scheduling. As a Type A personality himself, I am pretty confident he could spot an over scheduler a mile away. He saw that I was a momma who tended to go with the flow—whatever seemed important, I'd let it take as long as it took, live in the moment, and try to fix it all later. That doesn't work when you're self-employed. When you are your own boss, you need discipline! Your business can't run itself, and if you don't commit time to it, you'll find you don't have a business. Or a family.

I recognized the issue pretty swiftly, but not before it cost me a wonderful personal assistant who was frustrated with my lack of boundaries. I took the entire month of December off and regrouped. I tried to get into a rhythm, but it eluded me, so I decided to commit some time to study and get better at time management. No matter what rank you achieve in Young Living, never lose your humility and always be willing to take it on the chin when you have made an error. You have to be willing to accept criticism or you'll never grow.

These were the resources I digested:

- Dani Johnson's Time Secrets Series (danijohnson.com)
- Lisa Terkeursts' "The Best Yes"
- Dr. Henry Cloud and Dr. John Townsend's "Boundaries"

Have I got it all down now? Absolutely not. But there is a pause to my step. In January, I had the opportunity to schedule 16 classes with some lucrative groups, but instead I committed to only two classes a month. John and I are in mega debt payoff mode right now, and the extra income would have been a great blessing to us, but I feel like I'm honoring the Lord more by staying behind the scenes this season. It also allowed some new leaders to take the limelight on my team, and I'm realizing how much I love seeing them shine. I am also loving the rest that is coming by letting others lead.

After reading those books, I looked at ways to be more efficient with the time I was spending on my business. I hired a woman to help me with mailings and follow up and committed that extra time to going on a run each day. By making that simple change, I've lost 22 pounds in three months and am sleeping better.

Then, to save time burning DVD's and to save money in the cost of mailings, I decided to put more of my lectures and content online. We're launching the oilabilityteam.com page, and it will be accessible to any team member—even our members in Thailand and Canada—without the cost of mailing packages. I've written this book to pass knowledge along to leaders who are a great distance away and harder for me to hand train in person. When I realized that each class I teach, especially the one-on-one classes, takes time away from my children, I started holding group Teacher Trainings.

Those are some of the changes that have really helped me get on track. But to be totally honest with you, I had to apply some of those tactics to my home life as well. We power clean different areas of the house for 15 minutes a day, with each child assigned a room that's visible to the visiting public. I save my deep cleans (and cleaning of hidden areas, like back rooms and master bathrooms) for Saturdays. I am pretty OCD about a clean house, but I had to let perfection go if I'm running a business and homeschooling.

I'm getting better at sticking to a schedule with our schoolwork and not going on so many rabbit trails that it costs me an entire day of work. Putting my littles in quiet time for an hour each afternoon made it possible to give my leaders more respect by using that afternoon hour to return their messages which came in while my phone was off that morning during homeschooling time.

I mentioned earlier that my Diamond upline, Jay Carter, told me he had a system for staying on track. He made a list of seven things he wanted to do every day (usually three or four were personal things, like working out. Three things were business related). When he has completed the list of seven, he makes time for his family and for fun. I'll get so wrapped up in writing books and lectures, reading, studying, training that I often forget to include the fun. I've lucked out though, because my husband is the master of fun. He's the one who's always bringing home new movies to watch and planning ahead with root beer float nights for the kids, while I'm tucked away in a corner typing as fast as I can. One of my goals this year is to pull my head out of my books and focus on some of the things in front of me—before my kids are grown.

I don't want to wrap up this chapter without speaking to the other crowd too, though. You know who you are: the crowd that doesn't start. The crowd who sees the task of the business, gets overwhelmed, and watches other leaders rise from afar, knowing it could have been you, if you'd make the commitment to begin.

Here's my admonition: start. Please, hear my heart, leader. This is the one thing you should be committing time to. All the other distractions in your life—look at them for what they are. They take your time away from something the Lord has placed right in front of you to bless you. He has sent your rescue. This is the thing that will buy you time with your family, financial freedom, and the dreams and wishes of your heart—whatever they may be, like supporting a missionary, going on missions trips yourself, taking care of a family member who's had nothing, visiting a friend that's far away because you can, anonymously writing a ridiculous check to someone in need, your first true family vacation. Through hard work and consistency, Young Living is the vehicle that will take you there!

Never in my wildest dreams would I have imagined that I'd be standing in the streets of Venice in 2015, 11 months after getting my starter kit, as one of the top Young Living leaders in the entire world. I had won the honor as a Silver, not as a Diamond.

I stood there in those ancient streets with my three oldest teens, looking at things we'd only read about in our homeschool books. We stood in a clock tower with a bell made by Galileo and walked the streets Lord Byron walked and saw the body of Mark who wrote the gospel of Mark in the Bible. We stood in the stadium in Ephesus, Turkey, where Paul gave his sermon before he was arrested.

We made a thousand memories together. Our first vacation, our first flight, our first overseas trip, our first cruise—all rolled into two weeks. We ate dinner each night with Young Living Diamonds, my children frolicked on the ship with a dozen Royal Crown Diamond children, and my oldest son hung out with Gary Young's son Jacob and wore his Shutran for the girls on the ship. They were the silliest, most bizarre Cinderella memories, and somehow, I was actually in them this time, and not watching from afar.

This is shot of the four of us in the Doge's palace in Saint Mark's Square in Venice, in the medieval torture chamber above the prison catacombs. If you had told me I'd take my children to Venice because of Young Living, I would have laughed at you. Yet, there we were.

May I give you a practical, hands-on tip on how to apply time management at its best? Start in your home. The Bible says if we're faithful in the small things, God will trust us with the bigger things. What order should that be in?

1) Your Lord and Savior

2) Your spouse

3) Your children

4) Your job

If it's out of order, God is not going to trust you with more. It's called time economy, and you do not have favor if your priorities are out of whack.

Christians really seem to understand the principle of tithing. If you take 10% of what you make and give it to your home church, the Lord blesses the other 90%. It seems as if you don't have enough to cover the bills, but somehow, God stretches and multiplies that last bit and you never starve.

It seems to be lost on us that God does it with time too. Just like we tithe our money, we need to be putting our priorities in biblical order so God will bless the work of our hands. If we're faithful with the small things—our relationship with Christ, our spouse, our children, and our job—in that order—God will multiply our time, just like He does with our money.

If we're faithful with the small things, God will multiply our time.

I tried this out at home this week. I'm one of those moms who has 52 plates spinning in the air. Every second can't get wasted—we're homeschooling, I'm anchoring news part time for fun, running kids to activities, cooking unprocessed food, etc. If I want one-on-one child time or a date, it has to be budgeted. Just as I started setting aside time to pray over my business, I started setting aside blocks of time as alone time with God, as date time with John, and as time with my children.

To give you a few examples, we played laser tag at 10:00 p.m. in our yard, I made out with my husband when he walked in the door from work, and after I took my 16-year-old son on a driving lesson, we stopped for a slice of pie. They were all little things, but when they were the priority and I wasn't on my phone running my Young Living business, somehow I still had time to send the messages I needed to send, write the lectures that needed to be written, contact the leaders that needed leading, and it all worked. I have no explanation except that God multiplied my time.

How do you start? Set aside a time each day for your business. Commit to that time. Maybe it's 6:00 a.m. to 7:00 a.m., or 1:00 to 2:00 p.m., or 4:00 to 5:00 p.m., but in this season, only once a week, with a class twice a month on Friday nights, commit to it and stick to the parameters. When the clock crosses 5:01, shut the phone off and prepare for your husband or your children. Then devote that time to them and see what the Lord does to the rest of your clock!

Here's a photo of me with the love of my life, who we call "The Harn." We got engaged three weeks after we met, when I was 16 years old, and we just celebrated our 18th wedding anniversary. Your spouse has to be a priority. If your marriage isn't right, set your business aside and fix that first.

I can't tell you what adventures you'll have with this company! It really depends on you and what you put into it. But I can tell you that if you make the commitment to truly run this as a business, that I have yet to meet anyone on my team who has regretted that decision. For John and me, it's the best financial decision we've ever made.

How do you get there? From point A to point B? It starts with a why. Write it down. "I want to take my children to Venice." "I want to pay off my credit cards and live debt free." "I want to take care of my mom without being in financial peril." "I want to buy grass-fed beef." Set goals and then commit to the business. Set aside time for four classes a month. That's eight hours a month of teaching. Then set aside an hour a day—at any time- to do follow up and practice your lecture and respond to messages. Pick two leaders and start building under them. Commit to that time, with discipline, every day. Pray and keep Christ as your center and number one on your priority list. Then stand back and watch your business grow and hold on, because it will completely surprise you! Your life will not look the same a year from now!

CHAPTER 21

ATTRACTING AND MOTIVATING LEADERS

This is a pretty short chapter, because when you are practicing good leadership, you will naturally attract and inspire other leaders. There are a couple of practical tips I can give you for identifying and motivating leaders, but remember that *how you lead* will have the most impact.

Chase every 101 class with a, "Why Do Young Living as a Business," DVD. We have it available on oilabilityteam.com. It shows people why this is the best job in the world. See Chapter One to refresh your memory on the reasons why.

When you do follow up mailings, mail that DVD (along with Oily Lifestyle) to all the people who got a kit. Show them how to get their oils for free. When you follow up with people who do not have a starter kit yet, include those same materials. I have people that know little about the oils who started sharing simply because they were drawn to the business side of things.

HOW TO SPOT POTENTIAL LEADERS

How do I find leaders? I look for those who are frustrated at work. Those that don't make enough to get by. Those that have no plan for retirement, or nothing saved, or see no way out. I sit down with them and train them with the Teacher Training script and get them off the ground, walk them through their first class, and touch base weekly.

How do you raise a leader? You vision cast with them. Once they see that how they are spending their time will not get them where they want to go, they will pursue the business with tenacity.

Never judge from the outside. I can tell you my upline never, ever had any idea that I'd walk away from radio to sell oils kits. When I started sharing, it blew her mind! She said, "You're famous! You talk to five million people every morning! I never thought you'd do this. I didn't even think to ask!" But when I looked over my life, it seemed wiser to have time economy and be home with my children than to be so depleted from the morning hour of my shift. I love radio with every bone in my body. Anchoring news is in my blood, and it will always be there, but I love my husband and children more.

I mentioned in the Virtual Office tour that you need two leaders to start developing legs, so that's where I'd start. When you're a Distributor, a Star, or a Senior Star, it does not matter. But for Executive and Silver you need two strong legs. So go ahead and start building early with two leaders, two people who'd be blessed by the income and blessed by the oils. If you don't know who they are, pray specifically for the Lord to reveal them to you. Ask for names; ask for the right people to cross your path. When I first started, it was all about getting my oils free. But as our check grew, I couldn't walk into a Walmart without talking to the cashier. It's a smarter way of living, and anyone can share oils!

This is a shot of me with one of my Silvers-in-Six, Sheri Napier. We were on our way to teach a Beauty School and a Teacher Training. She had just driven from South Carolina to New York to teach for one day. That's commitment!

Once you see someone on your team has started sharing and a new member pops up under them, contact your new leader with the Teacher Training, which is in Appendix L on page 281 of this book. Run them through it, train them on the Virtual Office, and check in with them once a week to see how they're doing. Give them this book after they teach their first class. Build a relationship, and as their checks come in, they'll get more and more excited about where Young Living goes! Cast the vision with them.

CONFIDENCE IS KEY

I'd say the biggest key to developing leaders is boldness. Most business builders I see who aren't raising leaders don't have confidence in themselves. If you truly believe Young Living is a crazy incredible income source, and you see how far it can go, wouldn't you want to share it with everyone around you? Wouldn't you want your mom and sister and best friend to be financially free? So share boldly and see what doors open up! I promise you, you'll be very surprised at who takes leadership roles in your organization!

Tools I Use To Find Business Builders:

1) I share the business opportunity at each class with "Your Gameplan" (the mini)

2) I train my new leaders with the Teacher Training in "Appendix L: Teacher Training: How to Launch a Young Living Leader" on page 281 of the this book

3) If they are discouraged, I send them to "Sarah's Why" video on oilabilityteam.com under "Share." It's a tear jerker—and inspirational.

4) I take time to help them find their why. If you wake up every day and know your why, you're much more likely to fight for it. Why are they building the business?

5) Get them to events. If they are surrounded constantly by people who say this business is not possible, they will begin to believe it. Half the battle with business builders is simply mindset.

CHAPTER 22

HOW TO PRAY OVER YOUR YOUNG LIVING BUSINESS

This should have been the first chapter of the book, because it's at the top of my priorities list. But honestly, I can't teach you how to pray over your business unless you're sure you want one first, so it was pretty important to tell you the "why" of a Young Living business at the beginning. We're about to get serious about all that vision casting right now.

The single most important thing you can do for your business is pray for it daily. Let me repeat that. The single most important thing you can do for your business is to pray for it daily. If you're not a prayer warrior or you don't like to pray with others, or can't think of what to say, one of my favorite movies is "The War Room." To get some prayer strategies, go watch it!

This is a shot of one of our Oil Ability leaders' retreats in Myrtle Beach, South Caro-

219

lina. Fifty-three leaders were bowing together, praying specifically over their businesses.

Here are a few things I do that have really helped me.

START A PRAYER JOURNAL

You can dress it up and go to a bookstore and get something really nice in leather, or you can go to the corner store and grab a $1 notebook. Both work just as well.

Break the book into three columns: thanks, leaders, goals.

1. Thanks

In the first column, every single time you come across something you're grateful for, write it down. Keep that notebook close. For example, this week I trained my 60-year-old mom how to do follow-up on her downline. She called me twice in 24 hours to say that two people had gotten on Essential Rewards. She was giddy! Something she had done had impacted the lives of those families. The simple gesture of a mailing made all the difference. That went in my grateful column, grateful that more people will be impacted by the oils and that more people will be following Young Living's mission of getting oils into every home in the world. I was so grateful to hear the joy in my mom's voice, knowing that she had a made a difference.

2. Leaders

The second column is a bit trickier. It only works if you're keeping in touch with your team. At first, it will just be the people you come into contact with. Then it will be people at your classes and new leaders who are raised up. Get to know them and get to know their struggles. Write them down very specifically and pray for them. As your list grows, you may only be able to pray for three or four of them a day as you rotate through the list; and that's totally ok. Just commit to praying every day. I leave a little check box next to each name, because as the Lord answers those prayers, I love to see them checked off. It always floors me when I go back over a year and see how many checks there are. Sometimes you think the Lord isn't answering, but the truth is that you're just not watching.

3. Goals

Column three is the fun one! That's your goals column, the place where you write down, specifically, what you'd like to see happen in your business. And I mean *specifically*. Many of my leaders have frowned on this one because they feel like they have no place asking God for things, but I tell them that God LOVES to love His children! The Bible says to ask and you'll receive! So ask!

Many have pulled me aside at events and said they do not pray, because God does not answer them. Do you know what the trouble is? We're not paying attention! I have made it a habit to track the answers to my prayers, by writing the dates that prayers get answered in my journal. On New Year's Eve each year, I sit down and count the answered prayers. Last year, it was over 700 specific prayers that were answered. He answers! We just need to slow down the busyness of our life and ask.

PRAY SPECIFICALLY

How do you do it? Pray for OGV. Pray for leaders to be raised up under specific people you want to see blessed. Pray for full classes. Pray for many kits sold. Pray for motivation to accomplish tasks. Pray for clarity and wisdom on how to spend your business time that day. Pray for the right words to connect with your leaders. Pray for an open door to raise up leaders or grow your team. Pray for more people to get on Essential Rewards and then give a number. Pray specifically over certain leaders and areas in which they need to be blessed. Pray with another leader on your team and commit to regular prayer time with them.

My prayers look like this. Right off the bat, it is 30% praise for the things I'm seeing the Lord doing that week. Next come the 40% prayers over my team and my leaders, specifically. Last is the 30% vision casting with my Lord and praying specifically over our family business. End with thanks and gratitude at how the Lord is already moving.

Not sure how to pray? Just read right through your notebook. If it sounds silly, that's okay. God hears your heart. It's not about how you pray. It's that you pray. That's all that matters.

Commit and see what happens, and for even more fun, track it! One of my greatest joys is seeing the Lord move over my team!

If you do not have a personal relationship with Christ, there's a number you can call right now to speak with someone. Go online to www.needhim.org. You are not alone.

We'll end this chapter with a testimony from Brandee Gorsline, the woman who enrolled me in Young Living.

"I KNOW prayer is why I have been so successful! I am not as deliberate as what Sarah describes above, but I do pray over people and our businesses. I am blessed to have some of my best friends in the world on my team and I love them and their families, so praying for favor and abundance over them comes naturally. Can you imagine what our team will look like in a year if all the leaders took the time to pray like this? It's so exciting to think about! Goal setting with specifics is a proven strategy for success. It's amazing how often it turns out exactly as you planned. My team member, Mindy, had a goal of adding 22 team members in February, and on the last day of the month #22 logged on and bought a starter kit! It truly works and when backed with prayer and intention, WOW! There are only three commandments in the Bible: prayer, giving, and fasting. Can you imagine what would happen if we pray over our teams and our businesses and fast regularly for wisdom, action, and breakthrough? God wants to bless us in so many ways, and not just financially. My Young Living journey has been a blessing to me and my family in SO many ways, financially, friends, oils, health, and helping others. We need to remember that the enemy does not want any of this to happen, so we need to bathe our journey in prayer every day!"

CHAPTER 23

AVOIDING DISTRACTIONS

This is a big deal. Maybe you dive head on into your business, ready for it to explode. You're so serious about aromatherapy that you go for a certification and you read 192 aromatherapy and leadership books in a year. You go to every leadership training you can find. You even stop teaching classes so you can get more leadership training. Then you go train some more. You want everyone to experience the oils, so you build a massive make-and-take store. Maybe you pay rent to sell the oils retail somewhere. You're on fire, but your business isn't growing!

Who am I talking to? Umm ... me. I did all of the above. I hold six certifications in aromatherapy, and I read all those books. I had a huge store in the ten bins I toted around with me; this is where I gave my Young Living oils away and sold the bases, like a cream base or a roll-on base. This story was all me! I believe I would have been Diamond long before now, had I not been so distracted.

When I was on the Young Living Venice Global Leadership cruise, I was in a hot tub with a few other women. We were all Golds together, yet nine months later, they were all Diamond, and I was baby Platinum.

What happened? Distraction. Distraction will take your momentum and melt it into a puddle. You'll push and push and push—like a fish swimming against the current—and not get anywhere. You put in hours, but don't grow, and you don't know why.

Here's why. What you're doing isn't growing your business. Your attention is in other places. There are tasks each day that will grow you and tasks each day that will slow you down or do absolutely nothing to your magnify your business. What grows your business? Raising leaders, selling starter kits, and good follow up! That's it!

If it doesn't fall in either of those three categories, then don't do it. When you're raising leaders, if they're not on the leg you're building, it's counter-productive. Hand them this book, do a two-hour Teacher Training with them with the script in the back of this book, and let them loose. Work with the leaders on your weak legs. That's how you move up in rank; that's how you grow your income; that's how you get time freedom and financial freedom; and that's how you bless more people. Focus on you so you can get to the place where you can pour your attention into philanthropy. You're not there yet.

PITFALLS TO WATCH OUT FOR:

1. Spending more than you make

Hear me on this. If your check is $200 a month, you may have friends in Canada, but you don't make enough to travel to them. The Lord will not trust you with more unless you're faithful with the small stuff. You haven't grown enough to spend $700 on a flight to Canada. If you're set on that team, train them online. Mail them resources. Get creative. Find local leaders on other teams who will allow them into their classes. Mail my DVD's (oilabilityteam.com), but don't go there until you have the income to pull it off. That's not good stewardship.

I went without business cards for eight weeks because I just didn't have the income to do it yet. We were faithful, God provided, and I have knockout business cards now. Overspending is a distraction that can cause dissension in your marriage and pull your heart away from your business. Be careful!

This is a wonderful place to offer a rare resource. At convention, I met a friend and top Young Living leader named Steve Sheridan, who I consider to be the Dave Ramsey of Young Living. He's a gifted financial advisor. He and his wife Nancy have written a book called, "Journey to Health and Wealth: 10 Step Plan to Wellness, Purpose, and Abundance," which takes you through the financial side of Young Living, including emergency funds, debt reduction, and investing. It's wonderful, and it will give you a good road map on how to handle your income as it rises. Pick up his book and check out his website at www.j2hw.com. Steve has written an entire chapter in Gameplan 2 for Silvers and above—watch for it!

2. Wanting education up-front

I mentioned this is earlier, but I want to go into more depth. Do you think doctors and lawyers have 20 years' experience the first month they start their practice? No way. Most of what I learned, I have learned from listening to distributors and hearing their heart on their oils journey, then teaching them to answer their own questions by researching.

Is an aromatherapy certification good to have? Well, sure it is. But do you need it to grow your business? Absolutely not! That's what reference guides are for. That's why I make my CD's and DVD's available. Learn as you go and don't wait to start until you have an aromatherapy degree. That's a distraction and a waste of time as you are starting. As you grow, if you have the income, absolutely—go learn. You'll have time freedom and money. But right now, as you're building and trying to escape your 40-hour/week job in order to have time with your family, you don't need to nail aromachemistry. Wait for it. What am I saying? Trust the system. Learn your tools. Point people where they need to go and stand down. Don't be the expert. You are scaring away your leaders who think that they too must be experts to build. Always ask yourself if what you are doing can be duplicated.

If I could go back and do all those certifications again, I probably wouldn't. I did them because I was brand-spanking new at network marketing in 2014, and I thought that was what it took to build a business. But some of the fastest growth in my business happened before I ever even finished the education. I found some of my most powerful leaders before I took my final exams.

Is education important? Yes. Please don't read me incorrectly. I think personal development and reading books matters. I digest dozens of books a week just because I love learning. But should you put your business on hold because you don't "know" enough? Never. That could be the mistake that costs you your entire business. You will lose interest because you rank so slowly—and it's because you're not doing the things you need to do to grow.

What do you need to grow your business? A passion for oils! When you have a passion that is infectious, people will buy the kit! That doesn't require a degree. Anything else you need, you can look up, or better yet, train your downline to look it up themselves.

3. Getting involved in more than one network marketing company

This one is a doozy, and I see a lot of people make this mistake. On my own team I've lost more than 20 members who got discouraged that they weren't ranking fast enough with Young Living, but at the same time, they were trying to run another business.

I was blessed to have a great upline that warned me of this early on. It is tempting in the beginning to host a jewelry party, or a pots and pans party, or a books party to bring in some extra cash. But when you do that, you confuse your team.

I'm not saying to avoid your friends in other companies. Go to their parties; buy their pans, books and jewelry; support and encourage them. Just don't market their parties on your social media. Attend the parties, don't host the parties.

Do you think it may harm your relationships with your friends? It may in the short-term, but only with the friends you have that are doing MLM's— which is a very small percentage of your pool of potential oilers.

I truly don't believe it's possible to successfully run two network marketing companies. One of them will suffer, or you or your family will suffer. For Young Living, I spend time each week with my leaders, I run two Facebook pages, teach classes, do follow up, mail packages, and do recognition with my team. A couple of times a year, I'm also holding retreats and large Beauty Schools and Business Bootcamps. How can I do that for two MLM's? I can't do it well. If you commit to both, you will do both with mediocrity, and never rise to a rank of Diamond in either. You also confuse friends, as well as your leaders and oilers, who are watching and see you as not committed.

Focus on one thing and do it with excellence. Do not run two business-es. You will be the jack of all trades and master of none.

4. Building a storefront

This is a big one, and many of my own leaders have fallen into this trap. First, it's against Young Living's rules to sell their oils if the bottles are opened. If you do that, you can get into big trouble.

It's also time consuming. If you're making your own creams and roll-ons and selling them, then you're not training leaders and holding classes. If you want someone to experience an oil, give them a few drops of that oil, don't make a store. You'll lose valuable, precious time while you're on fire and you need this fire to assemble and amass your team.

You can give anything away that you want, and Young Living even encourages that by giving you share-it bottles in your starter kit, but you can't sell their oils which have been opened. So having a store and making products out of the oils is a liability and a big distraction.

This includes having a retail, brick and mortar, store. If you're already running a retail store, and you include this in what you're already doing, that's different. But to open a retail storefront, at the start of your business, with no know-how on how to do it, that's something your budding leaders will see and try to copy. It will take them a long time to rank.

Opening a retail storefront requires insurance, a rented space every month, paint, renovation, shelving, inventory, and more. One of the perks of a Young Living business is that you don't have to deal with all that, you don't have to stand in a store from nine to five! You can invite people to a class in the evening and work with them there, instead of losing eight hours a day sitting in a retail store. It's time efficient. You don't need to stock product. It's financially efficient. You just need a 3-page script and a starter kit. That's duplicatable.

5. Getting on Facebook and wasting time

Okay, confession time. I *totally* still do this. I get on hoping to write a few messages to my leaders, and hour later I've commented on Billy's new toad, liked my friend's pillow fight photo, and posted a pic of me eating ice cream. Wow. That's an hour of my life I'll never get back!

Here's my tip (this goes back to the chapter on Balancing the Business): make a list of three things you *need* to do that day, three tasks that are critical to your business. Don't allow yourself free time until those tasks are done. Period. Just don't do it. If those tasks are not on Facebook, don't get on Facebook. Don't put yourself in places where you'll lose time. Then when those tasks are done, reward yourself with brainless scrolling!

6. Not setting regular business hours for yourself

I homeschool five children, so I get up at 7:00, go on a run, and set breakfast on the table. I start with the little ones and school them from 8:00 until 10:30, which is time for a snack, and then they go off and work on their homework. I homeschool my older children from 11:00 until 1:00, after which, they do the rest of their work independently. I nap for an hour. Then I work my business from 2:00 until 5:00. After that, we have family time.

Those business hours are when I answer all my team's questions, run my leadership page, and train leaders. That's when I do follow up, mailings, and recognition. One night a week, I'm out of the house teaching, and one night a week, I do a team-wide leadership training online for 30 minutes. That's my life as a Diamond.

Even my little ones know not to disrupt me during business hours, or they will pay for it with a loss of their own personal time and some extra chores. That time is protected, and their time is protected, too. My phone is off during school and when I'm engaged with my children. You may try to write or call, but I will not answer. Set boundaries. Train your leaders that you're not available at 1 a.m., and that they shouldn't be, either.

Some days, I can't get all three hours of business in, because the children have dance or Boy Scouts. That's okay, because I'm consistent and I protect that time throughout the week; so that when we have seasons of recitals, my business does not suffer because of it.

One of the reasons our business has grown so quickly is because of committed, consistent time without distractions. Each morning or night before you go to bed, make a list of the three most important business tasks, and set aside regular time to make it happen and do them! Make no excuses. Stay on course!

7. Training other teams

I also want to make a quick statement on raising leaders and crossline training. First off, if you're thinking of crossline recruiting (taking people from other teams)—DON'T. Even if they're your close friend and you missed your chance to sign them for a kit by a week. Why? It's a lack of integrity. The Lord won't bless you if you're pulling from other people's teams. When I see a crossline request to join our team, I delete it. I don't even respond. We have plenty of training tools online (oilabilityteam.com) for them to grow where they are planted. It does not honor the leader who poured into them by signing them to steal them for my team.

What about requests to speak for other teams? As you rank up, you'll get these more and more frequently. People will be drawn to your success. I'd definitely recommend against more than one or two crossline classes a year. It will burn you out, and this means that you're not pouring life into your own leaders. It is another form of distraction. Keep watch for burnout. If you're in a stage of life without a lot of family responsibility and can pull it off, you may be able to do more. But recognize that for every crossline class taught, that's a class you've lost for your team.

Apply that same principal to your family. Each class you're out teaching for your own team is time away from your spouse and children. Choose your classes carefully. Choose locations carefully. Always ask yourself if this is a class you must teach in person or if you can achieve the same results online or by delegating it to another leader. Don't overbook yourself.

(I once taught four classes in 12 hours in three different states and pulled my children along with me. That is not good time stewardship.) Work in a way that's wise and that keeps your family above your business. This will bring you far greater blessings.

In the same breath, you can experience more growth by pouring your efforts into certain downline groups. If you have a leader who's knocking it out of the ballpark, send them encouragement, but let them lead. Don't step on their team. Focus your attention on the leaders who need more encouragement. If you have two legs that are under the OGV you need to rank, take six months and do all your classes under those legs and those legs alone. Don't get distracted. The faster you rank, the more people you can help!

8. Leadership training

For me, this falls under the same category as aromatherapy classes. It's great. You will grow, and personal growth is important. But if you're spending more time reading and attending seminars than you are in teaching 101 classes, or training leaders, you're doing it wrong.

I once asked Adam Green how on earth he got to Royal Crown Diamond by age 24. I call it classes, and he calls them "meetings." He said, "Meetings meetings meetings. Hold a lot of meetings, and then hold more. Then do it again." This is a pattern among all the Diamonds. Even at that rank, they are out there teaching classes. Constantly. If you keep that right in front of you and make it your number one goal, you'll move up in rank. If you're doing more leadership training and reading books than teaching classes, you are upside down and will grow slowly.

Don't get distracted. Education is good, but not to the detriment of your ultimate goal, which is to build a business that is sustainable and sets you free. That includes the freedom to learn and the freedom for personal development.

I commit a little time each day for personal development, 30 minutes a day, sometimes 60, if I have more free time. Most of it is done by audio CD as I'm driving. (My children are well-trained, too, because of it!) But most of my attention is on classes, because that's where it needs to be for you to grow. By the way, if you want this book on audio, check it out on Audible.

Keep distractions down and classes up, because that's the secret to thriving!

FOCUS ON GROWTH

There are only three things that lead to direct OGV growth in your business. In the network marketing world, we call them income producing activities, or IPA's. It's not that other things will not grow you—they absolutely will. But if you're in a season of hustle and gearing up for a rank up, these three elements need to be in every work week.

The first IPA is selling kits, and you do this by sharing the oils and teaching classes. You need to be consistently sharing to rank up. If you're not committed to sharing in your way at least 4-6 times a month, your climb up the ranks will be slow. I am convinced that if this is the only skill you master at the beginning, it will be enough for you to hit the first several ranks. You find leaders by teaching classes. You get people on Essential Rewards by teaching classes. This is your base.

The second IPA is getting people on Essential Rewards. As I said earlier, without getting people on ER, you restart your business every month. That is a LOT of work. Learning good follow up, building relationships and meeting needs—that's the most important skill you can master in this line of work. Meet them where they are. Offer what they need. Start in that place. That's how you build a lifelong oiler.

Finally, you need to train your leaders. Make sure your leaders now how to follow in your footsteps and do the three IPA's themselves. That's the power of duplication. Royal Crown Diamond Vickie Opfer has a wonderful book called "Heart Centered Sharing," In it, she outlines the 24/531 principle. If you trained two leaders, and they trained 2 leaders, and that duplicated just 12 times—(over a year)—you'd have an organization of 531,000 and would be a Royal Crown Diamond in one year. That's the power of duplication.

If you can stay focused on these three areas of growth, you will see results.

CHAPTER 24

ENCOURAGEMENT FOR THE CLIMB

I want to end with some encouragement. It's easy to close this book, look at your OGV, and quit. Even as a Platinum, I had days with so much frustration that I wanted to walk away, so let me pass along a few words that really encouraged me in those moments.

COMPARISON WILL KILL YOU

First, don't rate your beginning by someone else's middle. Their life is like an iceberg; their bulk of their story is under the water of ocean waves. You have no idea what it took for that person to get where they are, and their journey may have been incredibly difficult. Don't rate your starting line with their mile 26. You're comparing apples and oranges, and you're putting yourself in a place where you're speaking death over your business.

Is that a term you've heard before? Speaking death or speaking life? It's Biblical. The Bible talks about the power of the words that we speak. God created the entire universe with His spoken words of life. When you walk around saying you can't do things, or that your business won't grow, or that network marketing can't possibly work, or that you'll never attain a certain rank or income; you're speaking death.

If you had $170,000 deposited into your bank account on the 20th of this month because you were a Royal Crown Diamond, would you carry yourself differently? Would you speak with more confidence? Would you make different choices? Carry yourself as if you're already there. Have passion, purpose, abundance, and meaning to your day. Speak life over the work that you do, and then watch your work and your attitude transform!

EMBRACE YOUR PACE

Second, each person has their own rate at which they grow, and that's okay. If it takes you 12 years to get to Diamond and it takes someone else two years to get there, your way was not wrong and their way was not right.

Each person has unique gifts, treasures, and personality traits that allow them to grow at different rates. It doesn't make them better at network marketing. In fact, network marketing guru Dani Johnson in her GEMS training says that across all network marketing companies, most of those who reach the top ranks in their company have pearl personalities! These are the most laid back, peaceful, compassionate, loyal people out there. They aren't the ones in the spotlight or the ones that are loud—they're the ones that don't give up. Ever. They are tenacious, and they persevere. They are the ones that dominate this field. I am a ruby—a loud, obnoxious, uber-organized competitive limelighter; so some of us make it in too—but the pearls are more common! Rate each day against yourself, not anyone else.

It is my hope, if this book does nothing else, that it helps you see where Young Living goes. I hope you can walk away and really catch the vision. Young Living is the least amount of effort for the most amount of reward. It's time economy. If you were to commit 40 hours a week to your Young Living business, it would explode! But don't think that's the only way to succeed.

Commit what you are able.

Set boundaries, including boundaries over your business, and protect that time you've set aside just to work.

Don't give up, even when things don't go as planned. The only people who don't make it to Diamond are the ones that give up. When life throws you curve balls, collect yourself, get back on the horse, and keep moving. Pick up where you left off. That's how you become a Diamond.

Grow from your weaknesses and take criticism well.

Avoid the six pitfalls.

Know your why and revisit it often.

Pray specifically over your business, and pray over your leaders by name.

Connect relationally with your downline. Whatever you do, always keep the distributor at the center of your decisions. If your heart is always for them, the Lord will bless it.

Be a good steward of your time and your finances, and the Lord will give you more time and more finances.

PLANS TO PROSPER

I have no idea where the Lord will take our family business another year from now. But let me tell you what our family has seen in the past two years. I've stood in the fields of almost every U.S. Young Living farm. We took a trip every month from May through November last year. I've had a 20-minute private conversation with Gary Young. I've watched my daughter play with his horses for an entire afternoon, interviewed his employees, and opened all the doors to the farms and peeked in each room, just out of news anchor curiosity.

I've made friends in Australia who I text and speak with daily—and also in Texas, Chicago, North Carolina, and more. I have grown closer to my family and watched my mother buy a home and my sister and sister-in-law quit their jobs and retire because of Young Living. In less than a year, I have seen over 100 leaders on my team walk the same path and they have similar stories. It's not just me.

I have interviewed nearly every major figure at Young Living Corporate, just so my team would have a chance to meet them. I have laid my hands on a thousand people and spread oils on their skin. I have stood before rooms full to the doorways and lectured for hours when people had no room to sit, and I've given the same lecture with four people in the tiny house of an elderly couple who opened their doors for a night to love some weary moms.

I've taught classes kayaking on the Aegean Sea off of Greece and walked in catacombs in Venice with my children and Young Living distributors who were the top sellers in the world. I sat at a table with half a dozen Diamonds at the Drive to Win in Hawaii and had a 5-hour breakfast, picking their brains on the secrets to their success.

I now manage a team of over 3,000 people in all 50 states and several countries. We have team members who have made Silver or Executive in one month. The Oil Ability team added 430 people to our team in one month. That's not big by Diamond standards, but for a homeschool mom in the middle of nowhere, who moved across the country and didn't know anyone, and who had zero network marketing or sales experience—that's dynamic!

I was the one on welfare. I was the one who at age 20 was pregnant, working two jobs, and taking a 21-hour college course load. I was the one living in public housing with no furniture and with cockroaches. I was the one who got my children's Christmas gifts at the Salvation Army. That was me at the beginning of the story.

I have one thing to say about that—one thing that's mighty, prophetic, and spoken over your life, too. "'For I know the plans I have for you,' says the Lord. 'Plans to prosper you and not to harm you. Plans to give you a hope and a future.'" Jeremiah 29:11. Claim your future. Stand on the hope that is promised to you. The photo below is of me in a rental car with the wind in my hair. I have Oola Grow oil on my hands. This was taken

at the Young Living Drive to Win contest in Hawaii. I had wanted to go to Hawaii for my wedding 18 years ago, and there I am! That trip was an answered prayer. It was only the second vacation I'd been on in my life. The first was Venice, last year, with my oldest 3 kids. All of it was paid for, courtesy of Young Living.

Do I share my story with you to brag? Goodness, absolutely not. I share all this with you because I believe with all my heart that you can do it, too!

Part inside of you looks at this story, shakes your head and walks away. But, there's a part of you that knows that you have it in you to pull this off.

The time line doesn't matter.

The size of your friend circle doesn't matter.

The location doesn't matter, or the resources.

The only thing that matters is your will, your passion, your consistency, your focus, your confidence, and your tenacity.

So here's your challenge. You have 24 hours. Sit down and write your vision. Write your goals. Make a Gameplan. Open your calendar and schedule a class. Ask three people to invite others to your class. Don't just say you'll do it, or think you'll do it—make it happen. Set a date for your first class *today*.

Then, share your story to inspire someone else. You have some wild adventures ahead! The stuff books are made of!

PAUSE FOR GRATITUDE

Can I talk joy with you for just one moment? And how to get your head out of a place of negativity? It's hard to build a business from a place of discouragement when you feel you're not growing fast enough.

Wake up today with excitement at what is ahead! Have you ever just paused...with a grateful heart...at what the Lord has already provided?

The first month I hit Star, I was so very grateful to have my oils order paid for with my paycheck. A year later at Gold, I was so grateful for my amazing leaders-- the ones with fight, that caught the vision. A year later at Diamond-- grateful for a new home. For doors that closed. Grateful for my kids bedrooms that were not in my garage.

A year later, on the edge of Crown Diamond, I'm grateful for: my sister and sister-in-law's pregnancies; A new grandbaby; My first Diamond retreat; Finishing the second edition of Gameplan; The 50,000 of you that encourage me every single day. I have so much to be grateful for that my cup overflows!

When you are in that place where you're just tired and weary, and the rank seems so very far away, can I encourage you to simply pause, and look at what God has already done? He has already moved you a few inches. And miles more are ahead! Be so very grateful for the sun on your face; for a car that works; for a little one giving you a morning smile; for a dragonfly in your yard or a walk in the woods; that you don't have time to notice the pace, the disappointments, the no-show classes, or the things that aren't turning out as you planned.

You see, God does have a plan for you. He has a plan for your business. He's not forgotten you at all. He is already, even now, moving chess pieces on the board in your favor. Sometimes the growth is in the pause. It's in those places where you find rest and regroup. The growth is in the places of joy. It's in the places where the complaining disappears, and you choose to rejoice.

Find your voice of joy today. That place of joy is the place that your business will grow from. It's the root of your passion. Live in that place, and you won't be able to focus on despair or frustration. You HAVE this.

It's because *you* are a Diamond Rising!

PART SEVEN

It Works: The View from the Top

Wow, the Gameplan book has given me the courage to speak to everyone about Young Living. It has also given me the answers to so many questions that I had. It's the best book ever for new business builders!

Jenn Merriam

I was stuck at Gold for two years, now I have leaders on seven legs on fire after doing Gameplan bootcamp with them! I'm now on the brink of Platinum! Is it appropriate to say Gameplan is freaking awesome?!

Laura Erdman-Luntz

I did Gameplan with my team in March and we had 90,000 OGV growth in one month and got to Diamond!

Chelsa Bruno

CHAPTER 25

CHEAT SHEET TO GO FROM STARTER KIT TO SILVER

You did it. You just finished this whole book. That tells me you have the tenacity to do this business! This book is a hum-zinger! It's tough!! (Don't skip the Appendixes, they are the best part of the book!)

Now what do you do? Apply it! If you can't remember the last 100 pages, here's this book in a nutshell. Cross each line off as you complete it! (If you want a more comprehensive to-do list, go to oilabilityteam.com and grab our Gameplan Workbook. It's not fill-in-the-blank busywork. It actually customizes this entire Gameplan Strategy guide to fit your team, and help you put feet to your dreams.)

1) If you are brand-spankin' new, order your Premium Starter Kit online

2) Photocopy Appendix A, the simple 101 Script, from the back of this book and practice it.

3) Make a list of all of your contacts *everywhere*. Grab them off Facebook, your Christmas card list, and even former

co-workers. That's your warm market. It is what you will draw from to start filling classes.

4) Set up a Facebook event for a class. (Click on "More" at the top of your profile page, then "Events" to get to the page). Fill out the description. Use powerful verbs and make the lecture exciting! Put a photo on your event.

5) Ask three people off your warm market list to invite 50 of their friends to the class. They can't just share it to their page, they have go under the "Invite Friends" button in the event and invite people. Ask them to say something nice about you and the class. Make up a gift basket as a thank you.

6) Market the class for two to three weeks, with no more than one or two posts a day.

7) Open your doors and read the 101 Script to the people sitting on your coach. End with a strong close, and tell them where to get the starter kit.

8) Follow up. Call or mail a handwritten note to those who came. I don't do this by email, because that's too impersonal. Stay in contact. The average person can only say no seven times!

9) Rinse and repeat. Teach four to six classes a month if your goal is Silver-in-Six.

10) As someone on your team turns to the person next to them and sells their own kit, go to Teacher Training on page 281 and train them. Make sure you touch base with your new leader once a week. To get to Silver, build under two strong leaders. When your OGV crosses 10,000 and each leg is over 4,000, you have made it!

11) Don't hunt people. Don't get lost in the no's. Change the philosophy of how you see the business. You are collecting relationships, not starter kit sales. Don't take it personally when they don't order. Move on, and keep yourself so busy scheduling classes that you don't notice the no's. Keep the focus on education instead of sales.

12) Pray! Pray over your business and use Abundance oil abundantly. God has you and God has this. You were meant to be free. Go out there, world changer! Be bold, have confidence, and bless all those you meet.

You can do this! I believe it with all my heart. After digesting all that this book has (I told you it was dense!), remember it all comes down to three very simple things: teach classes, get people on essential rewards, and train your leaders. Focus on those three income producing activities. Don't ever forget them, no matter what rank you achieve, and your business will continue to grow and grow!

CHAPTER 26

STORIES OF SUCCESS FROM
THE OIL ABILITY TEAM

Do you think this is real? Do you think you can really do it? Perhaps it will help you if I share some true-to-life stories from our team. These stories aren't over yet, because each of these Oil Ability Team members is still ranking. But, the best way to end this book is with the end game: stories of hope.

Angela is an Oil Ability Elite Express winner and a school teacher with a lot of debt. She paid off over $30,000 of debt, as well as giving another $8,000 to charity in a single year. Her wedding was completely debt free. Her goal is to be 100% debt free by 2018.

Rachael, as a Young Living Elite Express winner, was able to retire from all three of her jobs. In fact, in August of 2016, she left her third job weeks before her wedding and is now fully supported by her Young Living income! She is no longer working 60 hours a week.

Sheena is an Oil Ability Platinum who ran a wonderful natural health store in Eldred, Pennsylvania. She first went to a five-person class, and then went to another oils class in a different town. Very soft spoken (but extremely competitive), she became convicted to take the business seriously when one of her downline members had a larger paycheck than she did. She went from Executive to Silver in 11 days (beating my team record of 18 days that stinker!), and is now retired and home full-time with her two boys.

Theresa is an Oil Ability Elite Express winner who has a son with severe autism and completely non-verbal son. She started taking her business seriously in May 2016 and nearly doubled her OGV in one month. This soft spoken mom now runs a vendor booth at a large scale event called the Windmill in upstate New York every weekend and is leading a powerful team beneath her. She has connected and won the love and respect of the Oil Ability team because of her ability to organize, write, and educate. She is currently in the process of building her first home, after more than a decade in extreme poverty.

Sharon is an Oil Ability Elite Express winner who endured 40 years of physical abuse from an alcoholic husband. She separated from him and moved across the country to be near her grandchildren, and took a $10/hour job in Ithaca, NY. After 16 months with Young Living, her paycheck surpassed her full-time income. She's now able to buy a home and be totally self-sufficient because of her Young Living paycheck. Sharon moved into a home in New York that she was able to buy entirely by herself.

These are some of the stories of the Oil Ability team, and they can be yours, too, because you have your Gameplan. You know how to do this!

Remember the three simple steps: hold four to six classes a month using the 101 script in the back of this book, do follow up after every class or event, and train your leaders. Every time someone sells a kit, read the Teacher Training in Appendix L on page 281 and give them a tour of the Virtual Office. Put Gameplan in their hands. Rinse and repeat.

Classes, follow up, leaders.

Get into a regular rhythm of your business cycle. If you can master those three things, you have what it takes to be a #Diamondrising. The only thing between you and becoming a Young Living Diamond is tenacity and consistency. The more often you teach, the faster you will rank, the more people you will help, and the sooner you will become free.

It's time to cross some things off that bucket list you have been making for years. Are the ways you are spending your time right now getting you to the places you want to be? If not, it's time to re-evaluate. It's time to put a new Gameplan into action.

It's time to start.

APPENDIXES

SARAH'S SCRIPTS AND MORE

The Appendixes in Gameplan are liquid gold. Why? There are three things that grow your business: sharing the oils, getting people on Essential Rewards, and training your leaders. This part of the book is loaded with tips, tricks, and scripts to get you off the ground; whether you are just beginning, or have plateaued, or are looking for fresh momentum for your team.

Appendixes A-G are all about sharing the oils. This is the foundation of your business! If you are not sharing, you cannot find leaders or build a solid Essential Rewards base.

The second part is getting people on Essential Rewards. This is the cement under your feet. It's how you avoid restarting your business every single month from zero. If you nail teaching classes but never master training on an oily lifestyle, you will not hold rank. Appendixes H-J are all geared toward helping you get people on ER.

The third activity that increases your income is trianing your leaders. Appendixes K-P are all tools to help you grow your leaders Royal Crown Diamond Vicki Opfer says if you can train two to train two, and that duplicates only twelve times in a year, you end the year with an organization of 531,000 and are a Royal Crown Diamond. The power of leader training cannot be underestimated. Your new leaders don't need to keep repeating the boot-camp videos, but they do need to step into a position of leadership by leading the training with two new people a month. This section helps with simple duplication.

APPENDIXES

SHARING THE OILS

GET PEOPLE ON ER

TRAINING LEADERS

SIMPLE 101 SCRIPT

Start with your story! What got you into oils? What were your "wow" moments? Share that first.

WHAT ARE ESSENTIAL OILS?

They are the most powerful part of the plant.

They are distilled from shrubs, flowers, trees, roots, bushes, fruit, rinds, resins, and herbs.

Oils consist of over 100 different natural, organic compounds.

In humans, many provide support for every system in the body: your skeletal system, muscular system, circulatory system, endocrine system and your hormones, respiratory system, and immune system. They support brain health and a healthy weight. They are used extensively for spiritual support in your prayer life. They have been used for thousands of years as beauty aids and for emotional support. An oil in a diffuser can soothe a child's tough day at school and provide a calming effect when you've had a stressful day at work. Oils can be used as an alternative to cleaning chemicals in the home. You can literally start swapping out every single chemical in your home to live a purer lifestyle, and you can do it without breaking the bank!

There are about 300 oils on the earth, but you only need ten to twenty of them to build a good kit.

You do not need to be an aromatherapist to use them. In most cases, just rub it topically into the skin. There are three main ways to get oils into your system: the English apply it topically—rub it on the skin; the French ingest and cook with it; the Germans diffuse and inhale, which can be the most effective method because it doesn't have to pass through the digestive system.

How do they enter—and how long do they last?

Tests have shown oils reach the heart, liver, and thyroid in three seconds when inhaled; they were found in the bloodstream in 26 seconds when applied topically. Expulsion of essential oils takes three to six hours in a normal, healthy body.

ESSENTIAL OILS HISTORY

They were first mentioned by name in the biblical book of Genesis, chapter 37, when Joseph was sold to the slave traders. They carried spicery, balm, and Myrrh! Genesis ends with the burial of Joseph's father anointed with Myrrh. Oils are mentioned 1,100 times directly or indirectly in Scripture.

Some of the oldest cultures on earth used essential oils. The Babylonians placed orders for Cedarwood, Myrrh, and Cyprus. The Egyptians used essential oils for beauty and embalming and they have the oldest recorded deodorant recipe made with essential oils. Pakistan and Rome used essential oils in the communal bath houses.

They were even used by Christ! Jesus was given Gold, Frankincense, and Myrrh. Frankincense is sometimes referred to as "the coconut oil of essential oils," because it has over 10,000 uses.

Essential oils were used by the Medieval Europeans, many of whom brought oils back during the Crusades.

It was only after World War 2 when essential oils were "rediscovered," and the science on their uses grows with every single year.

DO ESSENTIAL OILS WORK?

I have used oils for six years. Lavender smelled nice in my bath, but never had any significant effect on my body. I used to buy my Lavender for $4 a bottle online, at farmers markets, or at bulk foods stores. In the United States, there is no rating system for essential oils. It would be wonderful if there were—because then you'd know what you were buying! If you walk into a grocery store and look at a box of cereal, you'll see nutrition facts on the side. There are no "nutrition facts" on the side of oils. That means you have to trust the source. You have to know the company you are purchasing from.

Young Living is a global leader in essential oils, with over 1.5 billion dollars in sales annually. Those that use the oils keep coming back! There are 3,000 employees globally , 600 life-changing products, 16 corporate and partner farms, more than 20 international markets, 50 highly trained scientists, 12 independent partner labs, and four million global members.

What sets Young Living aside? Seed to Seal. It's our promise of purity. All of our oil is run though vigorous 8-point testing to insure purity. They also do third party testing with accredited, respected, independent labs. Young Living has never had to recall an essential oil in 23 years of business. You can trust their integrity. You can learn more about Seed to Seal at seedtoseal.com

This is why I don't buy from mom and pop oils shop—they don't have the team to do the testing that's needed to stay on top of hundreds of oils and blends.

Why can't you just buy oils at the grocery store? Purity. You get what you pay for. I have seen bottles of Frankincense for $7 at the grocery store—but it costs more than that just to distill! It's a red flag that the oil has been adulterated.

All oils in the world fall into one of four categories: Authentic, Manipulated, Perfume, or Synthetic.

1) **Authentic** means the oils are 100% pure, with no added synthetics, or other species in the bottle. These are Young Living oils!

2) **Manipulated** means the final product has been made to smell more pleasing and less earthy. Some of the heavier molecules have been stripped out, or another species introduced, to enhance the aroma.

3) **Perfume** oils are not pure. They are mixed with synthetics to enhance the aroma. These oils have no therapeutic action. Frequently, solvents are used to extract the plant.

4) **Synthetic** oils are not true oils at all. They smell nothing like the original plant, and are typically labeled as "scented products." These are synthetic.

Authentic is the only true pure oil. Synthetic oils would be like opening your fridge, taking a glass of orange juice and diluting it 95% before you drank it! (And diluting it with chemicals!) It wouldn't have the same benefits of a full glass of only orange juice. That's why you want authentic oils. Before you purchase, check to see if the company grows their own plants, has Seed to Seal, and controls the entire process—from the farm to the sealed bottle. Pesticides, pollution, previously farmed land; all of it can affect the quality of an oil. Why would you go the extra step of using an oil to get away from a chemical—only to use an oil laden with chemicals? It makes no sense.

Young Living's Seed to Seal process is a promise of integrity. There are no pesticides used, no chemicals, and no weed killers. The plants are harvested at their peak. They're then put through a vigorous testing process. Then they go from the farm directly to your home. Seed to Seal is not a slogan, it's a promise.

WHY DO SOME OIL COMPANIES SELL OILS MORE CHEAPLY?

Most essential oils are sold more cheaply because companies cut corners to save money. If you spray your crop with pesticides, you have more crop to distill. If you use a chemical solvent to extract the oil, you pull more out. If you dilute it with a cheaper oil, or a carrier oil, you stretch the oil you have distilled, and can easily sell more cheaply.

HOW OILS ARE MADE:

It takes a great deal of work to produce a tiny amount of essential oil!

- 60,000 rose blossoms provide only one ounce of Rose oil

- Lavender is abundant—220 pounds will provide seven pounds of oil

- Jasmine flowers must be picked by hand before the sun becomes hot on the very first day they open, thus making it one of the most expensive oils in the world! It takes eight million hand-picked blossoms to produce 2.2 pounds of oil

- A Sandalwood tree must be 30 years old and 30 feet high before it can be cut down for distillation. Young Living's Sandalwood trees must be 90% dead before they are harvested.

But a little goes a long way. Most oils are $10 to $30 a bottle. Depending on oil thickness (viscosity), a 5-ml bottle contains 90-100 drops, and a 15-ml bottle contains 200-240 drops. Each application is one to three drops, meaning even a small bottle will get you 45 to 90 applications. Thieves® cleaner is made of plants only and costs about $1.50 a bottle to make. You can't even get that in the organic section at the grocery store! It replaces a multi-purpose cleaner, glass cleaner, and floor cleaner. The organic versions of those can run you $4 to $6 a bottle.

ARE THEY SAFE?

There are certain oils that are photosensitive, meaning you don't want to wear them and go outside. These are mostly citrus oils, like Grapefruit, Lemon, etc.

When using on your skin, always watch for redness and dilute with a carrier oil. Dilute oils on children, because their skin is more permeable and absorbs the oils more quickly. What is a carrier oil? It's a fatty oil like olive oil or coconut oil, and its molecules are much larger than those of essential oils. Using a carrier oil with an essential oil slows down the rate the body can absorb the essential oil, because it has to ping pong through the large molecules of the carrier oil to get into your skin.

Be wary of putting the oils topically near your eyes. Some oils, like Peppermint, can cause a burning sensation. If you are placing an oil near your eye, apply the oil to a Q-tip instead of tipping the bottle toward your face.

You can become desensitized to an oil if you use the same one day after day, so I rotate my oils every three to four days.

What about internal use of essential oils? The National Association for Holistic Aromatherapy (NAHA), one of the top aromatherapy schools in the United States, doesn't advocate essential oils for internal use. Why? Most oils companies don't carry any GRAS (Generally Regarded As Safe) essential oils. But Young Living Vitality oils are GRAS certified and approved for internal use, just like a food additive. To check out the validity of GRAS oils yourself, go directly to the primary source— the FDA website.

NAHA also bases a lot of their decisions on the British model, which advocates topical use only. Many of the British studies are flawed, for example, done at extremely high doses or in ways the oils aren't used, like pouring a bottle inside the body.

Young Living utilizes all three methods of aromatherapy: British, French, and German. The French have been safely using some essential oils internally for decades. You have been consuming essential oils for most of your life—when you chew gum or put oregano in your pasta sauce. The key using essential oils internally is to make sure you're checking the labels first. Are they GRAS certified? Young Living's Vitality line has distinctive white labels, so you can easily recognize which oils are approved for internal use.

ON THE FLIP SIDE:

Look at the ingredient list of what you have in your bathroom and kitchen. Every day we put products on our skin, in our body, and breathe them; but many of these products contain damaging chemicals. The average woman applies over 300 chemicals every day to her body just through soaps, make-up, shampoos, and hair care products. Eighty of those products are applied before breakfast!

When you use Young Living's essential oils, you're using a product with one ingredient, like Lemon, Oregano, Tangerine – no synthetic additives and no yuck.

Is all this a bit overwhelming? Let me tell you how I started my oils journey: with a Young Living starter kit. It's the only item on the Young Living website that is half off! If you're a frugal momma like me, this is the best bang for your buck! It comes with 11 bottles of oil and a diffuser, a sample of Thieves® Cleaner and NingXia Red®, and bottles to share oils!

(Pass around the Premium starter Kit with diffuser, open the bottles and smell them)

- **Frankincense.** One of the top skin oils. Helps smooth the appearance of skin. A key ingredient in Young Living's "Brain Power" essential oil blend. Diffuse during prayer time to help with grounding and purpose.

- **Lavender**. Oil of relaxation. Diffuse for a calming, soothing aroma. Unwind by adding a few drops to a nighttime bath. One of the top oils to support healthy skin. Called the "Swiss army knife" of essential oils because of its many uses.

- **Peppermint Vitality**. Supports gastrointestinal comfort. Promotes healthy bowel function and enhanced healthy gut function. Helps maintain efficiency of the digestive tract. May support performance during exercise.

- **Citrus Fresh**. Diffuse to freshen the air. This blend is a mix of Orange, Tangerine, Grapefruit, Lemon and Mandarin oils. It's a replacement for chemical-based home fragrances. Spritz in rooms and closets and over linens. Dilute with V-6 carrier and use a perfume. It also helps to tone and smooth the appearance of skin.

- **Thieves® Vitality**. Helps support a healthy respiratory system and helps maintain overall wellness when taken as a dietary supplement. Add a drop to hot drinks for a spicy zing!

- **Stress Away**. Promotes wellness and may be an important part of a daily health regimen. One of the top emotion oils blends!

- **Lemon Vitality**. Its citrus flavor enhances the taste of food and water. A key ingredient in Thieves® and NingXia Red®. May help support the immune system.

- **PanAway**. Apply after exercise to soothe muscles. Has a stimulating aroma. Apply to back and neck for a soothing aromatic experience. Supports the appearance of healthy skin coloration.

- **Copaiba Vitality**. Promotes overall wellness. Supports the immune system. Also a great skin oil. Called the "Frankinsense of South America."

- **DiGize Vitality**. Top oil blend for supporting the digestive system. Add two drops, along with a drop of peppermint, to water for a stimulating beverage. Take in a veggie capsule internally. Use with Essentialzyme at every meal to support a wellness regimen.

- **Raven**. A cleansing blend of Ravintsara, Peppermint, Eucalyptus Radiata, and other essential oils. Raven creates a cooling sensation when applied topically to the chest and throat. Diffuse up to three times daily for a soothing aroma.

How do you order? Simply go to www.youngliving.com, click on "Become a Member," and use the number of the person who told you about oils as enroller and sponsor.. It's that simple. Welcome to the world of oils!

30-Second Script To Get Someone to Come to Class

You can only hold the average person's attention for about 30 seconds when you are in passing, having a short casual conversation. Online it's about three to four minutes. That's how long you have to convince them to get to an oils class. But why would they need it? And how do you unscramble your thoughts when you're standing right in front of them?

I'd really encourage you to listen to them first. Each person has a story and they have a reason why they might use the oils. Some may need them for emotions. Some may need them because they have a smell in their house that they need to get rid of (that was how I hooked my brother!). Try listening to them first, and then responding.

But if that isn't an option, and if I only have a few moments, I always take the chemical-free home angle, because no one wants poison in their house. Oils are a clean way to live.

Below is a quick script you can use to get people to oils classes, without even knowing them. It's important to have a running 30-second script in your head all the time, so you can fall back on it when you only have a few moments to convey the need for oils to someone. This script works WONDERFUL at vendor events, or anytime you're inviting someone to a class or piquing their interest to buy a starter kit.

Script:

The average person applies 300 chemicals to their body every single day, and 80 of those chemicals before breakfast! Most are from four things: soap, makeup, shampoo, and hair care. The biggest pollutants in our home are fabric softener, dryer sheets, air freshener plug-ins, and candles. You are literally poisoning your family every day with the stuff that you can't pronounce that is inside the products you use; like your bright blue dish soap, the cleaner you use for your kitchen counters, processed food, and more. Health and safety data only exists for 15% of all the chemicals out there, even though so many are known to cause asthma or endocrine disruptions.

Essential oils are a better way. They are totally pure, steam distilled or cold pressed from pure plants. There's nothing in them but that one oil; whether it is Lemon, Tangerine, Lavender, Peppermint, or others. There are over a million uses for essential oils—cleaning supplies, personal care products like toothpaste and deodorant, diffusing, oil-infused nutritional supplements. Come to a one-hour class that costs you nothing to learn how to kick the chemicals in your home to the curb. I will walk you through step by step. It's easy, simple, and it's a small change you can make to protect your family and take charge of what's in your house.

I then hand them my business card and collect their information. If I have an event online, I add them to it, and I'm off and running! Don't worry, they'll listen a lot longer when they are in the physical class!

THE OIL ABILITY MARKETING SYSTEM

A simple, free marketing system that works

1) Set up a time and place for a class

2) Set up a Facebook event two to three weeks ahead of the class.

   a) In that event, add a banner photo and a punchy description of the class, as well as address and time.

3) Ask three people to invite 50 people to the event. They need to go into the event and hit "Invite Friends" for it to work. Ask them to put one sentence in the event about you to build trust. Make them a thank you basket.

   a) I like to include some Thieves® cleaner, a Peppermint roll-on, and some of my DVD's. It costs less than $5 per person to pull that off.

4) Grab FDA compliant photos and lines from the 101 Script and market it every single day. Or pull a line from the script and market it that way.

5) After class, schedule another and set up a new Facebook event. Tap into your new downline (the people who attended your class) and ask three of them to invite 50 people to the class.

6) Rinse and repeat (Follow steps 1-4 all over again). This way, you have never-ending friend circles without hitting up your family and friends over and over. Make sure you always have at least three people inviting to each class.

7) Brace yourself for electric growth!

Remember:

Wording matters on your events. Use power-packed action verbs that take them somewhere.

   BAD: Please come to my essential oils class. I will have dessert. I will speak for two hours on oils. If you can bring someone, that would be good. We will have NingXia for an extra cost. If you can't come, I will teach another class.

GOOD: Would you like to learn how to kick chemicals out of your home? I'll walk you through step by step and give easy, simple, and affordable tactics anyone can use with the best essential oils on the planet. This class is totally FREE and will blow your mind! I come with an iced NingXia Red® bar for weary mommas! Gear up for a fast-paced, ground-up lecture on everything oils, and have some fun and pampering in the process. I can't wait to see you! I'll have freebies at the door for those that invite 50 friends on the Facebook event. It's time to take control of the yuck in your home and kick it to the curb!

If you need images for your events, go to the "Oil Ability with Sarah" Facebook page for compliant posts.

OIL ABILITY CLOSING SCRIPTS

Here are two strong closes to use at the end of your classes. Start your close after you have gone through the oils in the kit.

NAIL THE SALE

Why oils?

Because you need them in your home as part of a simple, chemical-free lifestyle. When you see what the oils do for your own body and how they help create a chemical-free home, it's impossible to walk into the homes of your friends and family members and see their bright blue dish soap or their chemical-laden shampoo that is in their bloodstream in 26 seconds and not speak about what you know! You share it because you love and care for your friends, and you want to see them living a healthy life. When you take care of yourself, you can fully do what God created you to do, what you were called to do.

How do you begin?

With a Young Living Premium Starter Kit. I'm a frugal momma, and it's the only thing on the Young Living site that's half off. If you take the diffuser off, you're literally getting 11 bottles of therapeutic grade oil for $70. You can't even get it that cheap at the grocery store. Each bottle has 90 drops of oil in it—that's 90 applications.

The kit also comes with bottles to share the oils with your family and friends, an AromaGlide roll-on fitment to apply the oils on the go, and samples of NingXia Red® for full system support. I want to see every single person in this room on NingXia! It's your first line of defense in immune support!

You also get a diffuser with the kit AND a lifetime wholesale membership. That means 24% off your oils FOR LIFE. Every single order you place is 24% off. To maintain a wholesale membership, you have to spend $50 in a calendar year of products YOU select. That's like two bottles of Thieves cleaner, which is the only stuff I use to clean my counters, my stove, my floors, and my windows. Without any chemicals, in one swoop, it eradicated my multi-purpose counter spray, my glass cleaner, and my floor cleaner. If you need a small step to start using oils in your home, use them to clean!

Get plugged in to our team resources to learn more about how to use the oils. Join our Facebook page, Oil Ability with Sarah. Pick up one of our team DVD's—Essential Oils 101. Get a Teacher Training if you want to learn how to share the oils and GET YOUR OILS FOR FREE! It's not hard to talk about them.

They share themselves naturally, because of your love and compassion to see the people around you healthy.

Where do you start?

That's as hard as going to www.youngliving.com, click on "Become a Member," and filling out the form. You'll need a sponsor and enroller number because Young Living is a multi-level marketing company. Many people tell me they can't buy from an MLM, but when you shop at Walmart, you're supporting a CEO's third home. When you shop at a MLM, you're buying local. You're supporting my family business. You're paying for gas in our car or food on our table. It's the best form of business out there, and one of the most important reasons is that you get to see your friends and family financially blessed. The Oil Ability team now has, in two years, more than 3,000 members in all 50 states and several countries. It's because the oils work. A company which sells 100,000 starter kits a month is selling them for a reason! People are tired of the chemical yuck around them, and they are taking control of their homes.

If you look around you—Chipotle is cutting all their GMO's. Panera has placed signs in their restaurants that they're cutting all the chemicals from their salad dressings. Kraft Mac and Cheese has cut their dyes. Heinz has cut all corn syrup from their ketchup. People are starting to flip over and read the backs of the bottles of products they put on their skin, eat, clean their homes with, and say, "no more." That's where oils come in. Can you live a completely toxic free life? No, but you can minimize your exposure. You can take control of your laundry soap, your dish soap, your cleaning supplies, your supplements, and say, "I want a less toxic life." That's where oils come in. The starter kit has 10,000 uses, from cleaning your home, to emotional balance, to fitness, and to personal care products like toothpaste and deodorant.

I'd like to issue the three-cabinet challenge. When you get home, I'd like to encourage you to start flipping over the bottles that you use in any three cabinets in your home, and then read the ingredients. If there's anything on there that you can't pronounce, it's time to start swapping it out. I wouldn't slather that stuff on my skin, or plug it into my walls and smell it; giving it access to the limbic lobe of my brain! I wouldn't cook with it and ingest it. I wouldn't wash my hair with it and have it in my bloodstream over my brain in 26 seconds. I wouldn't clean my counters and butcher block with it and then eat my food off that same block; or wash my clothes with it. We're at a place where people aren't just taking everything at face value anymore; that is, thinking that a product is safe.

You are the gatekeeper of your home. Only you control what crosses the threshold of your doorway. You alone are responsible for the health and safety of your family within the four walls of your house. You can say NO. It's time to start kicking chemicals out of your home. To get a starter kit, we've set up a station where you can enroll right now, and we are here to help navigate the website with you. We will walk you through every step. If you'd like to do it at home, we have bags filled with a picture of the kit so you can see what comes in it, as well as a FREE copy of this 101 lecture on DVD. Take it home, share it with someone who should have been in this class with you. It's my gift to you. Also in the bag is my business card with my contact information, so you have a way to get back to me. Feel free to contact me absolutely any time! It is my job to walk you through this and to be there as a resource for you. There are no dumb questions. Also in the bag is a paper which walks you through how to order online.

Thank you for generously giving your time to learn about essential oils! I believe with all my heart that you're about to have the best year you've ever had. You will not recognize your home a year from now, and I am SO excited for you!

You have survived essential oils 101!

THE BOLD CLOSE

(Tweak it and include your story!)

Let me get real with you for a moment as I wrap up—and tell you the true reason I teach so emphatically about this. Why does chemical free living matter so much to me? Because I have seen the other end of a chemical filled lifestyle, and I want everyone to know what they are putting in and on their bodies.

The number two cause of death in the United States is cancer. 1,620 people a day die of cancer. One in three cases in the U.S. are directly linked to poor diet, physical inactivity, weight, or chemical exposure. The American Cancer Society says only 5% to 10% of all cancer cases are from gene defects. That means 95% of cancer cases are under our control. It's what we allow into our homes.

The National Institute of Occupational Safety and Health studied 2,983 ingredients in our products at home, and found 884 toxic ingredients. 314 of them caused biological mutations. 218 caused reproductive problems. 778 were toxic to the human body. They knew 146 caused cancer tumors—but were allowed in the United States, even though they were banned in other countries around the world. Many of these chemicals are allowed in common cleaning supplies in the United States—things under your cabinets right now.

26 seconds after exposure, chemicals are found in measurable amounts in the human body. The average woman applies 300 chemicals to her body a day—80 before breakfast. Of the top ten most dangerous chemicals in our

home, number one is air fresheners, like plug-ins or candles. Second on the list; chemical cleaning supplies: drain and oven cleaners, furniture polish, as well as dishwasher soap and dish soap. Beauty supplies and personal care products—hairspray, gel, shampoo, and deodorant are laden with chemicals. Most deodorant has aluminum in it, and we slather it on the lymph nodes under our arms for 70 years. Many scientists believe aluminum exposure may be linked to Alzheimer's and Parkinson's disease. Two of the top pollutants in the family home is laundry soap and fabric softener—you wash your clothes, they sit on your skin and outgas in your closet all night long. That information is straight from the government, from the U.S. Environmental Protection Agency's Top 10 Killer Household Chemicals Study.

There are 100,000 chemicals on the market today. The Toxic Substance Control Act (TCSA) of 1976 grandfathered them in. What does that mean to you? Simply put: these chemicals have not had any safety testing, and we know very little information about their side effects. Dr. Samuel Epstein, chairman of the Cancer Prevention Coalition, says, "it is unthinkable that women would knowingly inflict such exposures on their infants, children, and themselves if products were routinely labeled with explicit warnings of cancer risks. But they are not labeled."

Since the 1940's, prostate cancer is up 200%. Thyroid cancer, 155%. Brain cancer, 70%. And the American Cancer Society estimates a 50% rise in cancer rates by 2020.

What happens when your body is chemically overloaded? You may see it in something as catastrophic as cancer. But most of us feel it on other ways: lethargy, inability to focus, sleep trouble, chronic inflammation, unexplained pain, skin issues, adult acne, hot flashes, stress, anxiety, and fear. If you face any of these issues, it's time to kick chemicals to the curb. You can control what you allow within the walls of your home.

I was invited to my first oils class, got my starter kit, and began right where you are now, taking this chemical-free living thing one day at a time; kicking one chemical out of my home at a time. You can do this. It's about taking small steps, and saying- no more. I will not allow these things in my home. You can't control all the places you are exposed—but you are the gatekeeper of your house.

Learn alongside our team. Let us guide you through the process in simple, easy steps. Step one is to start with the starter kit—a diffuser and 11 bottles of oil, some of the most common oils on the earth for supporting systems of the body. They each have just one ingredient; Lemon is just cold pressed lemon rinds. Frankincense is resin, properly steam distilled at the right temperature to make essential oil. Lavender is freshly distilled at the peak of the harvest—with thousands of uses in the home. Let us come alongside you and train you how to kick chemicals to the curb. You can DO this.

Start by heading to www.youngliving.com, click on "Become A Member" and enter the sponsor and enroller number of the person who introduced you to the oils.

Once you have put in the sponsor and enroller number, it will take you to a second page and ask for personal information where you'll set up your account. Write it all down so you're able to log in later. The third page asks which starter kit you want. My personal favorite is the Rainstone diffuser with the Premium Starter Kit. If your budget is tight, the Desert Mist diffuser works wonderfully too. I'd also encourage you to sign up for Essential Rewards. You get to pick the oils that come to your door every single month, you switch them out—and you get paid 10% back for everything you order in reward points. That's 10% back on your laundry soap, dish soap, and Thieves® cleaner—which is all I use to clean my house. It's one of the best choices I ever made. If you'd like to add those to your order, I recommend the Thieves® Essential Rewards Kit—because in one swoop, it contains just about all you need to get rid of nearly every chemical cleaner in your home. It's simple and easy. And if you're taking chemical-free living head on, it's the best place to start.

The final window asks for payment, and you're off and running. We're honored to have you as a part of this team. Look for a welcome package in the mail! Connect with us online at Oil Ability with Sarah on Facebook. Find more resources at oilabilityteam.com. Welcome to the Oil Ability family!

This is something you NEED to take seriously. No one is watching your home but you. You are the gatekeeper. I'd be willing to bet my life that there are things in your home right now—that you're exposed to every single day—that could be killing you. And the thing is, it's totally preventable.

What do you do until the box arrives?

Start small. Start slow. Start with what you're convicted on. Let me give you a simple tip. With your food, flip the container over and start reading the ingredients. If you can't pronounce it, don't eat it. It doesn't mean you can't have ice cream—just go for the ice cream with milk, sugar, eggs, and vanilla instead of an ingredients list of 35 items you don't recognize.

With your home, start with the biggest offenders first—laundry soap, dishwasher soap, cleaning supplies, candles, and plug-ins. Toss the candles and plug-ins. Swap them out with a diffuser and pure essential oil. Young Living has oil-infused Thieves® cleaner, laundry soap, and dish soap that's affordable and simple to use. Add them to your Essential Rewards order once you have that starter kit.

This is about small, simple, baby steps. Take it one month at a time as you swap things out in your home. Maybe the first month you focus solely on Thieves® cleaner and toss your cleaning supplies. You can start that today by grabbing a $22 bottle of Thieves® cleaner. Go home and wipe your kitchen down and fall in love—knowing you just boosted your immune system instead of taxing your liver.

The next month, swap out some laundry soap or dish soap. Month three, focus on your personal care products—deodorant and/or shampoo. Month four, beauty supplies—like face wash. Every day you leave your makeup on, your skin ages by seven days. Use a chemical-free option to wash it off. The Young Living ART line is my favorite.

I started this journey myself two years ago, with a Young Living starter kit, and have never looked back. We use oils every single day in our home. Every oil you use is a chemical you're not using.

You matter. Your family matters. Your friends matter. You can take control of your own health. Kick the chemicals out of your life and start living clean.

Checklist Sheets to Take to Vendor Events

Name: _____

Phone: _____

Email: _____

Check a box:

☐ I am interested in having you come teach a FREE class for me and my homies. (This class can be at ANY location)

☐ I am interested in showing up to a class you teach! I will bring my friends!

☐ I would LOVE to get my hands on a premium starter kit and start oiling

☐ Please please please teach me how to use oils! Just contact me and give me info!

☐ If you call or contact me, I will egg your house. But I do want to win that gift basket.

This is the address where you can mail to if I win:

_____

Name: _____

Phone: _____

Email: _____

Check a box:

☐ I am Interested in having you come teach a FREE class for me and my homies. (This class can be at ANY location)

☐ I am interested in showing up to a class you teach! I will bring my friends!

☐ I would LOVE to get my hands on a premium starter kit and start oiling

☐ Please please please teach me how to use oils! Just contact me and give me info!

☐ If you call or contact me, I will egg your house. But I do want to win that gift basket.

This is the address where you can mail to if I win:

_____

Name: _____

Phone: _____

Email: _____

Check a box:

☐ I am Interested in having you come teach a FREE class for me and my homies. (This class can be at ANY location)

☐ I am interested in showing up to a class you teach! I will bring my friends!

☐ I would LOVE to get my hands on a premium starter kit and start oiling

☐ Please please please teach me how to use oils! Just contact me and give me info!

☐ If you call or contact me, I will egg your house. But I do want to win that gift basket.

This is the address where you can mail to if I win:

_____

THE FAMOUS PURPLE BAGS

Eighty percent of your business is simply being prepared. What does that mean? If you don't have something on your person to give a potential oiler, you will lose the sale. Enter in the purple bag. These make it crazy easy for you to share, even if you're not physically teaching a class.

There are a few basic components to the 6x9 organza bag, and they can be swapped out, but here is what I put in mine:

1) A cover sheet explaining what's in the bag (these are available to download for free on our website, oilabilityteam.com)

2) Your business card so they have a way to contact you.

3) A Toxin Free Life CD or 101 CD (you can burn it for free on our website, or save yourself time and order them professionally printed for $1.25 each)

4) Your Gameplan, the mini book which reveals the business opportunity

5) Fearless, which explains the need to oil

6) A photo/graphic of the starter kit so they know what they are ordering

7) Instructions on how to purchase the kit (also available as a free download at oilabilityteam.)

All the resources listed above are linked on our website under Share>Purple Follow Up Bags.

These bags have saved me over and over again. I use them for people I randomly meet at the store or post office who express interest in oils. I hand them out to attendees in every class. I keep a few in my purse for friends that I bump into along my day, such as at soccer games. I use them in follow up mailings—for people who have expressed interest in a kit. I even use them for people who already have kits, but I would love to see them regularly oiling, and on essential rewards. (For follow up purple bags, I skip the "how to order" info and the starter kit picture and send them a Toxin Free Life cd and the Fearless mini about habit training and oils.)

I make up a bunch of bags at the beginning of the month and carry five of them in my purse with me everywhere I go. In July, 2017 alone, I picked up 13 different business builders (not just kit sales!) simply through carrying these on me and following up!

Why and how do they work so well? The magic of the purple bag is it does the talking for you. When you're in line at the grocery store, it's unrealistic to have a full conversation on the Young Living income disclosure guide. But you can hand out a Your Gameplan mini book to the cashier, she can read it over her lunchbreak, and you can touch base later. It doesn't need to be creepy or awkward. Simply use "If I, will you." "If I give you this purple bag, will you go through it? And is it ok to add to you to Facebook to check in? I want to make sure you're OK! You look like you're having a tough day." Facebook puts a distance between you—they can choose to unfriend you later, and haven't given you any personal information. But it also allows for a crisp contact without weirdness. If it's someone you already know, make sure you have their current phone number and touch base.

The contents of the bag will do the talking for you, but you still need to touch base to close the sale. Purple bags will not work if you walk away and have not collected their information to talk again again. Practice handing them out on a few of your friends, and get into the habit of regularly carrying them with you so you don't lose prospects.

Another way I use these on my team is to have "purple bag stuffing parties." I love to encourage my leaders to train their teams to have these bags on them. Last month, I held a contest for anyone who could get five of their leaders to a purple bag stuffing party. Twenty-seven leaders responded, we mailed out supplies to them or sent them links to order, and they had fun putting the bags together with their teams. They built friendships and trained on the business and developed a valuable business tool in under 90 minutes.

Having the conversation is most of the battle. If you can get the information in front of them, it's amazing how many people will say yes. You just need the tools on hand. Be prepared.

HOW TO ORDER A YOUNG LIVING STARTER KIT

Each person that comes to class walks out with an organza bag with an image of the starter kit, my business card, a freebie (like a sample of Cool Azul pain cream), and instructions on how to sign up for a starter kit. This is the sheet I print out and put in those bags:

How To Order A Young Living Starter Kit:

1) Go to www.youngliving.com, click "United States, English"

2) Click "Become a Member"

3) Choose "member" (not retail customer)

4) Use sponsor # _____ and Enroller # _____

5) Pick a user name, password, a 4-digit pin (write it down—you'll need it to log in!)

6) I recommend choosing the Premium Starter Kit with Rainstone Diffuser. What does the kit come with? 11 bottles of oil, a diffuser, NingXia samples, lots of literature on how to use the oils, sharing bottles, oils samples, and more!

7) Choose whether or not you would like to be an Essential Rewards Member. You'll have the oils you choose shipped to your door every month! It's worth every penny!!! Shipping is cheaper, and you qualify for bonus oils if you spend 190, 250, or 300PV. You also get 10% back in free oils (no matter what you spend) for the first 3 months, 20% back after 4 months, and 25% back after 25 months. You must spend 50PV each month to maintain Essential Rewards. You can change the date your order ships each month, and you pick the oils you want.

8) Select "continue shopping" if you'd like to add other items to your cart. I recommend the Thieves cleaner for $22—it's concentrated; you get 20 spray bottles of out of it! That's 50 cents a bottle for organic cleaner!

To learn more about your oils, log into your virtual office at youngliving. com, "sign in" and check out the short videos on the "Getting Started" tab. Welcome to Young Living!

Simple Oil Ability Follow Up Calling Script

1) Introduce yourself: "This is (name/rank), calling from your Young Living upline. Thank you SO much for getting a starter kit and being on our team! I was just calling to make sure you've opened the box and are doing OK!"

2) Make sure they've opened the box: "Have you tried the diffuser? Do you need help setting it up?"

3) Find their need: "What are your top three goals with oils? Tell me why you came to the class." Answer their questions by showing them how and where to look things up.

4) Tell them you want to put some resources in thier hands to help train them to use their kit. "I will be sending you a copy of Fearless in the mail, with a Fearless calendar" You can also say, "If you accept the ten challenges and take a photo of the calendar and text it to me, I will gift you $25 toward your Essential Rewards order."

5) Explain Essential Rewards: "ER is Christmas every month—as you go room by room in your home and kick the chemicals to the curb. You get 10% in rewards points the first three months, 20% starting in month four and 25% after 25 consecutive months. These are the promos—the freebies—for this month: (list freebies)."

6) Stay connected: "This is my contact information if you have any questions. I appreciate you! My goal is to help you get the most out of your kit. I am so thankful to have you on this team!" Give them a list of upcoming classes or #ylunites rallies.Then get a bundle in the mail to them!

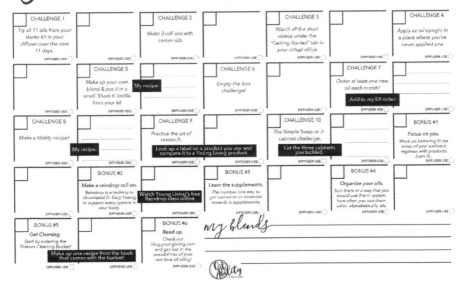

~Fearless~ CHALLENGES

CHALLENGE 1
Try all 11 oils from your starter kit in your diffuser over the next 11 days.

DIFFUSER USE

DIFFUSER USE

CHALLENGE 2
Make 3 roll ons with carrier oils

DIFFUSER USE

DIFFUSER USE

CHALLENGE 3
Watch all the short videos under the "Getting Started" tab in your virtual office

DIFFUSER USE

DIFFUSER USE

CHALLENGE 4
Apply an oil tonight in a place where you've never applied one

DIFFUSER USE

CHALLENGE 5
Make up your own blend & put it in a small 'Share it' bottle from your kit

My recipe:

DIFFUSER USE

DIFFUSER USE

CHALLENGE 6
Empty-the-box challenge!

DIFFUSER USE

DIFFUSER USE

CHALLENGE 7
Order at least one new oil each month!

Add to my ER order:

DIFFUSER USE

DIFFUSER USE

CHALLENGE 8
Make a Vitality recipe!

My recipe:

DIFFUSER USE

DIFFUSER USE

CHALLENGE 9
Practice the art of research.

Look up a label on a product you use and compare it to a Young Living product.

DIFFUSER USE

DIFFUSER USE

CHALLENGE 10
The Simple Swap or 3-cabinet challenge.

List the three cabinets you tackled.

DIFFUSER USE

DIFFUSER USE

BONUS #1
Focus on you.
Work on bettering three areas of your wellness regimen with products from YL.

DIFFUSER USE

BONUS #2
Make a raindrop roll-on.
Raindrop is a technique developed D. Gary Young to support every system in your body.
Watch Young Living's free Raindrop class online

DIFFUSER USE

DIFFUSER USE

BONUS #3
Learn the supplements.
The number one way to get someone on essential rewards is supplements.

DIFFUSER USE

DIFFUSER USE

BONUS #4
Organize your oils.
Sort them in a way that you would use them: system, how often you use them, color, alphabetically, etc.

DIFFUSER USE

BONUS #5
Get Cleaning.
Start by ordering the Thieves Cleaning Bucket!
Make up one recipe from the book that comes with the bucket!

DIFFUSER USE

DIFFUSER USE

BONUS #6
Read up.
Check out blog.younglgiving.com and get lost in the possibilities of your new love of oiling!

DIFFUSER USE

my blends

I rotate through my teams every couple of months. If there's a strong leader on that leg I sit down with them for an afternoon and train them to do their own follow up (and eat a lot of chocolate!) If there's no clear leader, I'll mail this package out myself. Then a couple months later, I may mail a different DVD and sample with a new handwritten note. It's all about building relationships.

FEARLESS TRAINING WITH A SAMPLE FEARLESS LETTER

Fearless is a powerful tool. When I started using it, my Essential Rewards totals were at 28%. Now, they are tapping 42%. How do I use it effectively? Expect something back.

I called over a thousand zeros on my team and asked why they weren't on ER, and the most common response was that they didn't think of using the oils. They had used the same products for 20, 30, or 40 years—and oils were an afterthought. There is a gap in the education process of training the LIFESTYLE. Fearless isn't a compilation of ways to use the starter kit. It's a tool to train label reading, researching, and practical aromatherapy all rolled into one. If you can train the lifestyle, you'll have a lifelong dedicated oiler. They need to know the why.

Fearless ends with ten challenges to get them oiling every single day and emptying their starter kit. Then it drives hard to Essential Rewards and offers the Simple Swap—a room by room breakdown of the dangers in their home, and what pure Young Living products to use instead.

HOW DO I USE FEARLESS?

After they get their kit, this is the first book I give them. It's an affordable, duplicatable business tool. I ask them to read Fearless and complete the Fearless calendar (available for free at oilabilityteam.com under "share" and "Fearless Tools and Resources." They send me a screenshot of their completed calendar. Then I gift them $25 toward their Essential Rewards order once I see it has processed. You can either send a check or call Young Living to place an account credit on their account. Invest back in them and see where it leads. When I offer the money back, I rarely get a no on completing the challenges. A single month of ER may yield the return of your $25, depending on the size of their order. And if you build the lifestyle, it's a blessing far greater than that.

SAMPLE LETTER FOR A FEARLESS MAILING AFTER THEY HAVE THEIR KIT

Hello there!

This is _____, your _____ upline. I am so thankful that you have a Young Living Premium Starter kit! This is the kit that rocked my world and turned it upside down in the best way possible. I have a totally different vantage point on how I build wellness for my family.

I want to make sure you get every drop out of your investment. I am committed to coming alongside you and training you how to use this kit! I have included two special gifts for you. The "Fearless" book held the top five spots on Amazon for six months in aromatherapy! It's a power packed little book that will train you in an oils lifestyle, which can be read in under two hours on a lunch break or during soccer practice. I also gave you a "Fearless" calendar to compliment the book. If you fill out this calendar and accept the ten Fearless challenges, I'd like to say thank you by gifting you $25 toward your Essential Rewards order.

To place that order, just log into your Virtual Office at youngliving.com by clicking the "sign in" button. You'll see the Essential Rewards tab on the left side of the page. The first three months, you get 10% back on every ER order you place. After three months it's 20% back. And after 25 months, it's 25% back. It's Christmas on your door every month as you kick chemicals in your home to the curb.

I believe in this lifestyle so deeply. It was a turning point for me. To take me up on my gift, simply screenshot your completed Fearless calendar to my cell phone, (insert your number), with your name, and I'll get it in the mail. Then look for a check in the mail from me after that order has been placed.

Thank you for the chance to pour into you!

ESSENTIAL REWARDS IN CLEAR LANGUAGE

I get asked at least once a day how the Essential Rewards program works, even by leaders, and when I see leaders with 288 PV or 187 PV, I want to kick a wall. So here's a simple explanation (for my own sanity).

1. Essential Rewards Freebies

If you spend 100 PV, 190 PV, 250 PV, or 300 PV, you get oodles of freebies! Example: The one this month—a free Everyday Oils Kit—for 300 PV is actually worth $270 (retail). With this amount of money, you can literally restock most of your starter kit, or your cleaning supplies, supplements and oils. The freebies change every single month. Look for January's to be released around December 31st. You cannot add to an order from earlier in the month to hit 300PV. It's got to be in one single order.

Earn gifts available only to members of the Essential Rewards program when you place consecutive Essential Rewards orders over 50 PV. Get rewarded when you consecutively order for 3, 6, and 9 months—and beyond. Plus, you'll get an exclusive blend after your 12th consecutive month!

2. Discounted shipping

Essential Rewards orders qualify for discounted shipping rates.

3. Cash back

For the first three months you're on Essential Rewards, you get 10% back. Beginning month four, you get 20% back, and after 25 months, you get 25% back. Most of my oils were free this way.

4. Kits only available on Essential Rewards

The NingXia Red® Essential Rewards kit, for example, costs $1.16/ounce instead of $1.60/ounce buying it in a Quick Order bundle. It's the cheapest way to buy NingXia, and if your whole family drinks it, like mine does, that's a big savings! The same is true of the Thieves® and Everyday Oils Essential Rewards kits.

5. The Requirements

You must spend 50 PV a month to place an Essential Rewards order, and you can always change the date to a better date for you. You must check your cart before your ship date and update it. The items in your cart from last month are left in the cart to order again. Why? Because most people use this to order the same supplements every month and don't want to keep adding them in month after month. Make sure you have what you want in your cart before it ships out.

Why should business builders be on Essential Rewards? Because you have to spend 100 PV to get your paycheck anyway, which is a good idea since it gets you familiar with the product. If you are on Essential Rewards, you get 10% back. That would mean you're actually only spending $90. And that's better financial stewardship. It's a wiser way to get paid.

Three other Essential Rewards questions I get every week:

1) Where do I order it?
   Under the Essential Rewards button only in your Virtual Office. I try to put my entire monthly order on it every month because it's free money back.

2) How do I claim my Essential Rewards points?
   Under the Quick Order button. All Essential Rewards points need to be claimed under Quick Order tab, not under the Essential Rewards tab.

3) Can I get the freebies under Quick Order?
   Yes. Hit the same benchmarks: 190, 250, or 300PV. You can get many of the freebies twice: once under Quick Order, and once under Essential Rewards. I frequently place an order under both the Quick Order and the ER buttons. You will only earn points under ER, and some of the freebies may be ER exclusive, just check that month's promotion.

the value of ESSENTIAL REWARDS

	3 MONTHS	6 MONTHS	12 MONTHS	2 YEARS	5 YEARS
50PV	$15	$45	$105	$225	$765
100PV	$75	$165	$345	$705	$2,325
190PV	$312	$681	$1,419	$2,825	$7,665
250PV	$495	$1,065	$2,205	$4,485	$14,995
300PV	$690	$1,470	$3,030	$6,150	$16,050

Based on points earned plus estimated value of monthly promotions

How to Use the Gameplan System

When I first wrote Gameplan, it was just a book. It was a simple highlight-it-and-shelf-it two-day read. But it has become so much more than that, because of you. I am honored to say because of your suggestions and your probing me to make this even better, it's now a complete duplicatable training system. the first put on paper in all of Young Living. It's affordable. And it keeps you and your leaders on the same page.

It started with the book. After running my team through bootcamp, they requested a workbook to mold the principles in the book to their teams specifically. Once we released it, there was a request on the Platinum page of Young Living to create a prospecting book for those that weren't ready for Gameplan yet. That's how the mini was developed: Your Gameplan.

I recorded the bootcamp videos to flesh out what was in the book and make it personable. And we ended up with a 25-day system: one chapter of the book, one set of workbook worksheets, and one video a day. 25 chapters, 25 worksheets, 25 videos. Rinse and repeat. Simple and easy, yet fully equipping your leaders with everything they need to succeed.

What I found after running several bootcamps with my team was that they would do the system, then get distracted. They'd look for the next best thing — the greener grass, when really all they needed to keep doing is duplicate. Doing 12 bootcamps a year isn't tricky, because you're not re-watching all the videos. You step into the position of leadership after your first bootcamp, and become the one leading your team. The same leaders are not doing bootcamp over and over and over again — they are stepping into the position of leader, and leading it themselves. Do bootcamp once. Lead it 11 times.

I knew after bootcamp we needed one more step to the system for long-term commitment and focus — and that's why I just wrapped up the "Gameplanner," which is unlike anything you've ever seen in a planner before. It marks a year of research and work. There's rank mapping, stat tracking for eight months in a sitting so you can watch trends on your team, places to chart classes, track OGV, focus on certain leaders and certain legs, watch those ranking up who are doing the work, keep in touch with your top leaders, track your oils collection, Fearless challenges to boost essential rewards, follow up and warm and cold market pages, and more. This is all the actions I've focused on and sketched into my planners for the past three years. It's based off market research on hundreds of different planners, over 1,000 of your planner requests, and includes every element of the Gameplan book, putting it into planner form. It's the definition of accountability.

How do I use the Gameplan system now that it's complete?

1) Hand out the mini ("Your Gameplan") like candy (this will help you find leaders!)

2) Do the Teacher Training in the back of the Gameplan book (this shows your budding leader how to market and host a class, do follow up, and explains how they are paid)

3) Coach them through their first 101 class using the script

4) Hand them the book and the workbook and direct them to the FREE Gameplan bootcamp at oilability.team.com

5) Have them pick two leaders and do the first four steps

6) Once they have trained their first two leaders, reward them with a Gameplanner to keep them on task. It is a full year of business accountability.

7) Rinse and repeat

For a year of accountability after they have completed bootcamp, there are two amazing resources for keeping them focused. The first, mentioned briefly above, is the Gameplanner. It allows them to track Gameplan bootcamps with their leaders, focus on teaching classes, doing follow up, tracking their stats, rank mapping to see how far they are from their next rank, and so much more. It is a powerhouse. I also recorded Gameplan as an audio book. When you listen to something, you use a totally different part of your brain. They can download it on Apple iTunes or Audible on Amazon and listen through their cell phone, and get Gameplan training as they drive. Solidify the concepts through audio learning!

What would happen to your family business if you committed to doing only income-producing activities for one year? If you held a class a week, did follow up once a month on your classes, and held twelve Gameplan bootcamps, training two to train two, and getting your leaders to duplicate? You'd have a totally new business in a year. You'd be building a legacy income. A Young Living business is built one brick at a time, with a little Essential Rewards mortar in between. Is it easy? No. Is it worth it? Yes.

I'll see you on the Diamond stage!

GAMEPLAN

The Complete Strategy Guide to go From **Starter Kit to Silver**

STEP 1
Read "Your Gameplan" (the mini)

STEP 2
Do the Teacher Training from the "Gameplan" Appendix

STEP 3
Market and Host the 101 Class from the "Gameplan" Appendix

STEP 4
Get "Gameplan" and "Gameplan Workbook" in your hands

STEP 5
Go to oilabilityteam.com and do the bootcamp *(25 FREE videos, 25 chapters in Gameplan, 25 workbook chapters)*

STEP 6
Train two people with the first five steps

STEP 7
Rinse and repeat.

To listen to a full 101 oils class for FREE - go to: **oilabilityteam.com**

TEACHER TRAINING: HOW TO LAUNCH A YOUNG LIVING LEADER

This section is the super-condensed version of all the leadership training in this book. Use it when you are training your leaders personally.

When I first train a leader, the most important thing is for them to understand where this goes. They have to stack Young Living against their current job and see that it's a better use of their time. Will they be where they want to be five years from now if they keep doing the same things they did today? If you have five minutes, run through the first two paragraphs of "Why Do a Young Living Business" (below) to encourage them to come to a leadership training. When they go home, have them go to oilabilityteam.com and click on the "Start Here" button and watch the free "Sarah's Why" video. It is a powerful video that will help them vision cast, and get their feet moving.

Once they are there, I'll go through this whole appendix with them, which takes about 60 minutes. Then cap it off with six homework assignments and end with a Virtual Office tour.

WHY DO A YOUNG LIVING BUSINESS?

Young Living allows you to build a willable income you can leave to your children and family. This isn't a 401k that can run out six months after you're gone; it's like having a downtown storefront with employees that continues to generate income even if you're not there. It is like baking a cake once and selling it, and the sale of that one cake gets paid to you, your kids and grandkids.

Other perks to Young Living: there is no income ceiling, you are your own boss, you set your own hours, you can take time off and still get paid, it doesn't matter when you get into the company, the product is consumable and it works! It's easier to share than a pan, some leggings, weight loss pills, or books and has virtually no overhead costs, save an affordable starter kit. You get to see people around you experience financial freedom (you cannot put a price tag on seeing your best friend leave a job that's cost her time and stress!), you get to build lifelong relationships with people who care about natural health, you are able to work with your friends and family (you pick your coworkers!), and build time economy; the greatest wealth there is. It does not matter how many people you know, and you don't have to be good in sales or speaking. Ready to learn more?

GETTING STARTED

How do you begin a Young Living business? It's easy! Print the 101 Script, open your calendar, grab some friends, and schedule a class! That's it! Rinse and repeat!

Check this out! It's the Young Living income disclosure guide. Need motivation? Here's a good place to start.

YOUNG LIVING 2016 U.S. INCOME DISCLOSURE STATEMENT

As a direct selling company selling essential oils, supplements, and other lifestyle products, Young Living offers opportunities for our members to build a business or simply receive discounts on our products.

Whatever your interest in the company, we hope to count you among the more than 2 million Young Living members joining us in our mission to bring Young Living essential oils to every home in the world.

What are my earning opportunities?

Members can earn commissions and bonuses as outlined in our Compensation Plan. As members move up in the ranks of Young Living, they become eligible for additional earning opportunities.

This document provides statistical, fiscal data about the average member income and information about achieving various ranks.

RANK	PERCENTAGE OF ALL MEMBERS	MONTHLY INCOME				ANNUALIZE AVERAGE INCOME	MONTHS TO ACHIEVE THIS RANK		
		Lowest	Highest	Median	Average		Low	Average	High
Distributor	94.0%	$0	$41	$0	$7	$12	N/A	N/A	N/A
Star	3.5%	$0	$811	$60	$77	$924	1	15	255
Senior Star	1.3%	$1	$3,512	$197	$240	$2,880	1	22	255
Executive	0.6%	$50	$12,139	$434	$514	$6,168	1	29	253
Silver	0.2%	$562	$25,546	$1,783	$2,227	$26,724	1	36	251
Gold	0.1%	$1,781	$46,800	$4,874	$6,067	$72,804	1	54	240
Platinum	<0.1%	$3,146	$85,997	$12,138	$15,324	$183,888	2	63	236
Diamond	<0.1%	$14,898	$140,333	$32,078	$39,566	$474,792	10	75	251
Crown Diamond	<0.1%	$37,227	$232,551	$64,256	$74,188	$890,256	14	83	236
Royal Crown Diamond	<0.1%	$58,392	$262,864	$135,248	$152,377	$1,828,524	17	166	230

The income statistics in this statement are for incomes earned by all active U.S. members in 2016. An "active" member is a member who made at least one product purchase in products in the previous 12 months. The average annual income for all members in this time was $25, and the median annual income for all members was $0. 51% of all members who enrolled in 2015 did not make a purchase with Young Living in 2016. 57% of all members who enrolled in 2014 did not continue with Young Living in 2016.

Note that the compensation paid to members summarized in this disclosure do not include expenses incurred by a member in the operation or promotion of his or her business, which can vary widely and might include advertising or promotional expenses, product samples, training, rent, travel, telephone and Internet costs, and miscellaneous expenses. The earnings of the members in this chart are not necessarily representative of the income, if any, that a Young Living member can or will earn through the Young Living Compensation Plan. These figures should not be considered as guarantees or projections of your actual earnings or profits. Your success will depend on individual diligence, work, effort, sales skill, and market conditions. Young Living does not guarantee any income or rank success.

YOUNG LIVING
ESSENTIAL OILS

Now, tell them to complete these homework assignments to earn a free gift from you, their leader:

1. Print this Teacher Training and pour over it. Buy a new folder and label it "Young Living Business" and store your training there.

2. Get your hands on a copy of the compliant 101 lecture notes. Write on them, make them yours (share how you got your starter kit), and call them George. Practice the lecture, and add the notes to your Young Living Business folder.

3. Watch a quick video to get over any fears you have of network marketing. This 4-minute video will give you a leg up on what it really is. Go to Youtube and type this in: "I still think it is a pyramid scheme". (Pyramid Scheme Cartoon by Pat Petrini)

4. Watch how you train. It's important to stay compliant. The FDA is not something to fear, just follow the rules. You will stay safe if you share the 101

script in this book. Do not diagnose or talk about oils for treating disease. Stay above the wellness line. Oils are for supporting systems, not curing cancer. There are thousands of ways of talking about the oils compliantly. People are looking for alternatives to a less toxic lifestyle. Chipotle has cut all GMO's, Panera is cutting chemicals from their salad dressing, Kraft has cut dyes from their mac and cheese, Heinz has cut corn syrup from their ketchup. People are reading labels and paying attention to what they put in their body. Young Living is a solution to that problem, whether it's chemical-free cleaning supplies, pure essential oils, or health supplements like NingXia Red or Pure Protein Complete. My family's business has tripled in half a year, even though our classes are taught compliantly. It's about supporting the body so it can do its own fighting, not curing disease.

5. Tour the Young Living Virtual Office. Access it by logging into your account at www.youngliving.com. If you do not know your username and password, call Young Living and they can email it to you. Watch all the videos provided in the "Getting Started" tab at the top of your dashboard and read through the documents on the "Member Resources" tab on the left side of the page. Review the "Rank Qualification" (how you watch you) tab and the "My Organization" (how you watch your team) tab. Then you will understand how to rank up.

6. Set a date for your first class.

HOW TO FILL CLASSES WITHOUT KNOWING PEOPLE

Our team's biggest successes are on FREE Facebook event pages. Under your photo on the header of your Facebook profile page, click on "More," then "Events" and set up an event. Then ask three people you know to go into that Facebook event and invite 50 people each. Make them a gift basket with some multi-purpose Thieves cleaner, one of my DVD's, and a Peppermint roll-on as a "thank you". You'll now have 150 people invited. Of those, 15 to 20 will actually show up if you market in the event once a day. If you are not having success filling classes, focus on relationships. One on fire oiler can fill a class for you. The average person knows 2,000 people by the time they are 20. Meet their needs.

Market the class for at least two to three weeks before the event. Why? People need a heads up. Standard network marketing numbers are that if you have a class of ten, two or three will get kits.

After that class, find the enthusiast—the one that got the kit and loves it—and ask to teach to their circle of friends. Ask three from the class to go into your next event and invite 50 people each. Always tap into new friend circles, and don't keep speaking to the same people. A word of caution: it grows FAST! If you are tenacious and stick with it, your business will not look the same one year from now!

TIPS FOR CLASS DAY

1) Get your diffuser going so they experience the oils right when they walk into the room.

2) Pass around a clipboard and collect their names, emails, and addresses so you can follow up later. This is the most important thing you can do! If you don't collect their information, you have lost every contact that came to the class.

3) Keep your lecture under an hour. Always start with your story! Facts tell, stories sell. Start by telling how you got involved with oils. Read the 3-page 101 script or pop in the DVD if you don't want to speak. End by having everyone smell the oils in the Premium Starter Kit and explain how the kit can be used.

4) End with a strong closing script and tell them how to order on the Young Living website. You will not sell any starter kits if you don't tell people where to go. Just tell them where you started your journey. It doesn't have to come off as salesy. It just has to be genuine. Have a laptop set up with internet access so they can order right at the class.

5) Give them a purple bag with a photo of the starter kit, step-by-step information on how to sign up, your business card, and a freebie. I always give the book Fearless so they know why they need oils, and Your Gameplan, the mini, so every attendee gets the business opportunity.

NOW FOLLOW UP!

Pick up the phone and call the people who came to class! I follow the mantra of 3-10-30. Check in three days after class, ten days after, and 30 days after.

You'll run across people who say they're not interested (drop them), those who say they are interested but got sidetracked (walk them through getting the kit), and those who say they can't afford it right now. (They're actually telling you they don't know they need it.) Find their biggest struggle, and make them something oily that will bless them.

Use the same 3-10-30 motto for people who have gotten a kit. What oils have they not used? Do they know how to use the diffuser? Get the Oil Ability audio CD's or DVD's in their hands, or get them plugged into new classes, and explain Essential Rewards.

THE BIGGEST MISTAKES EVERY STAGNANT BUSINESS BUILDER MAKES

1) Not having a strong close in your lecture

2) Tapping into the same friend circles (use the Oil Ability marketing system!)

3) Not doing follow up

4) Not treating a business as a business (wanting a $10,000 paycheck and holding one class a month)

5) Distractions. Wanting 50 years of aromatherapy knowledge before you feel like you can share oils. Pick up the Gameplan book and read Chapter 23 for encouragement in this area.

COMMISSION CHECK

The first question I usually get after sending this is, "How do I get paid?" You have to spend $100 a month to get a paycheck. I'd encourage you to sign up for Essential Rewards, a once-a-month autoship program (you can change the date and what's in your cart any time you want). Why is that a good idea? Because you'll get $10 back (10% of your PV) in free oils! So to get a paycheck, you're actually only spending $90, and that's a wiser way to get paid.

Your paycheck is mailed out from the Young Living headquarters on the 20th of the next month. All of January's sales will be in your February 20th paycheck. In the Virtual Office, you can go to "Member Resources" and "Direct Deposit Instructions For U.S. Members" to have your paycheck directly deposited into your bank account so you don't need to wait for snail mail.

Commission check breakdown:

You get a minimum of $50 for every Premium Starter Kit you sell where you are the sponsor and the enroller. That's the Starter Kit Bonus and the Fast Start Bonus. Then for the first three months, you get 25% of everything they buy. That's called Fast Start. (And it is SWEET!)

After three months, you get 8% of all they buy. If they enroll someone, you get a 10% Fast Start bonus for three months and then 5% commission of that new person's PV. If that person enrolls someone, you get 4% of that PV. That's called Unilevel bonuses. As a Star, Senior Star, and Executive, you may qualify for the Rising Star Team Bonus Pool, and once you reach Silver, you may qualify for the Generation Leadership Bonus. Both of these are generous shares from the company every month.

Four parts to the check:

Starter Kit bonus: $50 on every kit (half is technically the starter kit Bonus and half is the Fast Start Bonus)

Fast Start: 25% on all they buy after the kit (for the first three calendar months)

Unilevel: (starts on month four) 8% on those directly under you, 5% on your second level, 4% on the third, fourth, and fifth levels

Rising Star Team Bonus (Star, Senior Star, Executive) or Generation Leadership Bonus (Silver through Royal Crown Diamond): The former is based more on volume and the latter is based more on rank.

FIND YOUR NICHE

What if I don't want to stand in front of people? There are many ways of sharing Young Living! Do classes online or vendor events if you have no friend circles. Bring kits with you to sell on the spot and give them Fearless with an explanation of Essential Rewards. Make up samples of the oils and hand them out, then promote the Premium Starter Kit. Give one-on-one classes over lunch. Recruit people to share the oils and read this training to each person who shares a kit. Mail our Oil Ability DVD's to people and do strong follow-up. My team's best successes are when we invite four or five people to our living room and read the script. If you don't want to stand in front of people, pop in the DVD and let Sarah teach. End by passing around the Premium Starter Kit and telling them how to buy with your distributor number.

One last tip: Pray and give your business to the Lord. Every good thing comes from the Father of Lights!

Hopefully that answers most of your questions! No question is dumb! Network marketing isn't a lottery—it's a mathematical certainty. Get out there and share, and do it again and again, and you'll grow.

Tell your leader-in-training: When you complete those six homework assignments, you will have gone from learning the Virtual Office, to marketing, to hosting your own class, to doing thorough follow-up that get people their starter kits and onto Essential Rewards. Great job! That is one full cycle of your Young Living business. Since most of the fear in this is just getting through that first initial class, (it's fear of the unknown)—I'm now going to bless you with something that really catapulted my business. It's called the Gameplan book and workbook, and it lays out a strategy for what to do next. I just wanted you to see that you can launch your business on your own first, simply with the 101 Script and a starter kit. If you repeat that one action over and over again, you have what it takes to go Diamond. You are a #diamondrising!

God bless you. Time to see some miracles!

BOOTCAMP TRACKING

What would happen to your business in one year if you commit to direct income producing activities? What if you committed to teaching one class a week, doing follow up mailings monthly, and training your leaders with bootcamp once a month—for 12 straight months?

You would explode your OGV!

And you would never look back. Make that commitment to bootcamp now. On a calendar (or your Gameplanner) track the day of bootcamp you are on. The system is simple: there are 25 chapters in this book, 25 worksheets in the workbook, and 25 videos at oilabilityteam.com.

- Pick two people in your organization
- Work with them through the 25 sections—at your own pace (you do not need to re-watch the videos, just be an accountability partner).
- Write the section on the date when you complete it

When they finish, gift them a Gameplanner to keep them focused—but only if they immediately start training two of their own people.

Train two to train two—it works!

Duplication is where you will truly feel the power of Gameplan! Commit to 12 bootcamps and see where it leads!

RESOURCES TO CATAPULT YOUR TEAM

Since Gameplan was first released, the Oil Ability team has been on the forefront of ground-breaking sharing tools that make getting to Diamond even easier. For me, the goal is to make your path to Diamond shorter than mine was. Thousands of people have used these tools with terrific success.

When I saw the business opportunity (I mean TRULY saw it) -- and I knew where this went, I wanted it for everyone, no matter what their gift set was. Not everyone can comfortably stand in front of a room of 20 people Not everyone can read well. Public speaking is not everyone's way of sharing. An online format isn't necessarily everyone's way of sharing, either.

But I believe anyone can be free. So I started to develop tools that made it simpler to share. That's what this entire section is about. If you are afraid, this will take the fear out of the passion you have for oils. Let's work together to get oils into every home in the world.

BOOKS

Gameplan: A Comprehensive Strategy Guide to go from Starter Kit to Silver. This is the book that started it all; over 1.5 million copies sold in a year. Thousands have used Gameplan to explode their OGV and hit rank after rank. Once you finish reading it, pick two leaders and train two to train two. Have them read the 25 chapters in the book, do the 25 worksheets in the workbook, and watch the 25 free Bootcamp videos for the full system. The Gameplan you hold in your hands has been revised with over 50 pages of new content, and updated information for the Starter kit.

Gameplan Workbook: This is a companion workbook that makes the book come alive for your team. It puts action to your dreams and goals. This isn't just a fill-in-the-blank workbook. It helps you put action to your goals chapter by chapter. This is the accountability tool to help you train your team to duplicate!

Your Gameplan: This mini book is the first prospecting book in all of Young Living, designed to be affordable to share and to effectively draw members to your team. This explains Sarah's story from rags to riches, shows the Income Disclosure Guide, gives eight reasons for doing a Young Living business, and poses the questions, "Will their 40 hour a week job get them out of where they are? Can they cross things off their bucket list?" If the answer is no, it's time to re-evaluate. This is the book that gets them stacking up a Young Living business against how they are spending their time right now, then coming back to you to get trained.

Fearless, Confidence with Essential Oils in 2 Hours: This is the top oils training guide in all of Young Living. Why? It gently trains new oilers to research, label read, look critically at things in their home, accept 10 oiling challenges and oil with purpose and deliberation every day. It's an affordable training system for aromatherapy, the perfect place to start when someone gets their kit. It will take the fear out of using their oils, and educates them onto essential rewards. Pass these mini books out like candy with the free Fearless calendar at oilabilityteam.com. Sarah uses these in purple bags, in every class she teaches, in follow up mailings and care packages, and to members who are about to go inactive.

Gameplanner: This planner was put together after over a year of research and study of hundreds of other planning systems. It's the first revolving planner designed for network marketing. Every three months, it's pulled down off the website and new months are added, so if you have a leader explode in June, they can still get a full year of accountability. This is the glue that makes the entire Gameplan system stick for your budding leaders. It keeps them laser focused on teaching classes, getting people on Essential Rewards, and training their leaders. Each edition of the Gameplanner includes:

- rank mapping pages to strategically plan the path to the next rank
- stat tracking pages to catch your weaknesses before you feel them in your OGV
- Gameplan bootcamp tracking sheets to train your team
- Sheets to track mileage, and essential rewards orders for tax purposes
- A list of all the important dates in Young Living for the upcoming year
- Space for a vision board and debt pay-off goals
- warm and cold market lists

- daily business goals and schedule outline

- Space for planning weekly training and tracking contests

- prayer journal pages

- a full list of every oil Young Living has to help track as you build your collection

Plus beautiful full color photos of the farms and over 250 inspirational Gameplan quotes.

This planner is AWESOME. And it gets results. Sarah gifts these to every person on her team that trains two people with Bootcamp.

DVD'S

Intro to Young Living 2 DVD set: *Essential Oils 101* and *Why Do Young Living As A Business.* The 101 DVD is the first video; a ground up lecture where it all started; centers on the Premium Starter Kit. Sarah generated this for leaders that were too timid to teach. Just pop the DVD in, play hostess, and pass around the Starter Kit. It includes the bold close on the end. Why Do Young Living As A Business is what helped grow 800 Oil Ability leaders in 18 months. It's the Your Gameplan mini in DVD form. Sarah shows this 12-minute video after every class she teaches to pick up business builders. *50 minutes total*

Gameplan Live: This is the 35-hour Gameplan bootcamp in two hours. It's what Sarah teaches when she is on tour!. She uses it as a kick off when she does new bootcamps with her team, as a refresher to those that have been through bootcamp, or as a resource at team retreats. *2 hours*

The Complete Gameplan DVD Training System: This set contains over five hours of training; including a 60-minute compliance DVD (the only compliance training in all of Young Living), a new lecture called Oily Lifestyle, the full 101 class, a full Teacher Training DVD for you to use to train you leaders that are long distance, Why Do Young Living As A Business (the mini on DVD), and How To Fill Classes Without Knowing People. Also includes the Scavenger Hunt video, a four minute icebreaker video for your classes, featuring Sarah's five kids showing off what an oil-infused house looks like. This can be used in 101 classes to break up your lecture and introduce your audience to a personal tour of a chemical-free home. This video has gotten rave reviews and is a tremendous asset to your teaching!! *5 hours*

CD/AUDIOS

Essential Oils 101: This is an extremely powerful tool for busy potential oilers to listen to in the car. It's been called the best tool, save Gameplan, that the team has put together. Pass them out in purple bags. *45 minutes.*

Toxin Free Life: This is an entire class on the Thieves Starter kit that will rock your world. Use for people that are not ready yet for oils, to introduce them to a clean living lifestyle, or for those that have already been to a 101 class and are looking for more knowledge on different Young Living products. These can also be used in purple bags. 30 minutes

Gameplan: The Gameplan book is available in audio format via iTunes or Audible!!! Professionally recorded and read by the author. This is an amazing tool for those that have finished reading the Gameplan book. She gifts it to leaders as they finish bootcamp, to continue training their brain. You can listen on a cell phone, tablet, or computer. Find it on oilabilityteam.com or Amazon. *Over 5 hours*

Fearless, Confidence with Essential Oils in 2 Hours: Fearless hit number one on Amazon for Aromatherapy, and has remained in the top five for half a year. It's the top oils training guide in all of Young Living. Why? It gently trains people to research, label read, look critically at things in their home, accept ten oiling challenges and oil with purpose and deliberation every day. It's now available on iTunes or Audible. Read by the author and recorded in a professional studio. Let her radio voice lull you to absorb and apply aromatherapy knowledge! *2 hours*

FREE ON OILABILITYTEAM.COM

- "Textable" classes
- Free Essential Rewards marketing images
- Dozens of interviews with corporate employees at the farms and Young Living Diamonds
- One of the most powerful videos recorded on the business: "Sarah's Why" video, to fire up your team
- 101 and Toxin Free Life audio classes, to download and burn onto CD yourself!
- A full beauty school class
- Powerpoint slides to go with the 101 script in this book
- The Moses blessing
- Links to all the ingredients for the Famous Purple Bags.

- Updates on Sarah's speaking schedule and Gameplan Live events

You can connect with Sarah on Facebook. Oil Ability with Sarah Is a great place to send your leaders and team members for business education. Every Tuesday night, Sarah does a live Gameplan Roundtable at 8:30 p.m. eastern where you can ask your business questions and win prizes!

FOLLOW THE DIAMONDS

Gameplan is a unique book, because it's a compilation. It's not just one system, there's a wide variety of strategies in this book. I took all the training and put it in one spot, so it was easy to find and affordable to duplicate. I am not the youngest Diamond, the smartest Diamond or the fastest Diamond to rank—I am just a mom of five with a love of Young Living. And yet I still made it to the top of Young Living.

That's the neat thing about this business! It doesn't require a network marketing degree or aromatherapy certifications or glitz and glamor. It doesn't require a huge friend circle or an extroverted personality. It just takes fight directed in three specific areas: share the oils, follow up to get people on Essential Rewards, and train your leaders. Those are the only three things that produce direct income growth. Don't lose your focus, keep moving, and you will get there.

Gameplan is not the only book out there to help you on your journey. I back any tool generated by a Young Living Diamond, because they have walked the road you're on. They have what it takes to go to the top. If you are going to be trained, you should be trained by someone who has attained where your heart is heading. Make sure they have what you want before you engage. Do they have the experience to back the tools?

Listed below you'll find inspiration, strategy, and maybe a dose of courage to step into places you've been afraid to step. One word of warning thought–don't take any tool—including Gameplan—and use it as an excuse not to act on your business. I firmly believe that the talent lies in you, and not in any system, book, or tool. If there was a magic Diamond veggie cap, I'd be the first to put it in your hand! But it takes grit, focus and fight. Stay focused and build this thing brick by brick. You have what it takes deep within you! You are a DIAMOND RISING!

TOOLS FROM DIAMONDS

Books:

Monique McClean
> *shop.ohmyoils.com*
> 21 Days of Prayer
> Let's Talk Oils (Volume 1 and 2)
> Let's Talk Comp Plan

Erin Rodgers

oilsupplystore.com
Savvy Beauty Booklet
Starter kit brochures, postcards, get rolling kits

Jordan Schrandt

jordanschrandt.com, discoverlsp.com
Do The Hard Work
Funnel Your Focus
The Welcome Book
Young Living Lifestyle
We Miss You Book
Men of Young Living
Farmhouse Movement (magazine)

Melissa Poepping

thechemicalfreehome.com
Before Beauty: Your Ultimate Guide to Unstoppable
Confidence
Femme Fatal
Chemical Free Home–House Keeping
Chemical Free Home–Face & Body
Chemical Free Home–Baby & Mommy

Debra Raybern

growinghealthyhomes.com
Gentle Babies
Road to Royal
Road to Wellness
Art of Blending
Nutrition 101 (with Sera Johnson, Laura Hopkins, and Karen Hopkins)

Rhonda Favano

growinghealthyhomes.com
Conquering Toxin Emotions
Conquering Toxin Emotions workbook
Conquering Toxin Emotions Self Discovery Journal

Dr. David Stewart

discoverlsp.com
Healing Oils of the Bible
Chemistry of Essential Oils

Sarah Harnisch

oilabilityteam.com
Gameplan (available in print and audio book)
Gameplan workbook

Your Gameplan—mini
Fearless (available in print and audio book)
Gameplanner

Vicki and Chris Opfer

discoverlsp.com
Essential Sharing

Teri Secrest

terisecrestbooks.com
Eating Out of Heaven's Garden
How To Be A Stunning Success in Network Marketing
How Big Is Your Wave
A Biblical Perspective on Essential Oils

Karen Hopkins

growinghealthyhomes.com
ABC's of Building A Young Living Organization

Beth Whicker

amazon.com
Downline Whispering

Eric Walton

amazon.com
Downline Leadership

Bethany Shipley

bethanyshipley.com
Diamond Workbook

Amanda Brunngraeber

amandabrunngraeber.com
Dreaming Big Making Plans

Amanda Uribe

madesimplypure.com
Grow
Dig
The Harvest Planner
Journal

Jennifer Howard

amazon.com
Your Ultimate Life Plan

Katie Ganger

discoverlsp.com
Aroma Breathe

Jake Dempsey

drivenforsuccess.com
Driven for Success
#ladyboss Initiative

Chelsa Bruno

funeasyrecipesbook.com
Fun Easy Recipes

Scott Schuler

amazon.com
MAN UP: It's Hard to Resist a Bad Boy...
Even More So a Good Man

Connie McDanel

the-oily-essential-co.myshopify.com
Aroma Home
Aroma Clean
Aroma Family

Richard Bliss Brooke

richardbrooke.com
4 Year Career

Kimmy Brooke

kimmybrooke.com
4 Year Career for Women

Open Facebook Groups:

Madison Vining—My Happy Hangout
Jim Bob Haggerton—Essential Oil Club (EOC)
Echo Summer Hill—The RHINOlution
Jessica Laney Petty—RCD365
Stephanie Moram & Jamie Flaman—Keep It Oily Canada
Sandi Boudreau—Twelve Days of Diamonds
Jami Baker Nato—The Oil Collective
Vanessa Rae Romero—30 Day NingXia Red Cheers Challenge

Websites:

Lindsey Bernat Gremont
    homemademommy.net
Sandi and Kyler Boudreau
    outergain.com
Sarah Harnisch
    oilabilityteam.com
Vicki Opfer
    YLFamily.com

Casey Wiegand & Danielle Burkleo
> *thewellshopco.com*

LeeTen Tan Anderson
> *thescentsibletribe.com*

April Pointer, Danette Goodyear, Alyssa Francis, Melissa Poepping
> *ylfasttrack.com*   Password is ylfast

April Pointer, Jen Jordan, Leah Rockwell, Kristy Dempsey
> *operationsilverbootcamp.com*

Tom Nikkola
> *tomnikkola.com*

Men's Advance
> *www.eatsleepadvance.com*

Apps:

Jake Dempsey
> Oily Tools – *oilytools.com* (now run by Young Living)
> Oily Events – *oilyevents.com*
> Project Broadcast – *projectbroadcast.com*

DVD's:

Dr. Oli Wenker

biocodeacademy.com
Essential Oils Symposium (38 speakers)

Shannon Hudson

shannonhudsononyl.com
Sleek With Me
Hormones and You
Building for Diamond 101

Sarah Harnisch

oilabilityteam.com
Gameplan Live DVD
The Complete Gameplan Training System (7 DVD's)
Intro to Young Living DVD set

Online Coaching/Training:

Melissa Poepping   BASi6
> *melissapoepping.com*

Christie Rose   Instagram class
> *theoilysquad.com/instagram-101*

Dr. David Stewart   The CARE Program
> *raindroptraining.com*

Misc:

Kari Rae Lewis (mugs)
   makesnofrankincense.com

This list will be updated as new products from Diamonds become available at oilbilityteam.com.

YOUNG LIVINGEASE: LEARN THE LANGUAGE

YOUNG LIVING BUSINESS TERMS

Personal Volume (PV): Many products sold by Young Living have a PV amount. Not all products are dollar for dollar, so if you're trying to hit a certain rank, make sure you check the PV of an item and not its retail price. (Tax and shipping are not added into PV either). PV is one of the requirements for ranking within the compensation plan, and it accumulates throughout each commission period.

Organization Group Volume (OGV): OGV is the entire sales volume of a sales organization. This can be determined by calculating the sum of the PV of all the distributors and customers within a particular organization. OGV accumulates throughout each monthly commission period, and re-sets to zero with the start of a new month.

Personal Group Volume (PGV): For Silver or higher ranks in the compensation plan, PGV comes into play. It is determined by the sales volume of the organization directly supported by the distributor. Basically, it's all the volume outside of people who have ranked Silver or above. It is the sum of PV from the distributor down to, but not including, the next Silver or higher rank for each leg of the sales organization. If you are out there selling, you'll not have any problem hitting the 1,000 PGV requirement once you hit Silver (1,000 of your volume must be outside your legs). Let me explain to you how this works. If you have three people outside your legs that are spending 300 PV each, and you spend 100 PV to get your check, you will have 1,000 PGV. If you have nine people outside your two Silver legs spending 100 PV each, and you spend 100 PV to get your paycheck, you will have 1,000 PGV.

Sales Organization: Also known as a downline, this encompasses all members located beneath a particular distributor. This includes the distributor and all levels within his or her organization.

Level: The position of a distributor within a sales organization. Those distributors who are immediately sponsored by another distributor would be considered the sponsoring distributor's first level. Those distributors who are sponsored by a distributor's first level would be considered that distributor's second level, and so on.

Enroller: The person responsible for personally introducing a new distributor to Young Living. Enrollers are eligible to qualify for financial bonuses, including the Fast Start and starter kit bonuses.

Sponsor: A new distributor's direct upline and main support. The sponsor may also be the enroller.

Upline: Any distributor above another distributor in a sales organization.

Customer: A member who chooses not to participate in the Young Living compensation plan, but desires to purchase the product at retail price for personal use. Customers need to be sponsored and enrolled by a current Young Living distributor.

Unilevel: Unilevel is a form of commission that is earned through the compensation plan. Qualifying distributors earn 8% on the sales volume, or PV, of each distributor on the first level within their organization, 5% on the second level, and 4% on the third through fifth levels.

Compression: In circumstances where a distributor does not meet the 100 PV qualification to earn commissions, his or her volume, if any, is combined, or "compressed," with all the volume of distributors down to and including the next qualifying distributor in the sales organization with at least 100 PV. For instance, if in the third level a distributor places an order of only 30 PV, then the fourth-level distributor's PV in the organization who has ordered 100 PV compresses up with the third level for payout purposes. This creates a single unilevel to be paid out with a total of 130 PV for that commission period. Compression maximizes compensation in cases where there are inactive distributors in an organization who may not be purchasing regularly but may have others below them who are doing so.

PV Minimum: In order to qualify for retail earnings and enroller-based bonuses, and to be considered "active," a distributor must maintain a monthly order of at least 50 PV. In order to qualify for a paycheck, a distributor must maintain a monthly order of at least 100 PV. If an account becomes inactive by dropping below 50 PV for a period of 12 consecutive months, the account will be dropped.

YOUNG LIVING RANKS

Star: In order to qualify as a Star in the compensation plan, a distributor must achieve 100 PV and 500 OGV within a commission period. As a Star, the distributor qualifies to receive compensation on the volume of three unilevels in his or her organization (paid at 8%, 5%, and 4%, respectively) in addition to any retail earnings. Stars may also qualify to receive the Fast Start, Starter Kit, and Rising Star Team bonuses.

Senior Star: In order to qualify as a Senior Star in the compensation plan, a distributor must achieve 100 PV and 2,000 OGV within a commission period. As a Senior Star, the distributor qualifies to receive compensation on the volume of four unilevels in his or her organization (paid at 8%, 5%, 4%, and

4%, respectively) in addition to any retail earnings. Senior Stars may also qualify to receive the Fast Start, Starter Kit, and Rising Star Team bonuses.

Executive: In order to qualify as an Executive, a distributor must achieve 100 PV, 4,000 OGV, and two separate legs with 1,000 OGV each within a commission period. As an Executive, the distributor qualifies to receive compensation on the volume of five unilevels within his or her organization (paid at 8%, 5%, 4%, 4%, and 4%, respectively) in addition to any retail earnings. Executives may also qualify for the Fast Start, Starter Kit, and Rising Star Team bonuses.

Silver: In order to qualify as Silver, a distributor must achieve 100 PV, 10,000 OGV, 1,000 PGV, and two separate legs with 4,000 OGV each within a commission period. As a Silver, the distributor qualifies to receive compensation on the volume of five unilevels within his or her organization (paid at 8%, 5%, 4%, 4%, and 4%, respectively), personal generation commissions (paid at 2.5%), generation commissions on 2 levels (paid at 3%), in addition to any retail earnings. Silvers may also qualify for the Fast Start, Starter Kit, and Generation Leadership bonuses.

Gold: In order to qualify as Gold, a distributor must achieve 100 PV, 35,000 OGV, 1,000 PGV, and three separate legs with 6,000 OGV each within a commission period. As a Gold, the distributor qualifies to receive compensation on the volume of five unilevels within his or her organization (paid at 8%, 5%, 4%, 4%, and 4%, respectively), personal generation commissions (paid at 2.5%), generation commissions on 3 levels (paid at 3%), in addition to any retail earnings. Golds may also qualify for the Fast Start, Starter Kit, and Generation Leadership bonuses.

Platinum: In order to qualify as Platinum, a distributor must achieve 100 PV, 100,000 OGV, 1,000 PGV, and four separate legs with 8,000 OGV each within a commission period. As Platinum, the distributor qualifies to receive compensation on the volume of five unilevels within his or her organization (paid at 8%, 5%, 4%, 4%, and 4%, respectively), personal generation commissions (paid at 2.5%), generation commissions on four levels (paid at 3%), in addition to any retail earnings. Platinums may also qualify for the Fast Start, Starter Kit, and Generation Leadership bonuses.

Diamond: In order to qualify as Diamond, a distributor must achieve 100 PV, 250,000 OGV, 1,000 PGV, and five separate legs with 15,000 OGV each within a commission period. As Diamond, the distributor qualifies to receive compensation on the volume of five unilevels within his or her organization (paid at 8%, 5%, 4%, 4%, and 4%, respectively), personal generation commissions (paid at 2.5%), generation commissions on five levels (paid at 3%), in addition to any retail earnings. Diamonds may also qualify for the Fast Start, Starter Kit, Generation Leadership, and Diamond Express Profit Sharing Pool bonuses.

Crown Diamond: In order to qualify as Crown Diamond, a distributor must achieve 100 PV, 750,000 OGV, 1,000 PGV, and six separate legs with 20,000 OGV each within a commission period. As Crown Diamond, the distributor qualifies to receive compensation on the volume of five unilevels within his or her organization (paid at 8%, 5%, 4%, 4%, and 4%, respectively), personal generation commissions (paid at 2.5%), generation commissions on six levels (paid at 3%), in addition to any retail earnings. Crown Diamonds may also qualify for the Fast Start, Starter Kit, Generation Leadership, and Diamond Express Profit Sharing Pool bonuses.

Royal Crown Diamond: In order to qualify as Royal Crown Diamond, a distributor must achieve 100 PV, 1,500,000 OGV, 1,000 PGV, and six separate legs with 35,000 OGV each within a commission period. As Royal Crown Diamond, the distributor qualifies to receive compensation on the volume of five unilevels within his or her organization (paid at 8%, 5%, 4%, 4%, and 4%, respectively), personal generation commissions (paid at 2.5%), generation commissions on six levels (six levels paid at 3% and 1% paid on the seventh level), in addition to any retail earnings. Royal Crown Diamonds may also qualify for the Fast Start, Starter Kit, Generation Leadership, and Diamond Express Profit Sharing Pool bonuses.

FAQ SECTION

Every Tuesday at 8:30 PM Eastern, I do a Facebook Gameplan roundtable for 30 minutes on our Facebook page, at Oil Ability with Sarah. I get on with tens of thousands of you and answer your questions about the business and about the book. Some fantastic questions have come in the past year since we released the book. We compiled the most common ones and put them in this brand new second edition section of Gameplan. These are based on leaders who have led teams through bootcamp or are doing one right now. I have picked the most common business questions that I see.

Do you have ideas on who to share with when you've exhausted your friend circles and you have no one who wants to have a class?

Yes. This issue is not your friend circles, it's your way of approaching your friends. One on-fire oiler is enough to ignite a Silvership. One on-fire oiler will be a megaphone for your business. So start with the simple act of igniting one person. Build the relationship. Make it about them, not about the sale of your kit. Ask them what their needs are. Drop seeds. Loan out product. And then stand down and watch it work. Make sure your follow up is good.

See "No One is Coming to Classes—Now What?" on page 127 for more on this topic!

I will tell you too—that when we first start in network marketing, we're so excited we can scare many of our closest friends and family members away, just with our passion. It's ok to return to them, tell them you are sorry for your initial approach, and ask for forgiveness. Then work to rebuild that relationship, and eventually, a need will arise that will require oils. Be there in that moment, without being pushy. It's ok to re-engage with people you have scared off.

If you truly have not one person left in your warm market that wants the oils, I'd recommend vendor events to meet new people.

See "Attend Vendor events" on page 83

People have asked how much I have made, and honestly it's very little. How do I collect business builders when I have no story?

Tell them you are just seriously starting your business. Then share stories of people that have done it. They don't always need to hear of your success to get interested. Get good at using third party tools. *Your Gameplan* is great because it shares a truly rags to riches story, eight reasons why Young Living is the best job on the earth, then gets them stacking up what they are doing now against a Young Living business. See if you can get them to read that first.

I also love to point people to the website at oilabilityteam.com, the "Start Here" button and "Sarah's Why". That is a good way to ignite just about anyone.

But if they need more 'proof' that they can do this, just go into your virtual office and show them the 450 Diamonds that have already done it. (You can find that under "benefits" and "global recognition.")

Your story is coming. But for now, lean on others that have done it. This falls under the same category as having to know it all to do the business. Just get good at using third party tools. "I don't have the answer to that, but here's where you can look." Point them to reference guides for medical questions, Gameplan for business questions, the D. Gary Young book for purity questions as well as the Seed to Seal website. You don't need to be the expert or the success story. You just need enough passion to ignite a leader and show them it can be done. And you need enough passion to believe in them, even if you're still building your own belief.

Can you give me specific steps on how to grow my business?

Absolutely. This book.

How do you actually 'build' a leader?

Besides giving vision and training them, which is what this book is for, it really comes down to one word—serve. With my team, my leaders before me. Their kit sales matter more to me than mine, their few moments to vent matters more to me than what I am doing in that moment—the simple pause, the listening ear, the encouraging text. It goes so very far. If you launch your business with an ear for your leaders, it's amazing how far it will go. Use the same training so you're all on the same page, create a team culture and do rallies and events together, but above all, wash their feet—just like Jesus did. Serve. I picked up over 800 business builders in the first two years after getting my kit. I didn't have a system to follow. I just met needs and listened. Then grow together, right beside your leaders.

What do you gift your leaders when they rank up?

One of my goals when I was a teenager was to live on 10% and tithe 90%—the reverse tithe. I have had that focus for more than 20 years, and this is the first year that John and I have been able to make leaps and bound toward it. So my giving is probably a bit higher than the average leader. But I will tell you what I do, and you choose to take it and run with it, or take bits and pieces and make it your own.

I believe that until Silver, every uprank should get business tools. I think it's wonderful to hand out diffuser necklaces and pretty bracelets and spa days, but my number one goal as their Diamond upline is tools to make the next rank easier than the rank they just achieved. Once they hit Silver, my leaders have a pretty good idea where this goes. Many have left second jobs (or even their primary job), relieved the burden on their spouse and have more free time. They are not stopping until Royal Crown Diamond. They have caught Diamond fever. But it takes tenacity and tools to keep them focused.

This is what I do on my own team. Cherry pick what works for you!

Star:

      One Toxin Free Life cd
      One Essential Oils 101 cd
      One "Your Gameplan" mini book
      One copy of Fearless and a Fearless calendar
      One free month of Oily Tools subscription
      One Nitro

Senior Star:

      Supplies for making ten purple bags (flyers, cd's, mini's and Fearless)
      Two Gameplan books
      Two Gameplan workbooks (to train 2 to train 2)
      Intro To Young Living DVD (to play if they have timid leaders)
      A sample of Pure Protein complete and my Mango Smoothie recipe

Executive:

      Supplies for making 20 purple bags
      Two Gameplan books
      Two Gameplan workbooks (to train 2 to train 2)
      Gameplanner to keep them organized for 12 months. (Of the 43 Silvers on our team right now, 36 made Silver in Six because of focus and organization!)
      NingXia and Nitro packets

Silver:

      Six Gameplan books
      Six Gameplan workbooks
      Desert Mist diffuser
      Gameplan training 7-DVD set
      Private coaching session to strategize to Gold
      Fifty Fearless and Fearless calendars
      Aromacomplete case (if it's in the budget!)
      NingXia and Nitro packets and wolfberry crisp bars

What am I doing with these gifts? Giving them tools to grow. There are three things that lead to direct OGV growth: sharing (purple bags), getting people on Essential Rewards (Fearless and the calendar), and training your leaders (Gameplan and the workbook). The tools make it easier to rank up.

Did I do all of this when I was a Star? Absolutely not. I gave roll ons and coaching sessions and hand-written notes. Live within your budget. But as your check grows, set a portion aside to say thank you to your leaders. They will duplicate that generosity to their leaders. Are gifts necessary to grow? No. Will they make you rank faster? In some cases, perhaps, and in others, no. Are they an act of love and generosity to your leaders, and appreciation? Yes. That is why I give.

Do you have a list of resources to give people who are still convinced that buying their oils from a super market is a good idea!??

I will shoot straight with you here—you can only save so many people. If you have taught the 101 and explained purity, if you have told them that they get what they pay for—that they are using oils to get rid of chemicals, so why would they use an oil laden with chemicals—and they still think $7 Frankincense is a good idea, kick the dust off your feet and move on. Don't waste time and energy and live in a land of drama with people that are insistent that all oils are equal. You are in the oils business, and you know better. Plant gentle seeds with them and move on.

If it's the first time you're approached by a person, and they genuinely seem interested but there isn't enough "science" on Seed to Seal to make them comfortable, there is a tool generated by Jen O'Sullivan that I love. It's a chart of all the major oils companies in the world pitted against one another for purity, sourcing, number of farms, distillation methods, etc. You can find that chart at 31oils.com.

I find it a struggle handling questions of how to show those interested which oils to use for different issues. I feel like our tongues are so tied up by the FDA. I need help trying to help those that want it and still staying compliant.

Here is my trick: just use what's on the Young Living website. What they've written has been through a team of lawyers and it's safe to say. Young Living has knocked it out of the ballpark with YL Central. It has scripts, videos, PowerPoints, and all sorts of things you can share now if you don't have the words to say. Just log into your Virtual Office and click on "Member Resources", and you'll find it.

Let me put in one more word of encouragement here, too. Don't live in the land of fear. The Lord has brought this business to you, and He will make a way for you to share. It says in Scripture to be anxious for nothing. When we live in a land of fear, we aren't trusting that God made no mistakes when He put you on the team you're on, brought your leaders to you, filled your classes and gave you a passion for the things He created. You can do this! Just learn the lingo. Instead of diagnosing, say, "I don't know about that. I've never dealt with that before. Why don't you take home this oil and my diffuser and see how you feel?" That one line gets you off the hook. If you want to up your game, add in, "here's a place where you can begin your research" (and point to a reference guide). Now they are standing on their own two feet, as well, and looking things up.

I could use some tips on how to invite, teach, and lead men. Obviously, this is a very female driven company which is amazing! But I would love some guidance on how to help men be interested in the oils and the business!

Can I be totally frank with you? I do nothing different. Absolutely nothing. Men are faced with the same needs for respiratory support, immune support, personal care products and supplements. I teach my 101 class to men and women and get the same response. I'd say, after the class ask them why they came, and build relationships with them. Meet their needs with oils from the starter kit. That will get you farther than any "man" script!

About purple bags... when one is first starting out with the business do we include sample product? You have mentioned not spending more than you make. Is this something we add once our bonus checks start coming in?

Yes. I firmly believe in not spending more than you make. When I first started, I could not afford a $20 Vistaprint order for business cards, so I typed out my information, printed it on regular white paper and cut it out with scissors and handed it out. I took the first six months of my check and put it in my gas tank to get to classes. Your number one responsibility as you climb to Silver is to teach classes. You can't find leaders without classes. You can't get people on Essential Rewards without classes. You need to get that script in front of faces.

So how can you do purple bags on the cheap? Print the textable classes on your business cards and direct them to listen to it. Print off the freebies on the oilabilityteam.com website under purple bags and use those: the how to order sheet, the cover page. I'd hold off on samples until you have more income. If you feel convicted, put one drop of Peppermint in the palm of their hand while they are at class. That's my "wow" oil. That's a lot cheaper than giving away all your Share It bottles, ordering more, and buying carrier oils— and going through a bottle or two of oil each night of teaching. Be faithful with the small things, and the Lord will make you ruler over more.

Where do I sign people up to begin to build legs when I have no established leaders? How do I get people on ER so I can build under them and no one loses commission?

That's a great question! I got it so often that I added a whole section on Rising Star bonuses on the new edition of this book. Go check out "A

Young Living Strategy Guide on Where to Sign New Oilers" on page 181 for structuring.

To get people on ER utilize Fearless. See "Follow Up For Those Who Got a Kit" on page 116

What should a day look like when you are doing your business full time from home?

Eighty percent of your time should be spent prospecting. So if you're home full time, put that time to good use by teaching classes. The other 20% should be spent on behind the scenes stuff: training your leaders, teaching classes other than the 101 for your new members, doing follow up mailings, marketing your upcoming classes, possibly running a business or product Facebook page, etc. Always ask yourself if what you are doing is the best use of your time, and if it will lead to income producing activities. If they answer is no—why are you doing it? Cut back on those things and focus on the three things that build your OGV and make it last.

What does my day look like? I work about ten hours a week right now as a Diamond (but I do delegate a lot of my mailings to people that I pay). Eighty percent of my time is spent in training and teaching. I believe even as a Diamond that you can lose your rank when you stop teaching! The other 20% is what I just mentioned above, but mostly leader training and follow up mailings.

Follow up and social media: How do I follow up after doing a FB Live class?

The real work begins when the class ends, because follow up can be time consuming. But many, many Diamonds have been successful building on-line—it works. Start by going through your class and finding every "like" and every "comment". Message each person based on what they said or liked and start building the relationship. It may be something like "you liked the post about my dog in the class tonight. Do you have any dogs?" (Don't say 'want me to send you a sample for your dog?' Or 'want a Young Living starter kit for your dog?' You aren't there yet. You always start by asking questions to build relationship, not selling the kit.) Go for a back and forth exchange, asking questions about them, and lead into a sample, a tool, more knowledge, or the kit if they are ready for it.

How do I give a 1 on 1? A lot of my classes are 1 on 1 and it feels awkward since I'm talking to them like I would a class. It needs to be more intimate—but I'm not sure how to do that.

It may feel awkward to use a script when you are face to face with just one person, often a close friend or family member. But the great thing about scripts is that they are duplicatable—anyone can read a script. So if use one during a one-on-one, your new member will see that all they have to do to share is read a script!

There are two things that I've done to make it feel more natural and personal. First—practice. Seriously! Get that bad boy out and read it in front of a mirror 20 times. You'll have that sucker down pat. I'm not telling you to memorize it—that's not duplicatable. But if you have a good idea where you're going, you don't have to look down so much. Then what I do is highlight the first sentence of each paragraph and just glance down and then up again to give details.

The second thing is to start with your story. Don't use the script for that. Just share your passion. Why did you get a kit? Why have you fallen in love with it? Where did your journey begin? What prompts you to share them with everyone? Facts tell, stories sell. You start with your reasons, and they will fall in love.

What about people that really just want to be retail customers? There really are those people out there.

May we agree to disagree on this? I don't ever believe in selling one oil. Let me tell you why. Oils have been a course correction for my family. If anything, I don't live in fear anymore. I know I have what it takes on my oils shelf to calm my kiddos down and support multiple systems of their body when the need arises. But beyond that, I have kicked chemicals out of my home.

You see, oils aren't one bottle. They are a lifestyle. If you communicate that, you have nailed the entire reason why this network marketing company is the best in the world: consumable product. I don't need a bunch of pots and pans every month, or lots of books—but I use oils every single day, many times a day. I wash my hair with oil infused products and make smoothies for breakfast with Pure Protein complete. I have the diffuser running all day and all night, and include Vitality oils and supplements for wellness. It's part of the deal. You don't kick some poisons out of your home, but keep others. Don't train one bottle of oil. Don't train the starter kit. Train the lifestyle. That's the missing link in getting people on Essential Rewards and training them in the playground of oiling.

What do I say to them? "I can't train you how to clean out your cabinets with one bottle of oil. The Premium Starter Kit is a playground. It's got a diffuser— which is the fastest way to get oils into your system—and 11 full bottles of oil. Think you won't use it? Do you need respiratory support? Immune support? Joint and muscle support? That's what's in this kit. Snag it, and I am committed to training you every step of the way. We'll start with lifestyle training and Fearless. I know there's a part of you that doesn't want the garbage in your house. We'll do this together, one room at a time, one bottle at a time."

Why don't you do more themed classes (health, beauty, kids, pets, etc)?

Because they don't sell Starter Kits. There are four Premium Starter kits on Young Living's website: the oils kit, Savvy, NingXia, and Thieves. If you're not driving to one of those four kits, you're not setting up wholesale accounts. I have included a 101 and there is a Toxin Free Life Class on my website. As much as I adore Oils of Ancient Scripture (it's still my favorite class to teach!) I don't teach it often. If someone sits in that class, the likelihood of them getting a $185 starter kit, a $200 Ancient Scripture kit, and getting on Essential Rewards is pretty remote. Always funnel to the PSK's. That's where your longevity is.

How do I reengage business-minded members when they say they want to do this but then won't take any action?

Two tools I use are the mini—*Your Gameplan*—and the "Sarah's Why" video on the oilabilityteam.com website. That's under the "Start Here" button. Have them watch the video and read the mini, then meet with them for lunch and talk about their why. Talk about their need for freedom. Talk about where they are. Listen to their needs. Then offer gentle coaching to start teaching classes. If they won't commit, kick the dust off your feet and move on. Be so busy teaching 101 classes—and gathering leaders through them—that you don't have time to notice the naysayers.

If you call someone to invite them to a class you are hosting what do you say on that initial call? Then when you call back to remind them about the class and you get voicemail what message do you leave?

I never leave voicemail messages. It gives them a chance to opt out. I wait until I get an actual person, then I focus on the relationship. My first question isn't "My name is Sarah Harnisch, would you like to buy my starter kit???" (bats eyes). It's usually "talk to me about how you have been. What's going on in your life?" Then I tailor my oils response based on their need.

How do I get my spouse on board the Oil Train?!?

Oh this is a simple one! Show him the paycheck! Most spouses don't want you working harder and making less. Commit to one class a week and see where it leads. Then show him the fruit. Don't tell him how great oils are or how wonderful the business is—just show him results.

My struggle is getting three to invite 50. I know you are from a small town as well, but when those three people all know the same 50 people, how do you make that work???

You are overthinking it. It's not about the size of the town. It's about the art of the relationship. One person has a reach far beyond your little town. They know people all over the United States, and sometimes in different countries.

What happens when that one person gets excited about oils—and their home starts to look just like yours, with Thieves dish soap on the counter and shampoo in every shower? They get passion. And all it takes is the passion of one to build a team. That's where all the magic starts.

If you have 50 people in your town, that's a chance to build a pretty large organization with their contacts list. It's because they don't only know people in the town. They have been to school elsewhere, maybe had jobs far away, they have family members that don't live there, etc. All those faces could be part of your team. Don't see your town as a single town. See it as the city that could be your organization, if only you start a relationship with one.

If you walk out your door and see humans on the other side, those humans should be on your team. I think the bigger thing is fear. We fear what people will think of us, we fear rejection. We fear that we can't make this work. We feel the pressure of the need and desire to rank up, but get paralyzed by the art of building relationships and talking to people we do not know.

Here's the thing: you have a wide world of wisdom under your belt. You have been gifted something precious in the knowledge that you have of oils. It's knowledge that can help every person out there. When you do not share with them, you are robbing them of something precious that they need to care for their families. Your love for them must be greater than your fear of rejection. That's how you share oils.

I just don't know anyone. I live in a small town, and there's one church. There are eight distributors in that one church. What do I do? Everyone I know is oiling.

The real issue is that you must get better at asking questions. You do know people, but you are not connecting with them. How do I know that you know people? Is every family member and every friend and every social media contact on your team? If not, you have untapped resources.

The secret to connecting with people is asking better questions. Answer questions with questions. For example: "why is the kit so expensive?" I'd respond with "I spend money every week to take care of my family. This is just moving the money from a store into a place where there are healthier choices. Tell me one thing you struggle with—one thing you'd love to work on for your family's wellness, and let's start from that place." Ask a question. Then offer an oil from that place. The reason they say it's expensive is simply because they do not know they need it.

I have yet to see a family using Thieves that is craving the chemicals back in their home. It's simple knowledge to walk from yuck to purity. Meet them where they are and respond to their objections with questions. Find common ground and start there, then offer an oil. Here is another good question to ask, "what questions do you have of me?" Always put the ball in their court. Meet them in the place where they are, without judgement.

How do you handle it, or what do you say when a level 1 leg that's huge decides to stop her association with YL and go to another MLM? How do you recover that leg?

Your heart always needs to be for the distributor. When I first was building to Silver, I lost my level one leg twice as that leader decided to jump to another MLM. I believe with my whole heart that Young Living is the best company in the world, because we have a product that is consumable that people need every single day. It's easier to share than pans or books, because you need oils and oil infused products every day, all day long. But not everyone catches that vision and that's ok! If you try to force them into the business when their heart is elsewhere, you will lose more than a business builder—you may lose a friendship, too, and that is a far bigger cost. Dig farther down into your organization and find another leader—under that leader—that is willing to work. And work with them to keep that leg afloat.

I do explain how I feel, gently, one time, to that distributor that wants to leave. If they still have no interest in continuing, kick the dust out from under your feet, and move on. Then when you speak to them in the future, have no animosity. Love them in the place where they are.

How do I follow up with prospects from a vendor event, kiosk, or a casual meeting in the grocery line? How do I get them to respond to my voice mail, email, or hand-written notes (this also applies to current team members)?

Part of the issue with connecting is not giving an expectation during the initial contact. If it's a completely cold market person, it's usually awkward to ask for a cell phone number, address, or email. The average person gets 115 emails a day anyway, that's not an effective way to build a network marketing business. Your message will go in a pile. Instead, Facebook friend them. Give them something—like a purple bag, a sample, a mini or a Fearless. Then expect something back in the exchange. Tell them the date you'll call and check in with them. Then check in on that date. As soon as I walk away, I text their name to myself and set a reminder on my phone to touch base—then I don't lose them in my sea of friends on Facebook.

A Facebook 'friending' is very effective, because it's informal. If they truly didn't want to connect with you, then can unfriend you when you walk away and nothing is lost. There's a distancing with it that makes them feel safe— much more than giving out a cell phone number to a total stranger (though we get in the car with random strangers who work for Uber—so who knows, maybe it will eventually be acceptable!).

If you set the expectation that you've given a gift and will be checking in, they are usually expecting your call. I don't ever leave voicemail messages, because I don't want to appear to be a pest. I simply try again later if I can't get through. I will try for a couple of weeks at different times of day, and if I'm still not getting through, I let it go and move on to the next person. Be so busy making contacts that you don't have time to hunt down all the rogue leads.

When people say, "send me the link!," and then they still don't sign up... how do I keep following up then, without being pushy?

I just answered that above. I'll give it a few weeks, and if I'm still not getting anywhere, I let it go. But if they are not a totally cold lead (maybe they are a mom you see at soccer practice), I'll do what I call seed dropping. That means you'll have a few conversations that don't have the word essential oils in them. You're not actively pursuing them. After that, watch for a need. Offer an oil. And check in.

I have a really good example of it from one of my executives, Colleen. This is a text she sent me this morning:

"I signed a friend up over a year ago. I taught him about the oils, gave him pamphlets, DVD's, digital recordings, and talked to him occasionally about life and oils. He still decided to go inactive about four months ago. I finally got to see him a few weeks ago, and as soon as I walked into his home, I grabbed his oils and started using them. He has an 18-month-old who was not feeling the best. I also brought my Thieves cleaner and started using it. He immediately fell in love and started asking about it. As a parting gift, I left a few packets of NingXia, which his wife used last night. She felt depleted. I oiled her like I oiled his daughter. His wife woke up this morning and said "order that stuff. I don't care about the cost." He is calling Monday to go active with a Thieves Premium Starter Kit and is starting Essential Rewards with NingXia"

I can summarize her work with two simple hashtags: #carrythievescleaner #livewiththemtosellit

No, for real—this falls under the category of why I wrote *Fearless*. You need to train the lifestyle, not the Starter Kit. That's what makes that book so awesome. He didn't know how to use the products he had. If you train lifestyle, label reading, researching, Simple Swap, etc., you will grow on-fire oilers. Or go live with them for a night. That works too.

What's the best way to approach an existing business? Is there a script for sharing our products with chiropractors, dentists, massage therapists, etc.?

Yes. The 101 script.

Seriously.

I use it for EVERYTHING. Just because you are a chiropractor doesn't mean you don't need to know the 'who-where-what-when-why-how' of oils. Start with the basics. Start with your story. Lead with your heart. Lead with your passion. It's not the script they are after—it's you. If you can tell a story with conviction, purpose, passion, and confidence—it doesn't matter who is listening. Start from that place.

In places of business, I never offer professional accounts, because they lose their chance at a downline, and that's the greatest blessing. I simply get their family to fall in love with oils first. I work on that relationship with the owner. Get them reading *Fearless* and doing the challenges. Get the diffuser going in their home. Oil up their kiddos. In the interim, I encourage them to keep a diffuser going in their office constantly—that's the best sales tool you have in a business environment. And I keep a basket with purple bags right by it that says "want to learn more about this diffuser?" It will draw a LOT of attention. Put the sponsor and enroller numbers of the team members you want to build under in the bags, and build relationships with each person that shows up on your team.

How do I ask someone to host a class for me?

It depends who you are asking. If you're asking an on-fire oiler that you have already built a relationship with, it's simple. Tell them you want to train them how to use their kit. Ask them to invite a few friends and promise a hostess basket. I put some Thieves cleaner in mine, a roll-on of an oil not in the starter kit, a couple cd's with classes like *Essential Oils 101* or *Toxin Free Life*, *Fearless*, and a couple samples like Thieves cough drops or Cool Azul pain cream.

If it's someone who is not signed yet, then you have to take a step back and build the relationship first. If they are a friend, it's simple—ask them to do something to help your family business. Get an oil on their body based on a need that they have and ask if they will host. If they are not a friend, then you need to spend more time on the relationship aspect. A totally raw conversation might look something like this:

"Have you had any exposure to essential oils?"

"Yes, I think my mom's friend sells them."

"Tell me what's going on in your life right now. If you could list your top three wellness struggles, what would they be?"

"Stress is definitely one. I have a high stress job."

"Boy do I understand that! I am a mom of three! (Meet them where they are). I have something that you may like. Smell this. (offer Stress Away). Try it at work tomorrow and see if it takes the edge off your day."

Then check in—and see how they are doing the next day. That opens a door for them to get a kit. If they are not ready yet, offer to teach a class—either in their home or in yours, so you can give them some basic aromatherapy training. It's all in the art of the relationship and meeting needs. If you are meeting their needs, it does not matter whether you are getting them started with a starter kit or asking to set up a class—the language is the same. You want to educate, to train, and to meet them where they are.

Help! All the local farmer's markets require that you sell things that you have grown or made. Where do I find events that will welcome an oils booth?

Yes, there are a lot of vendor events that are crafts or pro only. But they are not your only option. You will have to get creative and do some more homework to find events that will work for you. Look into concert settings, conferences, trade shows, state and county fairs, and definitely call the Chamber of Commerce for your town and the ten towns around your town. They will have ideas of festivals and upcoming events. I just did an event this weekend that was set up at a christian concert with 2,000 women. They wanted a vendor hall—and there I was.

There was also a vendor event that told one of my leaders 'no'—that it was "crafts only", so I asked if I could make my case before their jurist panel. After appearing before them, they allowed to let my leader in—and she built from 8,000 OGV to 42,000 OGV in 18 months with that once a week Saturday fair. Get creative in how you ask, make a strong case, always have your eye out for festivals and fairs, and make some phone calls to make sure you're not missing local events.

How do I get my team to come to monthly classes/meetings? They always have excuses, do I just let them go?

Develop the skill of listening and vision casting. When I first get to know a leader, I ask their why. What do they want in their life? Where are they going? What is their bucket list? What do they want out of this business? Then gently, from time to time, remind them of their why. Remind them of the reason they began in the first place.

It's also really good to encourage attendance at events. Events always pump up my team. It may be a Gameplan Live event near you, or Go Pro, or an event from a Young Living Diamond like Elevate or Ignite. Set them on fire. And do it with all the other leaders around them. That's social proof, when they get to see everyone else fired up too, and hear their stories of how they have ranked. They begin to believe it's possible.

I believe the greatest weapon that Satan has in his arsenal against us is busyness and distraction. That's what leads to a lack of focus and puts your team on the road to giving up. Plan or attend #ylunites rallies, do events, do team classes, do retreats with your leaders. Let them grow in community with one another so they are constantly poured into by people that believe in this business. Encourage them to get some daily mindset training (see "Train your brain" on page 140) They need to get their head in the realm of possibility. When you get them dreaming, they will fight. A leader without vision goes nowhere.

What do you say to people who are content with other oils? It breaks my heart to know they're using inferior oils.

Your heart is big and your motive is good. But not everyone is ready to hear. I know you've heard me say it so many times—but it goes back to the art of building the relationship first. Eric Worre is one of my favorite network marketing trainers, and he once said that when you first start your business, you're so excited about it that you are like a puppy that is potty training. You piddle in every corner of the room. You spew information out to every person in your friend circle without concern of where they are. Sometimes you have to go back and fix those relationships. Apologize, stand down, have a few conversations without bringing up oils, wait for their need and make an offer—but only if they are ready.

I did this with my brother. For two years I sent him samples and big baskets at Christmas. He wasn't having it! When I came to visit, his hand went up in my face and said "don't mention Young Living." I had piddled in his corner! I did not meet him where he was. I only offered my need, not his need. But a later conversation led to getting the smoke smell out of his basement, which then became a starter kit, and he is now an Executive halfway to Silver.

They may not be ready for what you have to offer right now. And that's totally ok! Keep moving, and wait until the right opportunity to meet their needs.

What's your favorite oil for getting people's attention fast in line at the grocery store or at vendor events?

Peppermint is my wow oil. A sniff of peppermint is a memorable experience that it gets attention fast. I put one drop in the center of their hand and let them experience it for themselves.

What do you say to when you follow up with contacts you got at a vendor event?

"Thank you for coming to ___ event! I am so glad that our paths crossed. Young Living has changed my life. Tell me why you checked that you'd like more information on the card I gave you. What's going on right now with your health and wellness?"

Listen, respond, offer a sample, send a purple bag, make contact for the kit. Let your passion, belief, warmth, vision, and desire for them to be blessed with oils come out in your tone of voice. Relationship all stems from authenticity.

Do you struggle with authenticity? Try inviting *you*. Re-recruit yourself. Look in the mirror and use your own script on yourself. What would get your attention? Use those words. People need to hear the passion in your voice. They need to see that you are certain. That you have composure. That you can guide them where they want to go. You portray that through your voice, eye contact, tone, passion, belief, and most importantly—your story. Use it as a tool to connect.

What do you say to follow up after handing out the *Your Gameplan* mini?

I thank them for coming to the class. And then I stand down and ask for their story. "What would you do if you made an extra $1,000/month? What is your bucket list? Why would you do this? What is your biggest dream?" Ask leading business questions, then ask if they have 30 minutes to do a Teacher Training where you can show them how simple this is—without large friend circles, lots of time, or a big bank account.

I have stalled out. I am not sure I am able to do this business. How do I get momentum and motivation again?

You lose motivation when you get comfortable with a rank. You lose momentum when you slip into leadership mode. If you let your team do the work and forget that 80% of your time in this business NEEDS to be spent prospecting. Sharing with new people is how you built to the rank that you have already—you must never stop doing that one activity!

If you go months without selling a kit, that's how you lose your mojo. It's said that 7-figure earners invite as many as seven to ten people a day to take a look at their opportunity. That's seven people a day that you're building relationships with, dropping seeds, leaving purple bags, and oiling up. Keep the initial conversation short and lead them to a tool, like the mini, the textable classes, *Fearless*, or the CD's that they can listen to in their car.

You should always be inviting. The day you stop doing that, your business slips. You are either growing or you are shrinking. If you're not prospecting, you're shrinking. The key is consistency. You can't invite people one day a month. It's got to be something you get into the practice of doing regularly, because it's more important than any other thing you do for your business. It leads to kit sales and keeps you moving forward.

Help! I believe this works, but what would you say to those of us so mentally and emotionally exhausted from life—divorce, etc. that do not have anything left to give past their day job, children and surviving?

Oh weary warrior, I was you. I was the momma up at 3 a.m. to work, 52 weeks a year. I was the beaten down traveler. I was the mom of an autistic high-needs son. I was at the brink of collapse. I know that place like it was so real and so raw that it was yesterday. There are moments when I still pause and ask myself if I'm truly free of those burdens!

As I write this, I'm on the Diamond Retreat in Banff, Canada—looking out at the Rockies. I pinch myself and wonder if this life truly is the life the Lord has laid out for me. Can it be real? Will I stay humble—and give the glory to the Lord, or soak it up for myself? Can I stay momma and still be a millionaire? I have so many thoughts running through my head. Our life has been completely changed and altered forever because of the hands of Gary Young and the incredible corporate staff at Young Living.

May I offer some gentle wisdom? There is no release where you are. There is only decades more of pain, frustration, insecurity, exhaustion, and loss of hope. If your feet stay in those waters, you stay in a place of stagnation and weariness. You are looking at decades more of emotional turmoil, mental exhaustion and physical collapse. I know deep in my heart that is not the life you want for yourself.

Start by putting good things in your mind. Separate yourself from the things that tear you down. Look over your life at the things that drag you into the deep, dark places—and stand back. It may be a difficult marriage, friends with no vision, or wayward adult kids. Step back. Allow yourself personal distance. Spend more time with those that inspire you. It was once said that you are the combination of your five closest friends. Who do you let in?

Once you have cut toxic relationships out, start pouring into YOU. Start filling your head with mindset training that will give you hope. I gave you a list of my favorite mindset training in Chapter 13, "Keys to Confidence" on page 137, and there is a list of Diamond resources in "Appendix O: Follow the Diamonds" on page 297 too. Start on Youtube—do something free, and get lost in hope. I'd also encourage you to get your nose in the Bible. That's where I find my greatest source of hope! Just start reading, even if you don't know what you are doing. The lines of that book have ancient wisdom and truth that have pulled me from some of my darkest places. Read it cover to cover, then do it again.

You can slowly put one foot in front of the other. But it takes one thing: courage. You have to see this life for yourself. You have to imagine your check, the freedom from emotional baggage, you have to WANT it for yourself. It's not hard to fight once the vision is in place. So head to your Gameplan workbook and work on your vision board. Allow yourself to dream. You may have been hurt ten thousand times. But you don't need to stay there. You are the one that controls where your feet and your mind go. Start walking.

You know what is on the other side. If I could, sweet one, I would pick you up and carry you there myself! This momma from the projects knows pain and rejection and hurt. If I had a magic Diamond veggie cap that would release all that pain and toss ranks at your feet, I'd hand it to you right away. But the truth is, the first step is knowing you were made for more. The first step is allowing yourself to picture freedom for your family. The first step starting to dream. Writing it out. Letting your mind go to the places of where this goes. Vision leads to belief. And belief leads to action. And then action makes your vision truth. But the first step is to move from where you are. And only you can make that choice.

You see, everyone has fight. You don't need a loud personality or a large friend circle for fight. It was born into you. But that fight won't come out without a plan. The plan is inside you, if only you will move from the places where you stand right now. You CAN do this, no matter how much you hurt. Do not be content with pain.

Pick up your mat and walk. There is peace on the other side of the climb.

Index

Index

Index

Index

Index

ABOUT THE FOUNDERS OF THE OIL ABILITY TEAM

John and Sarah Harnisch are a husband and wife Young Living team that went from starter kit to Diamond in less than three years, with no prior sales or network marketing experience. Sarah has anchored news for 18 years, has a degree in English and Japanese, is a homeschooling mom to five amazing kids, and grandmother to one adorable grand daughter. She loves running, gardening, horseback riding, deep cleaning the house and throwing everything away, and playing laser tag in the dark outside with her sons and daughter. John is a Lego-building software developer that retired from a Fortune 500 company. He is also an avid reader, tech expert, and Minecraft guru. He loves a chilly fall day, family movies with popcorn, and getaways with Sarah. Their passion is raising as many Diamonds as possible.

Congratulations

on completing the

GAMEPLAN

Sarah Harnisch, Young Living Diamond

Author of Gameplan

28165374R00193

Made in the USA
Columbia, SC
06 October 2018